"The information found in this text is intri*
Instructional Design for Organizational Justice otters a fresh perspective on
learning, training, and performance for those instructional designer practitioners with
a range of experience, from novice to mid-career, and who may be interested in creating
equitable performance-based learning and development interventions in their craft to
support adult learners."

—**Joanie Chavis**, *Head of Research, Instructional, and Engagement Services
and Liaison to Extended Learning in the Department of Library
Services at North Carolina A&T State University, USA*

"*Instructional Design for Organizational Justice* will be an invaluable resource for
instructional designers of all experience levels across multiple industries, as well as those
in the position of being able to influence the workplace environment. While I do not
teach as much as I used to, as an administrator, I would use this text to help support my
efforts to promote a culturally responsive, inclusive, and equitable work environment."

—**Jozenia Colorado-Resa**, *Ph.D., Assistant Dean for Accreditation and
Academic Operations at the University of Oregon, USA*

"I've worked in instructional design for nearly two decades, and I love the fresh outlook
that this book provides. The LeaPS ID model encourages collaboration beyond the same
old players (ID team and SME), showing where we can break down silos and encourage
input from diverse vantage points. Anyone who reads and applies the methods in this
book will be able to create more inclusive and effective learning material that engages
their audience in meaningful ways."

—**Emily Cox**, *M.Ed., Senior Experiential Learning Designer at
Bryan University, USA*

"In the ID world, one of the biggest paradoxes is that we often, on the job, do not have
the resources (time, money, or people) to complete full instructional design models
from analysis to evaluation like we are taught in school. This book acknowledges that
there are other cultural forces involved in our decisions and day-to-day work that must
be taken into consideration and shows the wider context of the systems that we work
within. All new IDs will benefit from learning the LeaPS ID model as they venture into
the workforce."

—**Nicole DeJong,** *M.Ed., Associate Vice President of Product Design and
Development at Dignity Health Global Education*

"Giacumo, Villachica, and Stepich offer us a refreshing yet thought-provoking approach
to ID. Their book forced me to question the value of efficiency at the expense of justice.
Today's world is increasingly divisive, and it is easy to feel helpless in turning the tide.
Justice and equity are notable goals; however, they are typically considered the work of
others. *Instructional Design for Organizational Justice* spells out how these goals can and
should be our work with its prescriptive approach, case studies, reflective questions,
and guides. It reminds us of the power we have and lays out how we who develop
instructional solutions for others can be truly inclusive."

—**Judy Hale**, *Ph.D., Principal, Hale & Associates*

"I can see this book being applicable to all levels of our performance improvement and instructional design curriculum. I can for sure see it as a required text for our Instructional and Performance Technology doctorate program. We try to choose books the students will use during their program and then long after. We try to help them build their professional library—this will surely be one of them."

—**Holley Handley**, *Ed.D., Assistant Professor of Instructional Design and Technology at the University of West Florida, USA*

"This book is an excellent resource for leaders and faculty who seek to successfully implement equitable learning, training, and performance strategies in their organizations and professional practice."

—**Constance H. Harris**, *Director of Online Learning at the University of Baltimore, USA*

"I can attest that this book is full of tips, tricks, examples, and guidance for instructional designers of all backgrounds and experience levels. The book is an invaluable resource for anyone in the field, offering both sound guidance and effective insights to creating equitable instructional design. A must-read for well-seasoned IDs and aspiring IDs alike. The topic is incredibly relevant for instructional designers today. I am glad that you all tapped into this and shared our experiences from grad school as real-life examples for individuals to engage with. Great work, I'm excited to see this published!"

—**Jessie Laurence**, *M.S., Research and Accessible Learning Experience Design Consultant at Boisie State University, USA*

"As far as I know, there aren't other books on instructional design that consider and include diversity, equity, and inclusion (DEI) distinctions across all stakeholder groups. *Instructional Design for Organizational Justice* is your source material and perspective from an evidence-based point of view. The arguments for doing so are compelling and readily actionable. The authors draw on their vast work and life experiences to underscore and illustrate how their LeaPS (Learning and Performance Support) ID model can effectively accommodate the range of stakeholder groups involved in any ID project. I am heartened by the authors' approach and the broad benefits that can accrue by such intentional efforts."

—**John Lazar**, *M.A., Founder and CEO of John B. Lazar & Associates, Inc.*

"A must-read for instructional designers, this book addresses a critical aspect of education and training that has long been overlooked: diversity, equity, and inclusion. One of the standout features of this book is its comprehensive map for equitable instruction. In an industry that has historically struggled with issues of diversity and inclusion, this textbook serves as a much-needed guide. It challenges us to think critically about the impact of our designs on learners from all backgrounds and to strive for fairness and justice in education and training. The inclusion of simulated cases and reflection questions is another highlight of the book. These practical exercises enable readers to apply the concepts they've learned in real-world scenarios, enhancing their understanding and skill development. It's a hands-on approach that makes the book not just a source of knowledge but a toolkit for instructional designers. This hands-on approach demystifies the instructional design process, making it accessible to both novices and experts."

—**Paige Lunny**, *M.Ed., PMP, Project Management and Instructional Design Consultant*

"A step-by-step guide for marrying DEI practices and Instructional Design. Not only will you come away with a deeper understanding of how to design performance materials to be culturally responsive, but you will be provided with the tools and templates necessary to enact change in your organization today. Specifically, you will learn why and how to incorporate your diverse learners in the design process. This book is refreshingly approachable, with something to offer to everyone, from students of instructional design to researchers to learning and training experts. Written by practitioners, this book is filled with case studies, templates, and reflection questions designed to challenge the reader to improve their ID skills."

—**Madeleine MacDonald**, *M.S., Senior Learning Consultant for Environmental Resources Management*

"*Instructional Design for Organizational Justice* provides a unique and expansive view of learning design. Not only is this a comprehensive book, but it presents a societal and cultural context for doing instructional design work. The goal is to promote the type of inclusivity and diversity essential for the twenty-first-century workplace."

—**Connie Malamed**, *M.A., Founder of Mastering Instructional Design*

"This textbook is invaluable for Instructional Designers committed to culturally responsive design. I recommend it to any Instructional Designer interested in becoming a more culturally responsive practitioner. I look forward to applying these principles as I become more knowledgeable in advocating for greater DEI in my learning solutions."

—**Osemome Ndebbio**, *B.A., Learning Experience Designer at Boisie State University, USA*

"In higher education institutions, instructional designers (IDs) are often caught in liminal spaces somewhere between faculty or subject matter experts and administrative leadership. IDs are the consummate conciliators, fixers, and glue who can bring stakeholders together, manage projects, timelines, and transform subject matter content. Oftentimes when IDs take on this myriad of roles, there is little slack left to advocate for diversity, equity, and inclusion. Even more rare in institutional instructional design meetings is the discussion of justice, something that has historically been ignored. What is particularly powerful in this book in addition to the LeaPS ID model are the reflection questions. These questions are topics that we as IDs often think deeply about but do not say out loud or make part of our standard opening procedures. These are questions like, 'Is it your responsibility as an ID to ensure that an organization's learning and development interventions are culturally responsive and inclusive? How would you answer this at your organization?'"

—**Kae Novak**, *M.E.T., Assistant Director of Learning Design at Front Range Community College, USA*

"This textbook presents a robust design process that successfully integrates instructional design research and diversity, equity, and inclusion issues. The approach combines theoretical rigor with practical advice, yielding a valuable resource for students of instructional design."

—**Clark Quinn**, *Ph.D., Executive Director of Quinnovation*

"Authors Lisa A. Giacumo, Steven W. Villachica, and Donald A. Stepich should be applauded! Their stated purpose for writing their new book was to support emerging and experienced instructional designers who want to draw upon an instructional design (ID) process, which is merged with a diversity, equity, and inclusion framework. This book does that via an introduction to their Learning and Performance Support Instructional Design (LeaPS ID) model, which integrates inclusive design practices in creating performance-based learning and development interventions that are culturally responsive and equitable."

—**Guy Wallace**, *B.A., Retired Performance Analysis & Instructional Architect*

"As someone responsible for preparing learning professionals to effectively meet the various challenges they face in the field, I am always looking for resources to support my students' ID knowledge and practice. I was excited to find that this book presents both a model (LeaPS) that integrates DEI and ID practices, and real-world examples (e.g., case studies) and applications (e.g., templates) of these practices. For the case studies and templates alone, this book is worth taking a look at implementing in your courses. But there is even more on offer here. This book also covers important project management and interpersonal skills required for the success of ID projects (including those projects your students engage in as part of their coursework!). Each chapter ends with a case study and reflection questions, providing an appropriate level of depth for both beginning and more experienced practitioners."

—**Katherine Walters**, *Ph.D., Clinical Assistant Professor and Graduate Program Director at the University of North Carolina at Greensboro, USA*

Instructional Design for Organizational Justice

Instructional Design for Organizational Justice prepares instructional designers to use culturally relevant, performance-based learning materials and environments that improve organizational and workplace learning experiences for today's diverse, globalized contexts. With socially just leadership and DEI initiatives growing in institutions across sectors, today's instructional design programs must prepare graduate students to be more culturally relevant, equity-minded, and inclusive in their professional practice. This textbook explores the implementation of systematic, systemic, and performance-oriented designs alongside the use of organizational justice theory to facilitate more equitable, inclusive performance improvement and workplace learning interventions.

The book introduces the Learning and Performance Support Instructional Design (LeaPs ID) Model. Applicable to instructional designers, educational technologists, learning experience designers, learning engineers, and human resource development professionals, this original, iterative process:

- integrates common ID heuristics, design-based thinking, culture, equity, inclusion, and other inputs external to the organization and ID project;
- portrays a realistic, scalable, iterative, agile approach to the ID process;
- aids in the design of environments in which adult learners can observe, practice, and receive feedback, building the knowledge and capacity required for their desired performance; and
- is illustrated by a wealth of examples, templates, and processes developed in the field to support adult learners and collaborate with subject matter experts.

Relevant to business, government, military, non-profit, non-governmental, and higher education settings, this unique and comprehensive volume lends itself to uncovering values and motives essential to successful agile project management as well as to diversity, equity, and inclusion initiatives and social change.

Lisa A. Giacumo is an associate professor in the Department of Organizational Performance and Workplace Learning in the College of Engineering at Boise State University, USA.

Steven W. Villachica is a professor emeritus in the Department of Organizational Performance and Workplace Learning in the College of Engineering at Boise State University, USA.

Donald A. Stepich is a professor emeritus in the Department of Organizational Performance and Workplace Learning in the College of Engineering at Boise State University, USA.

INSTRUCTIONAL DESIGN FOR ORGANIZATIONAL JUSTICE

A Guide to Equitable Learning, Training, and Performance in Professional Education and Workforce Settings

Lisa A. Giacumo, Steven W. Villachica, and Donald A. Stepich

NEW YORK AND LONDON

Designed cover image: © Getty Images/Andriy Onufriyenko

First published 2025
by Routledge
605 Third Avenue, New York, NY 10158

and by Routledge
4 Park Square, Milton Park, Abingdon, Oxon, OX14 4RN

Routledge is an imprint of the Taylor & Francis Group, an informa business

ISBN: 978–1-032–41763–9 (hbk)
ISBN: 978–1-032–41966–4 (pbk)
ISBN: 978–1-003–36061–2 (ebk)

DOI: 10.4324/9781003360612

Typeset in Palatino
by Apex CoVantage, LLC

Dedication

To our mentors, colleagues, friends, clients, and students who have taught and continue to teach us how to be caring professionals and better instructional designers.

Contents

Preface

INTRODUCTION

Our purpose for writing this book was to support emerging and experienced instructional designers (IDs) who want to draw upon an instructional design (ID) process which is merged with a diversity, equity, and inclusion (DEI) framework. The book introduces the Learning and Performance Support Instructional Design (LeaPS ID) model, which uses inclusive design practices as a guide to creating performance-based learning and development interventions that are culturally relevant and equitable. The book includes instructional and non-instructional strategies that IDs can use to support adult learning and performance needs. The book also includes heuristics (e.g., rules of thumb for decision-making, mental shortcuts) to aid in learning and applying the model. The primary objectives of the book are to:

- Produce an innovative ID textbook with actionable strategies and guidance with templates.
- Introduce an ID model that applies principles of inclusive design to create learning and development interventions that meet the requirements of both effectiveness and equity.
- Enable IDs to engage in reflective practice as a way to both create effective instruction and enhance their own professional development.
- Intentionally refocus conversations in ID to the importance of being just, culturally relevant, equity-minded, and inclusive.

WHAT'S THE PURPOSE OF THIS BOOK?

Currently, there are no ID textbooks available to support practitioners who range in experience from novice to mid-career, who are entering the field, or for those who have some experience and desire to formalize their practice with creating performance-based training and learning environments that are culturally relevant and equitable. Yet researchers agree that these are central approaches used by performance improvement (PI) and ID practitioners (Asino & Giacumo, 2017, 2019; Benson et al., 2023; Breman, Giacumo, & Griffith-Boyes, 2019; Breman & Giacumo, 2020; Eglash & Bennett, 2023; Giacumo, forthcoming; Giacumo & Asino, 2022; Giacumo & Breman, 2021;

Giacumo, MacDonald, & Peters, 2021; Giacumo, Villachica, & Yount, 2020; Liu, 2021; Peters & Giacumo, 2019, 2020; Villachica, Giacumo, & Mammenga, 2023). Further, the practitioners that we serve through our work at Boise State University, and the external business consulting projects we have led for over 30 years, confirm that these principles, practices, instructional strategies, and approaches that we have developed and use are valued.

Our focus on creating learning environments and ID deliverables that are culturally responsive and equitable with the purpose to deliver desired performance outcomes, that are aligned with strategic business objectives, provides a very timely, innovative, and unique lens that cannot be found in other textbooks. No previous ID models have been created that address design justice practices and performance-based learning and development (L&D) practices as a way to enable DEI and PI. This integration and contextualization uniquely lends itself to uncovering values and motives essential to successful project processes as well as DEI.

Our approach integrates design thinking and traditional ID approaches to meet contextualized performance needs. The focus on building, supporting, and transferring knowledge and capacity to skilled performance is novel. Other textbooks omit this focus on supporting the transfer of learned skills and knowledge to real-world performance environments. This book is innovative because we provide guidance and example templates to help emerging and developing professionals implement processes to achieve the concepts we cover. This is a better approach for scaffolding and guiding learning and performance.

Many popular ID textbooks serve a combined audience of IDs who create learning materials for workplaces in business, government, military, non-profit, nongovernmental, and higher education settings. Our work will also serve this combined audience. Not only can we support professional IDs to create instructional and learning interventions for learners to build knowledge and meet accreditation, regulatory, or other industry standards, we can also show how IDs can deliver task-centered training and even compliance training that actually changes performance through successful transfer into the workplace. This is also a different approach to ID, which means that our book will improve upon past formally trained professional ID approaches to workplace learning design and, ultimately, performance.

This book is likely not as useful for traditional compulsory educational and theoretical learning or instructional needs. It may also not be as useful for situations in which the teacher or instructor is an expert in the subject area to be taught, content, learning, and design. In this book, we focus specifically on the design of L&D opportunities offered in workplaces, professional education, and other organizational contexts.

WHAT THE BOOK IS AND WHAT THE BOOK IS NOT

This book is:

- About a scalable, highly contextualized model.
- Based on our own experience.

- Based on the work of model builders and other ID "pioneers."
- A how-to book for practitioners.
- A timely and innovative perspective on justice and DEI in ID.
- Written primarily as a textbook.
- Written to fill a gap in textbook offerings.
- Useful for a variety of individuals.

This book is not:

- A guarantee.
- Useful in "traditional" compulsory educational and theoretical learning.
- A theoretical review.

In this book, we share a scalable model and one way to approach ID for performance-based professional education and workplace learning in organizations. It's not the only way, and we certainly don't claim it to be a panacea. However, it's worked great for us and hundreds of our own consulting projects in a variety of organizational settings, for diverse clients and learners. We have developed this approach through using our own evidence-based practices over the past two decades. Our evidence-based practice is grounded in our work histories, research, scholarship, prior educational experiences, and personal journeys.

We've based our ID practices standing on the shoulders of giants whose work we've drawn upon throughout our careers. Parts of our ID practice come from pioneers of performance-based instructional approaches, including: Brethower & Smalley (1998); Wallace (2020, 2021); Foshay, Silber, & Stelnicki (2003); Pollock, Jefferson, & Wick (2015); and Rothwell, Benscoter, King, & King (2016). Other parts of our ID practice come from instructional systems design (ISD) model builders such as Dick, Carey, & Carey (2009); Smith & Ragan (2005), Morrison et al. (2013), and Larson & Lockee (2019).

We acknowledge that using the methods and processes in this book alone will not guarantee L&D interventions are culturally relevant, inclusive, equitable, and just. Individuals themselves will also need to reflect and examine what they bring to the table in the form of hidden biases and work to overcome them or mindfully choose priorities while making decisions in projects to achieve culturally relevant, inclusive, equitable, and just outputs. We also understand that an organization's culture and leaders will also help determine individuals' abilities to design systems and outputs that are culturally relevant, inclusive, equitable, and just.

Further, we do not attempt to engage in a deep study and examination into equity, justice, and inclusion in this practitioner textbook. We feel a deep study such as this is better aligned with a research-oriented book. Likewise, we do not intend to share an exhaustive philosophical discussion and historical account regarding what all leads up to the current state of affairs in our discipline. We do feel that would be a very appropriate book focus, perhaps as an edited book with chapters describing a wide range of perspectives regarding a revised history and in-depth reflection on where the field needs to head in the next decade.

We don't engage in any philosophical discussion regarding the merits of liberatory pedagogy or its relevance to practitioners in organizations who support workplace learning or professional education for adults. We agree with Freire (2005): learners should be treated as individuals with dignity, they should not be viewed as mere receivers of instructional and non-instructional interventions; learners should be involved with co-creating knowledge in organizations and workplace learning contexts, and help identify their own learning paths. We acknowledge that learners, as organizational members at all levels, are needed to create robust learning and development interventions. We are fully committed to the idea that good organizational leaders and managers at all levels would ideally work hard to create unity, compassion, organization, and inclusion in their work, with their direct reports and project members, as well as with those professionals tasked with supporting L&D in organizations, in part through dialogue.

We also acknowledge there is relational tension inherent in situations where people contribute their time, energy, and talents in competitive environments in exchange for differentiated levels of financial compensation, a variety of benefits, and other valued commodities or incentives. We also acknowledge that design is not culturally neutral, and learning is mediated by culture and individuals' perceptions. Therefore, organizational leaders and designers seeking to create interventions which are more culturally relevant, inclusive, equitable, and just have a responsibility to work very intentionally and also differently from how they have in the past.

Thus, we offer the guidance in this book, grounded in both theory and practice, to support those who would endeavor to lead and create L&D opportunities in organizations that are culturally relevant, just, inclusive, and equitable. We do so with awareness, compassion, and faith in readers' abilities to apply what they find useful and modify or build on our contributions at will to design L&D opportunities that are theoretically informed and better support culturally relevant, inclusive, equitable, and just organizational practices. We will likely do the same, and hope to share future versions of this introductory work!

The Opportunities and Performance Gaps We Seek to Meet

This textbook fills an important gap in existing resources for PI and ID practitioners who are entering the field and formalizing their performance-based learning design practice. Additionally, other gaps in textbook offerings that we seek to address include the following guidance:

- How to use organizational justice theory to facilitate more just, equitable, and inclusive PI and workplace learning interventions.
- How to work with clients, subject matter experts (SMEs), and on teams.
- How to scale project scope.
- Heuristics that IDs use in projects to make decisions.
- How to engage in a more agile ID process.
- How to integrate design-based thinking with traditional ISD and the added value of this integration.
- How to scale an agile, culturally relevant, iterative ID project.

- A unique step-by-step process approach that builds on the LeaPS ID model.
- How to design culturally relevant instructional materials to facilitate learning.

The Individuals Who Might Find this Book Useful

Individuals with backgrounds in professional education, workplace learning, training, adult learning, curriculum and instruction, ID, learning design, educational technology (EdTech), instructional systems design, human resource development (HRD), business communications, eLearning design, workplace learning, and performance improvement (PI), who wish to actively promote culturally responsive, inclusive, and equitable interventions in performance-based L&D, might find this book useful.

Our goal is to support those who manage and build organizational training programs or courses, as well as other formal and informal learning interventions in organizations. These courses or professional development opportunities may be offered by centers of excellence or corporate universities of mid-sized to large organizations, boutique consultancies, and professional societies such as ATD, The Guild, AECT, IBSTPI, ISPI, and similar societies.

University professors interested in adding a service learning component to their courses may be interested in using our approach to help their students manage service learning ID projects that build the sponsor's capacity to meet their mission and serve their community. The introductory ID course the authors teach has employed a service learning approach that pairs virtual student ID teams within qualified sponsors' non-profit organizations. Students complete authentic, real-world service learning projects with real-world clients. Lastly, this book may have secondary appeal to education administration professionals who train teachers and university instructors.

COURSEWORK WITH SIMULATED CASES AND REAL CLIENTS

This book came out of our research, scholarship, and combined 40 years of experiences consulting clients and working with graduate degree-seeking learners. We used a prior version of this book, which we called the *ID Course Handbook,* while teaching graduate courses. It was the primary reading assignment for a 100 percent asynchronous online course. In the most recent iterations of the course, students worked independently on simulated client project cases as practice exercises and then with real clients on virtual teams to create common L&D deliverables during a 15-week graduate course (e.g., design documents, instructor-led training, job aids, slide decks, discussion activities, instructor guides, learner handouts, implementation plans). We intend to keep using this book to support our adult learners' completion of future project-based courses with the same simulated practice and live client project experience. Therefore, we are confident that our readers may choose to use the book to frame and support their work with live clients and/or in simulated projects as well.

There are many different ways you can integrate this book into your introductory ID course, other ID courses, or your own personal professional development project. However, we share one way that has worked for us. We have broken the simulated and live client projects into three chunks. We have organized these chunks into repeated learning cycles. Each chunk starts with a selection of readings, this book being the only required reading. We ask learners to create something to represent their reflection of the material they read such as a journal entry, blog entry, vlog entry, infographic, instructional video, or something else they might come up with. Then, we present a case video with relevant information and ask learners to independently complete at least one of the template(s) we provide. Finally, we match a mixed-ability group of learners with a client and ask them to complete the templates according to the client project scope. In the past, we have had our learners identify clients and project scopes. We have also identified clients and project scopes for our learners and allowed students to sign up for the client and project scope of their choice. Currently, we do both. We would love to hear how you would use this book, too.

OUR ORGANIZATIONAL STRATEGY FOR THIS BOOK

We organize our book in two ways. At a high level, we introduce overarching themes we've found helpful for conceptualizing performance-based L&D design that's culturally relevant, inclusive, equitable, and just. Then, we show how to implement these ideas in project work. We shift between introducing overarching themes and providing practical application support throughout the book as part of a holistic design process view.

That being said, we do recognize that as professional consultants we may be called in to start or exit a project at any point in the holistic process. We have found that the larger an organizational context becomes, the less likely one person will be assigned to complete all components of a truly iterative and comprehensive ID process. Likewise, we've found that in smaller projects it's a little more common for consultants to be called upon to complete more, or even all, components of an iterative project. Therefore, the book could be used in parts to focus on one component or another. We could see where individuals using this book might only complete project work related to front-end analysis work (e.g., chapters 1, 4, and 5), formative evaluation (i.e., chapter 3), or design and development work (e.g., chapters 6, 7, 8, and 11), or program planning (e.g., chapters 8, 9, 10, and 12), or implementation (e.g., chapters 12, 13, and 14). Certainly, these aren't the only chunks we see possible and desirable. We could also see where different combinations would serve different purposes and project scopes. We believe the selection, chunking, and grouping possibilities are as endless as any single organization's needs.

At a micro level, we have organized each chapter to include a brief introduction. We then explore related theories, models, frameworks, and approaches, which can be applied in practice, anonymized case examples from our own consulting work with clients, discussion questions, and references for further reading. This modular approach makes the book useful for a variety of different audiences and needs. In every chapter we center issues related to creating culturally relevant, inclusive, equitable, and just services and products. We incorporate some lived cases representing cross-cultural contexts and those of historically marginalized groups into the book with corresponding discussion questions to help others consider their roles in supporting more just, equitable, and inclusive organizations. This way, you have an opportunity to see how you can ensure your project work takes these issues into account throughout your decision points.

Again, we don't claim to present the only way to work. We invite readers to use what works for them and to modify ideas as appropriate for their own practice and unique contexts. Given our consulting experience and extensive work with emerging and advancing professionals in L&D both within a university context and within corporate businesses, we are confident that what we share in this book is a good starting point for continuous development and specialization in performance-based learning.

WRITING STYLE

We strive to use active voice to make this book easier to understand. At times, we use a conversational style because empirical research findings suggest that readers will be able to relate to it better and retain information. We feel this approach fits well with our framework and approach to sharing our experience, with the intention to allow readers to think about what might work for them and with examples of how to go about approaching their projects without trying to prescribe a recipe.

OUR BIOGRAPHIES

We each have different identities, and extensive, varied, work and personal histories. The practical approaches and rationales in this book are artifacts of our experiences, how we see the world, and how we work to gain the insights we need to design interventions that are intended to support individuals' L&D experiences that are culturally relevant, inclusive, equitable, and just in organizations.

Before we go any further, we'd like to introduce ourselves. We are not sharing our positionalities to participate in any discussion related to who deserves a voice in this area. Instead, we share so that readers know who we are and where we are coming from so that they can make more nuanced decisions about what we would share in this book.

Lisa A. Giacumo, Ph.D.

I grew up in the northeast United States and spent one year in France. I then lived and worked extensively in the US northeast, southwest, Pacific northwest, and for just over a year in the UK. My ID and PI consulting work has largely been situated in corporate contexts spanning more than one nation, usually including North America, but also including Pakistan, Haiti, Mozambique, Jordan, Ethiopia, and Namibia. I have done this work in many different types of organizations (i.e., non-profit, non-governmental, international non-governmental, educational, military, and for-profit) and sizes, from startup to multinational. My roles have been committed to providing diverse individuals with access to products and services intended to increase social equity. My personal and professional experiences are situated in many different locations, cultures, and organizations, allowing me to form extensive connections with individuals from all over the world, which have shaped me over time. I embrace these opportunities as methods to continuously learn more about myself, others, and social equity needs in the world. I draw upon these lived experiences and connections to continuously grow and evolve my own personal identity and professional outlook.

I am a white, neurodivergent female, over 45 years old, who at different times has experienced both middle and low incomes. Thus, I have experienced the consequences of both privilege and oppression originating from historically European and current North American settler cultures. I share these identity characteristics as a means to advocate for representation, as in relation to my privileged position I often see them devalued.

I wish to spend my short time on this earth, my intellectual bandwidth, and my energy towards eradicating oppression of groups of people who have been historically marginalized, or erased, and underrepresented in organizations. As such, my research and scholarship activities are centered in organizational performance and workplace learning contexts that span the globe, are cross-cultural, in support of marginalized populations, and integrate technology, digital devices, and both instructional and non-instructional interventions.

Currently, I am an associate professor in the Organizational Performance and Workplace Learning (OPWL) Department at Boise State University. I graduated with a PhD in EdTech from Arizona State University. I earned an MS degree from the University of Albany, SUNY, in curriculum development and instructional technology. I hold a BA degree in French Studies, International Perspectives of Third World Countries, and Education, from the University of Albany, SUNY.

Steven W. Villachica, Ph.D.

I have consulted and worked in business, government, and non-profit settings for more than 40 years. I joined the faculty of the OPWL Department in 2007 and retired in May 2022. I taught courses in instructional design, needs assessment, and workplace performance improvement.

Prior to joining Boise State, I worked as a performance consultant with DLS Group, Inc., to create large-scale performance support systems, performance-based eLearning and instructor-led training, job aids, and a host of award-winning performance improvement solutions for pharmaceutical companies, law enforcement agencies, securities companies and regulators, the Intelligence Community, and others.

In the 1990s, DLS Group adopted a Rapid Application Design (RAD) approach in creating these deliverables. This approach employed collaborative analysis and design, rapid prototyping, tryouts (usability testing), timeboxing, and specialized tools and templates. Modern theories of design and organizational justice further these ID practices that hold learners should play an active role in the creation of the learning and performance support materials they use in workplace settings.

As a co-investigator in the Process Management Lab, I currently work with OPWL students and graduates to provide affordable process planning, redesign, and implementation services to the non-profit community while developing process facilitation and consulting skills in the next generation of professionals.

Donald A. Stepich, M.S.W., Ph.D.

After almost 15 years as a professional social worker, I completed a doctoral degree in education and spent the next 25+ years teaching ID-related courses, including instructional design, needs assessment and evaluation, to graduate and undergraduate students at three different universities. Currently, I am a professor emeritus of the Organizational Performance and Workplace Learning Department at Boise State University.

ACKNOWLEDGEMENTS

We'd like to thank Lynn Kearny for the artwork that she created; both the Working Metropolitan Hospital image, created specifically for this book and Gerry Rummler's Anatomy of Performance Model image. We'd like to thank the International Society for Performance Improvement (ISPI), which owns the copyright for Rummler's Anatomy of Performance Model, for their permission to use it in this book. We'd like to thank Matt Donovan and GP Strategies for permission to use the Learning Ecosystems artwork in this book. We'd like to thank Brandalyn Athons for the graphic design she created for the example task analysis flipped into a job aid and Boise State University for the branding. Also, we thank our many colleagues who reviewed our manuscript, provided feedback, and offered testimonials.

REFERENCES

Asino, T., & Giacumo, L. A. (2017). Culture as a design "next": Theoretical frameworks to guide new design, development, and research of learning environments. *The Design Journal, 20*(sup1), S875–S885. doi:10.1080/14606925.2017.1353033

Asino, T., & Giacumo, L. A. (2019). Culture and global workplace learning. In Kenon, V., Palsole, S., Ong, R., & Duff, N. (Eds), *Wiley handbook of global workplace learning*, (pp. 395–412). John Wiley & Sons.

Benson, A. D., Beavers-Forrest, B., Giacumo, L., Harris, C., Horton, A., & Liu, J. C. (2023). Culture, learning, and technology and the promise of diversity, equity, and inclusion: Leading AECT into a more inclusive future. In Miller, C. T., Piña, A. A., Molenda, M. H., Harris, P. L., & Lockee, B. B. (Eds), *AECT at 100* (pp. 533–557). Brill.

Breman, J., & Giacumo, L. A. (2020). Instructional design case: Cross cultural instructional design project for a global workplace learning and training context. *Handbook of research in educational communications and technology*. Springer. doi:10.1007/978–3–030–36119–8

Breman, J., Giacumo, L. A., & Griffith-Boyes, R. (2019). A needs analysis to inform global humanitarian capacity building. *TechTrends, 63*(3), 294–303. doi:10.1007/s11528-019-00390-6

Brethower, D., & Smalley, K. (1998). *Performance-based instruction: Linking training to business results*. Jossey-Bass/Pfieffer.

Dick, W., Carey, L., & Carey, J. O. (2009). *The systematic design of instruction* (7th ed.). Pearson.

Eglash, R., & Bennett, A. (2023). Anti-racism for freethinkers: Cultivating a mindset for curiosity and scientific inquiry in the context of racial equity and social justice. *TechTrends, 67*(3), 456–466.

Foshay, W. R., Silber, K. H., & Stelnicki, M. (2003). *Writing training materials that work: How to train anyone to do anything*. Pfeiffer.

Freire, P. (2005). *Pedagogy of the oppressed: 30th anniversary edition*. Continuum.

Giacumo, L. A. (forthcoming). Diversity and inclusion in design for learning and human performance technologies. In Carr-Chellman, A., Reiser, R., & Dempsey, J. (Eds), *Trends and issues in instructional design and technology* (5th ed.). Routledge.

Giacumo, L. A., & Asino, T. I. (2022). Preparing instructional designers to apply human performance technology in global context. In Stefaniak, J. (Ed.), *The Instructional Design Trainer's Guide* (pp. 170–179). Routledge.

Giacumo, L. A., & Breman, J. (2021). Trends and implications of models, frameworks, and approaches, used by instructional designers in workplace learning and performance improvement. *Performance Improvement Quarterly, 34*(2), 131–170. doi:10.1002/piq.21349

Giacumo, L. A., MacDonald, M., & Peters, D. (2021). Promoting organizational justice in cross-cultural data collection, analysis, and interpretation: Towards an emerging conceptual model. *Journal of Applied Instructional Design, 10*(4). doi:10.51869/104/lgi

Giacumo, L. A., Villachica, S. W., & Yount, M. (2020). *LeaPS ID model explainer.* https://www.youtube.com/watch?v=c8GY7JCg6N8

Larson, M. B., & Lockee, B. B. (2019). *Streamlined ID: A practical guide to instructional design.* Routledge.

Liu, J. C. (2021). Inclusiveness in instructional design & development of informal learning experiences: From cultural lenses. *The Journal of Applied Instructional Design, 10*(3). doi:10.51869/103/jcl

Morrison, G. R., Ross, S. M., Kalman, H. K., & Kemp, J. E. (2013). *Designing effective instruction* (7th ed.). Wiley.

Peters, D. T., & Giacumo, L. A. (2019). A systematic evaluation process: Soliciting client participation and working in a cross-cultural context. *Performance Improvement, 58*(3), 6–19. doi:10.1002/pfi.21845

Peters, D. T., & Giacumo, L. A. (2020). Ethical and responsible cross-cultural interviewing: Theory to practice guidance for human performance and workplace learning professionals. *Performance Improvement, 59*(1), 26–34. doi:10.1002/pfi.21906

Pollock, R. V. H., Jefferson, A. M., & Wick, C. W. (2015). *The six disciplines of breakthrough learning* (3rd ed.). Wiley.

Rothwell, W., Benscoter, B., King, M., & King, S. B. (2016). *Mastering the instructional design process: A systematic approach* (5th ed.). Wiley.

Smith, P. L., & Ragan, T. J. (2005). *Instructional design* (3rd ed.). John Wiley & Sons.

Villachica, S. W., Giacumo, L., & Mammenga, J. (2023). Real projects for real community clients: Combining eService-learning and project-based learning. In Strait, J. R., Shumer, R. D., & Nordyke, K. J. (Eds), *Taking eService-learning to the next level: Addressing social problems in communities in times of crisis.* Information Age.

Wallace, G. W. (2020). *Conducting performance-based instructional analysis.* Guy W. Wallace.

Wallace, G. W. (2021). *Lesson mapping and instructional development using a facilitated group process.* Guy W. Wallace.

CHAPTER 1

An Introduction to Culturally Relevant and Equitable Instruction

INTRODUCTION

Instructional designers (IDs) serve as the architects of an organization's learning and development (L&D) programs, materials, and applications. Working with a client and others, architects create plans for buildings based on the people who will use the buildings, the purposes the building will serve, the site where the building will be located, and the budget and resources allocated to the project. They do this work as consultants, whether they are internal employees or external vendors.

In the same way, IDs usually work with others to create plans for *L&D interventions* based on the people who will use the programs, materials, and applications, the purposes they will serve, where they will be situated within the organization's overall plans, and the budget and resources allocated to them. In general, the purpose of these interventions is to help individuals within the organization build their knowledge and skills and, perhaps, change their attitudes. This is done to meet the performance objectives of both the organization and the learners. IDs do this by applying adult learning theories, relevant conceptual models, and evidence-based instructional methods to specific learning situations.

> Throughout the book, we will use the term *intervention* to mean the variety of possible learning and development programs, materials, and applications. This includes in-person classes; both synchronous and asynchronous online classes; self-paced learning; job aids and EPSS that can be used while on the job; on-the-job training; mentoring; coaching; and so on.

As learning architects, IDs are also in a position to "shape the culture of their workplace, cultivate new mindsets, develop and change behaviors and drive strategic initiatives" (Adefela, 2022). This aspect of instructional design (ID) has become prominent as more organizations have recognized the value of diversity, equity, and inclusion (DEI). Formal definitions of the three components of DEI are provided in the Glossary

DOI: 10.4324/9781003360612-1

at the end of the book. As an introduction, these three components can be related in the following way:

- *Diversity* is an inherent characteristic of human groups. People in any group will be diverse on a number of dimensions, including age, gender, race, nationality or ethnicity, religious beliefs, socioeconomic status, (dis)ability, sexual orientation, political perspectives, and so on.
- *Equity* is a goal describing fair and just treatment for all people. We want everyone to succeed, including those people who have not always had the opportunities and resources required to succeed.
- *Inclusion* is a practice. It's what we do to accommodate the inherent diversity among people and work towards the goal of equity.

Diversity, equity, and inclusion are often thought of in terms of sociology; however, this book is about them as they apply to ID. After reading this chapter, you will be able to:

- Articulate a rationale for incorporating DEI into all components of the ID process.
- Define several basic terms that will be used throughout the book.
- Explain two general principles that can guide the work of incorporating DEI into the ID process.
- Describe the LeaPS ID model as a way to work through the ID process with a focus on DEI.

WHY INCORPORATE DEI INTO ID?

DEI-related values have become more prominent. This can be seen in the recent emergence of "chief diversity officers" in organizations as varied as Walmart, Eli Lilly, Hilton, New York Life Insurance Co., Indiana University, MD Anderson Cancer Center, Wells Fargo, and CNN Worldwide. Chief diversity officers have been described as C-level executives who create strategies, plans, and programs to "ensure an equitable work environment for all employees" (Doyle, 2021). It isn't a surprise that researchers also describe an increased need to focus on DEI in post-COVID19 university ID landscapes (Liu, 2021). Thus, we've noted a growing research focus on ID practices that lead to more culturally relevant interventions (Young, 2021; Ren, 2022) and an interest in developing more justice-minded practitioner leaders (Kopcha et al., 2021; Ikeda et al., 2021; Bisson et al., 2022).

There is a good reason for this trend. For example, Hunt et al. (2018) published an industry report on behalf of McKinsey & Company consulting services, which described their "growing awareness of the business case for inclusion and diversity" (p. 1). This focus on DEI is not solely altruistic. There's global evidence for a correlation between increased gender and cultural diversity in leadership roles and increased profitability in organizations—along with decreased diversity and profitability in organizations with low gender and cultural diversity in leadership roles (Hunt et al., 2018). An article in the *Harvard Business Review* described mounting research evidence showing that this focus is advantageous for business results (Gompers & Kovvali, 2018).

Likewise, a growing body of research has tied workforce diversity to organizational innovation and performance outcomes (Khan et al., 2021). Some researchers have found evidence that suggests employee diversity can improve organizational performance and outcomes (Gomez & Bernet, 2019). Other researchers have found evidence that increased diversity in board members can lead to better governance (Conyon & He, 2017; Liu, 2021) and improved financial performance (Loh & Nguyen, 2018).

Further, researchers have also found that organizational justice can affect a variety of aspects of organizational performance (Ambrose & Cropanzano, 2003; Moon, 2017) and workplace learning (Oh, 2019; Sartti, 2019). Organizational justice theory is used to measure the level to which *all organizational members* perceive an organization's procedures, policies, and interactional environments to be *fair, equitable, respectful, and dignified* (Greenberg, 1990).

This is important; for example, as organizations become more fair and just, members become more engaged and productive (Giacumo, MacDonald, & Peters, 2021). Shared perceptions of a fair and just organization have also been shown to influence organizational citizenship and decrease counterproductive behaviors (Latham & Pinder, 2005). Researchers have also found relationships between organizational justice and increased job satisfaction, increased organizational loyalty, and decreased turnover (Fatt, Khin, & Heng, 2010). Giacumo et al. (2021) have begun to provide guidance on how organizational justice can be applied to IDs' data collection, intervention creation, and project implementation work. Thus, a new textbook providing guidance on how emerging and developing IDs can integrate a novel ID model and approaches that support greater DEI practices in organizations to achieve desired learning and performance results is appropriate and urgent.

This body of research suggests that DEI influences both employee performance and organizational performance. Taking this one step further, we believe that these results are closely related. This is based on the premise that what matters most in any organization is its people (e.g., Forbes.com; eLearning Partners.com). Emphasizing DEI can lead to a kind of self-fulfilling prophecy in which employees who believe they are valued *by* the organization are more likely to make valuable contributions *to* the organization. In the context of learning and development projects, diverse employees on a project design team will bring new perspectives and can result in those employees making valuable contributions to the team based on their "lived experiences" (i.e., direct, first-hand involvement in events and activities that lead to knowledge, perspectives, and insights that are unique to those employees). This might include finding ways to make the intervention more relatable, supportive, accessible, fair, respectful, and understandable to employees like themselves, perhaps because of the approach, structure, features, and/or the examples used to explain part of the content. It might also include finding ways to improve the work environment for *all* employees, a result that has been called the "curb-cut effect" (Blackwell, 2017). The small ramps (i.e., curb cuts) were built into city sidewalks to make it easier for people in wheelchairs to cross streets safely. But they also make it easier for people pushing strollers, or using other wheeled objects, carrying packages, using canes, crutches, or walkers, along with others who want to avoid the trip hazard of curbs. The point is that something that begins as a solution for some can serve as a solution for all. This kind of creative problem-solving is important to all organizations and can be enhanced by emphasizing DEI.

At the simplest level, ID refers to the "systematic process of translating principles of learning and instruction into plans for instructional materials and activities" (Smith & Ragan, 1999). However, we believe that instructional designers also have a civic responsibility (Yusop & Correia, 2012) to:

- Focus on the "common good" (i.e., something that provides benefits for and is naturally shared by all members of a given community, compared with things that solely benefit the private good of some individuals or sectors of society) in their work.
- Be informed and help shape interventions in positive ways.
- Avoid unintended consequences, particularly for those people who have been unrepresented, or underrepresented, or discriminated against in the past.

This is not a new idea. For more than 30 years, ID authors have suggested that societal impact should be an important consideration in learning and development. For example, the "Organizational Elements Model" developed by Kaufman et al. (1998) distinguishes between an organization's "outputs"—what it produces"—and its "outcomes"—the effects those products have on the customer *and the society* (emphasis added).

GUIDING PRINCIPLES

Costanza-Chock (2020) and others (Giacumo et al., 2021; Strommel, 2021) suggest that equitable learning experiences and improved organization performance can be facilitated through an ID process that includes, as part of the design team, learners who will be directly affected by the resulting intervention and who have routinely been excluded, intentionally or unintentionally, in the past. It also requires purposefully accounting for institutional practices that have presented barriers to participation by certain groups. At the same time, IDs have a responsibility to create effective instruction and help their clients meet their strategic goals.

The LeaPS ID model is meant to marry the dual requirements of interventions that are both equitable and effective. Subsequent chapters will provide information about how to be intentionally inclusive throughout the ID process. But first, this section describes two general principles that help form the foundation for each component of the LeaPS ID model.

Principle #1: Inclusive Design

The Inclusive Design Research Centre (IDRC) describes inclusive design as "design that considers the full range of human diversity with respect to ability, language, culture, gender, age, and other forms of human difference" (Inclusive Design Research Centre, n.d.). Inclusive design is not a new idea. It can be traced back to the 1950s and the push for "barrier-free" design of physical environments and was later applied to the design of digital products and services. It surfaced again with the collaborative analysis and design approaches associated with James Martin's (1991) Rapid Application

Development and IBM's Joint Application Design (August, 1991). From the beginning, the goal has been to create designs that everyone can use safely and without the need for adaptations. Our goal in this book is to apply principles of inclusive design and design justice specifically to the instructional design process.

The IDRC emphasizes three dimensions of inclusive design:

1. *Recognizing diversity and uniqueness.* This refers to emphasizing the importance of the users' self-determination and self-knowledge and keeping the uniqueness of each individual in mind.
2. *Inclusive process and tools.* This refers to creating diverse design teams that include "individuals that have difficulty or are excluded from the existing designs." It also requires including users as meaningful participants in design and making design and development tools as accessible and usable as possible.
3. *Broader beneficial impact.* This refers to going beyond the intended beneficiary of the design to "leverage the curb-cut effect."

Inclusive design is closely related to "design justice," which has been described as a human-centered "design with" strategy that advocates for inclusion of diverse stakeholders, ideally as members of a design team (Costanza-Chock, 2020). Design justice emphasizes "collaborative, creative practices" that center "the voices of those directly impacted by the outcomes of the design process" based on the principles that "everyone is an expert based on their own lived experience" and that "we all have unique and brilliant contributions to bring to a design process" (Design Justice Network, 2018). A key element of both inclusive design and design justice is the intentional inclusion of individuals who represent a range of identities and perspectives, particularly those who have been excluded in the past. It is this emphasis on a range that forms the foundation for expanded collaboration as described in this book. This requires a design team that includes working towards meeting the needs of diverse stakeholders and learners as meaningful participants throughout the ID process.

Instructional design has always been a "team sport." IDs have long collaborated with clients, content experts, media specialists, trainers, and others to create learning and development interventions. The LeaPS ID model expands this collaboration based on the concepts of "inclusive design" and "design justice." This section describes three guidelines for creating this kind of "expanded collaboration." It's important to note that each guideline refers to being "intentional." The reason is simple—the best way to avoid unintentional exclusion is to practice intentional inclusion.

Guideline 1. *Intentionally Include Individuals Representing Diverse Identities and Groups*

The goal is to go beyond the usual cast of characters and to intentionally include, in particular, people with diverse identities, representative of groups that have routinely been excluded in the past, either intentionally or unintentionally. Cultural relevance should not be focused on geolocation or ethnicity alone, but on identity (an individual's sense of self). One way to intentionally expand a design team is to look for "affinity groups," described as collections of individuals who share a common characteristic or interest as part of their identity. Affinity groups can form around a wide variety of common characteristics or interests.

In workplace settings the most useful affinity groups often form among people who feel discriminated against, underrepresented, marginalized, or who desire more connections or support within the workforce. For example, affinity groups may form based on gender, race, nationality, sexual orientation, socioeconomic status, religion, (dis)ability, and so on. Affinity groups have their own "culture" with values, attitudes, beliefs, social norms, practices, and a language that are shared by the members of the group and that contribute to a shared sense of "identity." Members of an affinity group can support one another and provide networking and mentoring opportunities. As part of a learning and development project team, affinity group members can also represent the group, helping others on the project team understand the experiences and concerns of the group (Geist, 2023). This can result in interventions that meet the dual requirements of equity and effectiveness.

Guideline 2. *When Possible, Intentionally Include Individuals with Diverse Identities as Full Participants on the Design Team, to the Point of "Co-Production."*

"Full participation" is an inherently abstract concept, one that is difficult to put into practice. But it can be made more tangible by distinguishing the following four levels of participation (adapted from Stark et al., 2021):

- *Level 1 Consultation.* Stakeholders are asked for opinions, ideas, or concerns, but there is no formal involvement via focus groups, surveys, etc.
- *Level 2 Involvement.* Stakeholders take part in defined activities such as adding to an agenda or the design of instructional methods or activities.
- *Level 3 Participation.* Stakeholders take an active role with more input on decision-making, but the agenda is largely defined and directed by IDs.
- *Level 4 Co-production.* Equal collaboration between IDs and stakeholders, with joint decision-making related to goals, methods, and outcomes.

Guideline 3. *Intentionally Respond to the Cultures these Diverse Individuals Represent*

This goes beyond acknowledging diverse cultures to using the input provided by the individuals as integral parts of the team's work. This requires the skill of facilitation, defined by the Association for Talent Development (ATD, n.d.) as "the act of engaging participants in creating, discovering, and applying learning insights."

Throughout the book, we will use the term *culturally relevant and equitable* to refer to the goal of learning and development interventions that are inclusive, fair, and just for all.

Co-production is the ideal. It takes advantage of the perspectives and insights provided by diverse stakeholders, including learners and the cultures they represent. This means that the resulting intervention is likely to be more effective in two ways. The first is that it will better meet the needs of a broader group of stakeholders and the actual circumstances in which they work. The second is that the stakeholders are more likely to support and use the intervention that they co-produced.

At the same time, co-production presents challenges, primarily because it requires more time and resources. It requires time to assemble a diverse design team; to incorporate more participants in framing the problems and the solutions; to brainstorm various solutions; to resolve differences of opinion among diverse participants; and to arrive at consensus or agreement about how to proceed. So co-production isn't always possible because of time or budget constraints. And it might not be suited for small projects in which the costs outweigh the benefits. It also requires an organization that is open to a collaborative design process that co-production calls for.

So as an instructional designer, work towards interventions that are culturally relevant and equitable. Apply the principle of "expanded collaboration" to the extent possible.

Principle #2: Performance-Based Learning and Development

In simple terms, performance-based learning and development (PBL&D) refers to standardized interventions. Standardized interventions are specifically designed to help individuals acquire the knowledge and skills required to perform particular job-related tasks to a standard of expectations. The focus of PBL&D is "learning by doing." According to Brethower and Smalley (1998), PBL&D reduces the gap between novice and excellent performance. To this end, it employs three main components that are typically presented in sequence (pp. 3–4).

- *Guided observation.* This refers to a series of demonstrations that show learners "why something is done, what is accomplished, and how it is done" (Brethower & Smalley, 1998). Good demonstrations highlight what is critical, difficult, and complex (Merrill, 2002). In addition, good demonstrations show how to recognize situations, make decisions, and solve problems—highlighting the more nuanced and otherwise invisible aspects of a task.
- *Guided practice.* This refers to a series of graduated exercises that allow learners to "practice specific processes that accomplish specific results" (Brethower & Smalley, 1998). As the series progresses, the nature of the tasks increases in difficulty, complexity, or standard of performance. Merrill (2002) notes that learners should receive real-time coaching (immediate identification and correction of errors and missteps). In addition, learners should receive delayed feedback after they perform the task. This kind of "post-mortem" describes both the extent to which the performance met specified standards and how to improve the performance.
- *Demonstration of mastery.* This refers to a test or assessment in which learners show that they have "mastered" the task; that they can perform the task and, thereby, generate the products or services needed in their work (Brethower & Smalley, 1998). Such

mastery tests show clients and other organizational stakeholders that, at the end of the intervention, learners are able to perform their job tasks in ways that meet business goals.

Consistent with the "learning by doing" theme, learning exercises, support materials, and tests are as job-like as time, budget, and ingenuity allow" (Brethower & Smalley, 1998, p. 7). Job tasks include anything requiring decision-making that's relevant to performance in professional education, or other organizational, volunteer, and work settings. Learners master *decision-making* in relevant job tasks by performing them until they can show they can complete the tasks and meet stated standards without receiving any help.

PBL&D offers several notable advantages.

- *It prioritizes critical "need-to-know" skills over "nice-to-know" information.* The focus of all three components is on making decisions in "authentic" situations (or as close to authentic as safety and economic feasibility allow) and meeting the performance standards used in the work setting. Infrequently used information is often included in job aids (print or online) that can be used on the job.
- *It's efficient.* Each of the three components typically lasts only as long as needed— demonstrations that provide just enough guidance to allow learners to begin practicing and enough practice, with coaching and feedback as needed, to enable learners to master the necessary *decision-making skills.* This allows learners to achieve high levels of performance quickly and return to the work setting. Real learning begins when learners start performing job tasks during practice exercises. Seen in this way, practice exercises are simulations relevant to decision-making and job tasks.
- *It promotes learning transfer by providing safe and authentic learning environments for learners to build job skills and apply them to the work setting in ways that produce valued behavior change on the job.* PBL&D typically includes activities that can be used towards the end of the intervention and/or back on the job to support skill retention. This requires the coordinated efforts of learners, supervisors, and managers.
- *It's applicable to any delivery mode,* including: instructor-led (or classroom) training; structured on-the-job training; blended learning/virtual classroom training; eLearning; self-paced workbooks; and so on.

At the same time, PBL&D presents several challenges. Specifically, it requires:

- *A focus on delivering workforce performance that meets specified measures.* Seen this way, the purpose of learning is to produce work setting behaviors that meet specified standards. These measures either appear in a previously conducted needs assessment or are specified early in an L&D project in collaboration with the client and other organizational stakeholders.
- *Adequate organizational sponsorship.* This means clients and other organizational stakeholders who will work with IDs to create, implement, and maintain the intervention.

- *Access to extant data and job incumbent*s who may participate in observations, group and individual interviews, and surveys along with access to subject matter experts (SMEs) who are exemplary performers.
- *Time and effort* to coordinate iterative reviews and tests of interventions.

THE LEAPS ID MODEL

Instructional design is a systematic and systemic process for creating learning and development materials. It is systematic in that it is organized and methodical. The outputs of previous activities become the inputs for subsequent ones. It is systemic in that it is made up of interrelated and interacting parts working together to achieve a common goal (a "system").

The LeaPS ID model is based on two important assumptions. The first is that someone in the organization has already conducted a needs assessment that has identified a skill gap that PBL&D can address. In specifying desired performance, the needs assessment provides detailed and achievable measures describing successful work setting behaviors—what learners who successfully complete the training will do on the job. If there is no needs assessment, then IDs, clients, and other stakeholders need to specify these measures early in the project. Discussions to set these measures should occur when these individuals begin discussing the proposed training. The second assumption is that the organization will provide a client who can sponsor the training project. More information about these two important assumptions appears in Chapter 4 and the discussion of a training requirements analysis.

As shown in Figure 1.1, the LeaPS ID model describes this systematic and systemic process as a set of three interrelated components, represented by circles: Empathize & Analyze; Design & Develop; Implement & Evaluate. The process is carried out within three larger, surrounding systems, represented by rectangles: project management; inclusive design in organizations; and government, economy, and cultures.

The bottom part of the figure shows the three components overlapping in different ways. The three components are dynamic. They shift back and forth to meet the needs of a particular project. For example, one project might progress in a largely sequential way: empathize/analyze followed by design/develop followed by implement/evaluate. Another project might progress with overlapping activities: design/develop taking place at the same time as empathize/analyze. And another project might progress with repeating activities: empathize/analyze might be followed by design/develop with a return to empathize/analyze perhaps because of a question or concern about some aspect of the design. The essential point is that the LeaPS ID model (and the ID process, more generally), is not always linear and sequential. And it's not static. It can be adapted to meet the requirements of a particular project and can be further adapted as the requirements of a project change.

If the LeaPS ID model seems complex and difficult to understand at first, consider this analogy. The LeaPS ID model is like a large metropolitan hospital. Both a hospital and the LeaPS ID model are "systems"—sets of interconnected parts working together towards a common purpose. As illustrated in Figure 1.2, a hospital is made up of a number of interconnected departments in which people with different skills, using a variety

Learning and Performance Support (LeaPS) ID model

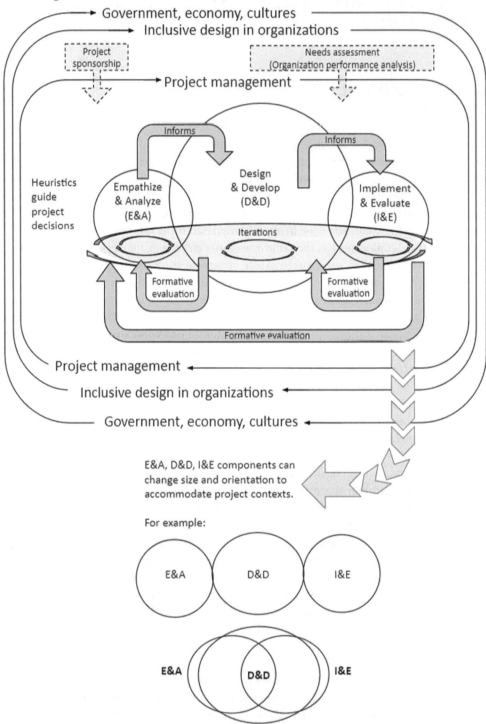

FIGURE 1.1 Learning and Performance Support (LeaPS) ID model.

of tools, engage in ongoing, purposeful, and dynamic interactions, all with the common goal of patient health. In the same way, the LeaPS ID model is made up of a number of interconnected components in which people with different skills and using a variety of tools engage in ongoing, purposeful, and dynamic interactions, all with the common goal of improving organizational performance. Note that the goals are slightly different and the "departments," people, and tools are different. But the essential similarity is that both involve a set of interrelated and interacting parts that work together to achieve a common purpose. In both, the interactions may involve different people and tools at different times or the same people and tools at multiple times. Either way, the interactions are ongoing and dynamic, depending on the requirements at the time. Chapter 2 will introduce the "cast of characters" who might be involved in an ID project.

As a system, the LeaPS ID model is made up of interconnected components and surrounded by three larger systems that influence and constrain the particular ID project.

Four Components

Empathize & Analyze

The purpose of this component is to understand, as fully as possible, the situation in which the particular ID project will be carried out, the players who will help carry it out, and the people who will use the resulting intervention. This includes:

- *Empathize.* As thoroughly as possible, understand the learners who will participate in or use the intervention. The purpose is to reveal the existing diverse identities,

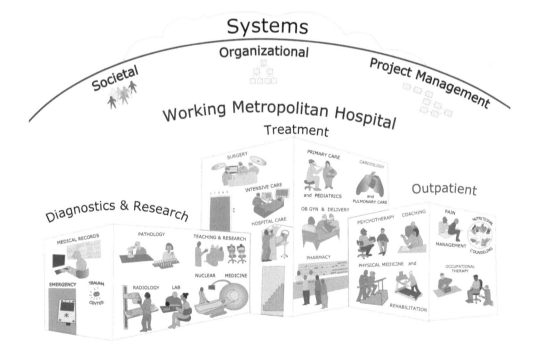

FIGURE 1.2 A working metropolitan hospital. Used with permission from Lynn Kearny, artist.

relevant motivations, pain points, goals, knowledge and skills of the learners, along with the norms, practices, language, concerns, etc. of the social, cultural, or affinity groups those learners belong to.

- *Analyze.* As thoroughly as possible, understand the existing problem the proposed intervention is meant to solve and the organizational situation in which that program will be created and implemented. This is done with a training requirements analysis, task analysis, and environmental analysis that considers the three larger systems that will both influence and constrain the project.

Empathizing and analyzing are dynamic and overlapping. Information will often result in additional questions, which will lead to new insights about the learners or the organization, which will lead to more questions, and so on.

Design & Develop

The purpose of this component is to create a set of specifications (a "design document" or "blueprint") for the planned intervention, prototype, or test, and finalize a set of materials based on those specifications. This includes:

- *Design.* Create the specifications, based on a collection of "design decisions" made in consultation with clients/sponsors, learners, and other relevant people. This is done with a learning/performance requirements analysis (overlaps with the training requirements analysis from the Empathize & Analyze stage), planning for learning/performance outcomes and objectives, implementation, an assessment, and transfer of learning to performance.
- *Develop.* Create the materials described in the specifications. Primary activities include materials such as job aids, instructor and participant guides, photos, tables, drawings, and other visual materials, handouts, eLearning materials, apps, and assessments.

Design and development are dynamic and overlapping. Developing the materials is likely to change details in the plan and reconsidering the plan is likely to change details in the materials. A common analogy for this is building a house. Work begins with blueprint plans. But on-the-ground construction often changes details in the blueprint, and some plan details (related, for example, to the structural requirements of a local building code) may require changes in on-the-ground construction.

Implement & Evaluate

The purpose of this component is to put the developed materials to use and evaluate the results against the performance requirements from the Design & Develop component. This includes:

- *Implement.* The purpose of these activities is preparing to "go live" with the developed materials, delivering them using the specified media and instructional approaches.

- *Evaluate.* The purpose of these activities is to assess the developed materials as described by the assessment plan in the other two components in order to revise those materials. Primary activities for formative evaluation include:
  - Reviews of developed materials.
  - Tryouts of the materials.
  - Pilot programs.

Iterations and Formative Evaluations

The LeaPS ID model includes formative evaluation feedback loops for the deliverables produced throughout the components. This is done to emphasize how feedback loops are utilized by IDs to re-envision, adapt, evolve, and change plans based on new information that becomes available as project timelines progress. These include:

- *Iterations.* The purpose of these activities is to solicit both input and feedback on the deliverables that are created as part of the activities IDs undertake during each component. Interviews, participatory activities, and co-design activities are common input mechanisms. Client reviews, expert reviews, and learner tryouts are common feedback mechanisms.
- *Formative evaluations.* The purpose of formative evaluations is to monitor and make improvements to deliverables that have been created throughout the ID process. The goal is to ensure delivery of culturally relevant and equitable interventions that work for all learners.

Three Larger Systems

An essential idea is that ID is itself a system and includes the principles (including systems theory), strategies, tactics, common practices, etc. that guide professional practice. This ID system is embedded within three gradually larger systems. These larger systems both guide and constrain the smaller systems they surround. A key point is that an ID emphasizing DEI might work to stretch the "design affordances" or opportunities that each of these systems offers.

Project Management

This system encompasses the instructional design process and refers to the collected relationships, budget constraints, oversight responsibilities and mechanisms, communication channels, etc. that apply to a particular project. The goal of project management is to provide work that meets client and stakeholder requirements—on time and within budget.

Inclusive Design in Organizations

This system encompasses the project management system and refers to the policies and practices, larger budget considerations, oversight responsibilities and mechanisms, lines of communication, etc. at work in a particular organization.

There are two important points here:

1. The organizational system has both formal and informal components. The formal component refers to established (i.e., usually written) organizational policies and procedures. The informal component refers to the (i.e., often unwritten) practices and language (e.g., common terms, acronyms, shorthand expressions) commonly used in day-to-day operations and interactions.
2. Individuals in the organization are influenced by both the organizational system and the particular society/culture in which they live outside of the organization. These multiple systems might conflict with one another.

Government, Economy, and Cultures

This system encompasses the organizational system and refers to the society and culture in which the organization operates.

There are two important points here:

1. Culture has both formal and informal components. The formal component refers to governmental laws and regulations, oversight agencies and standards, etc. within the region and nation in which the organization operates. The informal component refers to the norms, beliefs, values, practices, language, etc. within the region and nation in which the organization operates.
2. Individuals are influenced by multiple, and sometimes conflicting, cultural systems, influenced by their community, ethnicity or nationality, religion, job, etc.

Heuristics Are "Rules of Thumb"

IDs apply heuristics throughout the LeaPS ID model. These are mental shortcuts or reminders that can guide thinking about a topic or problem. Subsequent chapters will often include heuristics related to the chapter's content.

Here are several heuristics related to the LeaPS ID model:

- ID is a team sport.
- Work towards the dual requirements of interventions that are both equitable and effective.
- Work towards inclusive design through intentionally expanded collaboration.
- Work towards "co-production" whenever possible.
- The ID process is dynamic, changing to meet the changing requirements of a specific project.
- To meet schedule and cost, IDs share operating assumptions with the clients. Then they collect data to either verify or reject the assumptions.
- In any situation, there are typically several ways to do ID right. There are many ways to do it wrong, too.

CASE STUDY

Each chapter in the book will include a case study that asks you to put yourself in the shoes of an ID. The purpose is to provide you with an opportunity to think back over the content in the chapter and how it applies to a particular situation. The case studies are based on actual events, with the details changed for the purpose of anonymity.

Over the last two years, National Security Force (pseudonym) has repeatedly lost all of its new female employees after only a few months on the job at one of their locations, Base Q (pseudonym). However, Base Q was able to retain male employees who came on board at the same time as the females, who were not retained. Base Q has a zero-tolerance policy for gender discrimination, sexual harassment, and sexual assault. When questioned, the male supervisors were unable to identify a problem in the Base Q organizational environment system. Instead, the male supervisors pointed to the individual females' behaviors (e.g., inappropriate use of government resources, insubordination) as the cause for the current separation patterns. Base Q is interested in improving their organizational performance such that they have an equivalent retention rate for new male and female employees. Base Q executive leaders have asked the learning and development department to provide consultation, recommendations, and appropriate learning interventions.

- What would you do to begin assembling a design team to work on this project? In what ways would you try to go beyond the usual cast of characters? Are there particular "affinity groups" that you would look for?
- How do you think employee perceptions of fairness might be at issue? What would you do to begin exploring this question?
- What challenges do you see in applying the principles of "performance-based learning and development" in this case? What would you do to begin building the kind of organizational support required for PBL&D?

REFLECTION QUESTIONS

Each chapter will also include questions to help you build a reflective practice. These can be used as thought exercises or as questions to guide discussions with others. Reflect on ID practice or project decisions that you might have faced or could face in the future. This is an opportunity for you to think back over projects you've worked on, problems you've encountered, and practices you've used, and to identify principles or guidelines that can be used in future ID projects.

- When there's tension between groups of people, or cultures, or ways of working in an organizational system, how can you best facilitate responsive and equitable decisions?
- If organizational members are meeting their learning, development, and performance goals, is it necessary to increase DEI or to change your design process and approaches?

- What should you do if your client or sponsor asks you to create a solution without getting input from the diverse individuals who are affected by a project?
- Is it your responsibility as an ID to ensure that an organization's learning and development interventions are culturally relevant and inclusive? Why or why not?

REFERENCES

Adefela, A. A. (2022). The intersection of L&D and diversity, equity and inclusion. *Training Industry Magazine* (Winter), 38–39. https://trainingindustry.com/magazine/winter-2022/the-intersection-of-ld-and-diversity-equity-and-inclusion

Ambrose, M. L., & Cropanzano, R. (2003). A longitudinal analysis of organizational fairness: An examination of reactions to tenure and promotion decisions. *Journal of Applied Psychology, 88*(2), 266. doi:10.1037/0021–9010.88.2.266

Association for Talent Development (ATD). (n.d.). Talent development glossary terms: What is facilitation? https://www.td.org/talent-development-glossary-terms/what-is-facilitation

Bisson, L. F., Jamison-McClung, D., Grindstaff, L., Katehi, L., & Leon Siantz, M. L. D. (2022). Leadership and organizational structure. In *Uprooting bias in the academy* (pp. 81–95). Springer.

Blackwell, A. G. (2017). The curb cut effect. *Stanford Social Innovation Review*, Winter. https://ssir.org/articles/entry/the_curb_cut_effect

Brethower, D., & Smalley, K. (1998). *Performance-based instruction: Linking training to business results*. Jossey-Bass/Pfieffer.

Conyon, M. J., & He, L. (2017). Firm performance and boardroom gender diversity: A quantile regression approach. *Journal of Business Research, 79*, 198–211. doi:10.1016/j.jbusres.2017.02.006

Costanza-Chock, S. (2020). *Design justice: Community-led practices to build the worlds we need*. The MIT Press. https://library.oapen.org/bitstream/handle/20.500.12657/43542/external_content.pdf

Design Justice Network. (2018). Read the principles. https://designjustice.org/read-the-principles

Doyle, A. (2021). What does a chief diversity officer do? *The Balance*. https://www.thebalancemoney.com/what-does-a-chief-diversity-officer-do-5212087#:~:text=A%20chief%20diversity%20officer%20is%20the%20principal%20architect,as%20well%20as%20diversity%20training%20programs%20for%20employees

Fatt, C. K., Khin, E. W. S., & Heng, T. N. (2010). The impact of organizational justice on employees' job satisfaction: The Malaysian companies perspectives. *American Journal of Economics and Business Administration, 2*(1), 56–63. doi:10.3844/ajebasp.2010.56.63

Geist, S. (2023, March 28). The benefits of affinity groups in the workplace. McGregor Boyall, *Human Resources & Talent Management Blog*. https://www.mcgregor-boyall.com/resources/blog/the-benefits-of-affinity-groups-in-the-workplace/

Giacumo, L. A., MacDonald, M., & Peters, D. T. (2021). Promoting organizational justice in cross-cultural data collection, analysis, and interpretation: Towards an emerging conceptual model. *The Journal of Applied Instructional Design, 10*(4). doi:10.51869/104/lgi

Gomez, L. E., & Bernet, P. (2019). Diversity improves performance and outcomes. *Journal of the National Medical Association, 111*(4), 383–392. doi:10.1016/j.jnma.2019.01.006

Gompers, P., & Kovvali, S. (2018). The other diversity dividend. *Harvard Business Review*, 72–77. https://hbr.org/2018/07/the-other-diversity-dividend

Greenberg, J. (1990). Organizational justice: Yesterday, today, and tomorrow. *Journal of Management, 16*(2), 399–432. doi:10.1177/014920639001600208

Hunt, V., Prince, S., Dixon-Fyle, S., & Yee, L. (2018). *Delivering through diversity*. McKinsey & Company. https://www.mckinsey.com/capabilities/people-and-organizational-performance/our-insights/delivering-through-diversity

Ikeda, R., Nham, K., Armstrong, L., Diec, F., Kim, N., Parada, D., Sanchez, D., Zhen, K., & Robinson, V. (2021). Designing for liberation: A case study in antiracism instructional design. *The Journal of Applied Instructional Design*, *10*(4). doi:10.51869/104/rik

Inclusive Design Research Centre. (n.d.). Philosophy. https://idrc.ocadu.ca/about/philosophy/

Kaufman, R., Watkins, R., Stith, M., & Triner, D. (1998). The changing corporate mind: Organizations, vision, missions, purposes, and indicators on the move toward societal payoffs. *Performance Improvement Quarterly*, *11*(3), 32–44. doi:10.1111/j.1937–8327.1998.tb00098.x

Khan, M. S., Saengon, P., Charoenpoom, S., Soonthornpipit, H., & Chongcharoen, D. (2021). The impact of organizational learning culture, workforce diversity and knowledge management on innovation and organization performance: A structural equation modeling approach. *Human Systems Management*, *40*(1), 103–115. doi:10.3233/HSM-200984

Kopcha, T. J., Asino, T., Giacumo, L. A., & Walters, K. (2021). Preface to the special issue: Attending to issues of social justice through learning design. *The Journal of Applied Instructional Design*, *10*(4). doi:10.51869/104/kop

Latham, G. P., & Pinder, C. C. (2005). Work motivation theory and research at the dawn of the twenty-first century. *Annual Review of Psychology, 56*, 485–516. doi:10.1146/annurev.psych.55.090902.142105

Liu, J. C. (2021). Inclusiveness in instructional design & development of informal learning experiences: From cultural lenses. *The Journal of Applied Instructional Design*, *10*(3). doi:10.51869/103/jcl

Loh, L. Y. H., & Nguyen, M. H. (2018). Board diversity and business performance in Singapore-listed companies the role of corporate governance. *Research Journal of Social Science & Management*, *7*(10), 95–104.

Martin, J. (1991). *Rapid application development*. Macmillan.

Merrill, M. D. (2002). First principles of instruction. *Educational Technology Research & Development*, *50*(3), 43–59. doi:10.1007/BF02505024

Moon, K. K. (2017). Fairness at the organizational level: Examining the effect of organizational justice climate on collective turnover rates and organizational performance. *Public Personnel Management*, *46*(2), 118–143. doi:10.1177/0091026017702610

Oh, S. Y. (2019). Effects of organizational learning on performance: The moderating roles of trust in leaders and organizational justice. *Journal of Knowledge Management*, *33*(2), 313–331. doi:10.1108/JKM-02–2018–0087

Ren, X. (2022). Autoethnographic research to explore instructional design practices for distance teaching and learning in a cross-cultural context. *TechTrends*, *66*(1), 47–55. doi:10.1007/s11528-021-00683-9

Sartti, D. (2019). Balancing organizational justice and leader–member exchange to engage workforce. *Journal of Workplace Learning*, *31*(3), 231–246. doi:10.1108/JWL-09–2018–0116

Smith, P. L., & Ragan, T. J. ([1999]2004). *Instructional design* (3rd ed.). John Wiley & Sons.

Stark, E., Ali, D., Ayre, A., Schneider, N., Parveen, S., Marais, K., . . . & Pender, R. (2021). Coproduction with autistic adults: Reflections from the authentistic research collective. *Autism in Adulthood*, *3*(2), 195–203. doi:10.1089/aut.2020.0050

Strommel, J. (2021). Foreword. In Thurston, T. N., Lundstrom, K., & González, C. (Eds), *Resilient pedagogy: Practical teaching strategies to overcome distance, disruption, and distraction*. Utah State University. doi:10.26079/a516-fb24

Young, P. (2021). *Human specialization in design and technology: The current wave for learning, culture, industry, and beyond*. Routledge.

Yusop, F. D., & Correia, A. P. (2012). The civic-minded instructional designers framework: An alternative approach to contemporary instructional designers' education in higher education. *British Journal of Educational Technology*, *43*(2), 180–190. doi:10.1111/j.1467–8535.2011.01185.x

CHAPTER 2

Introducing ID Projects

INTRODUCTION

Organizations undertake instructional design (ID) projects to create, implement, and maintain instructional, learning, and performance support materials. In doing so, individual instructional designers (IDs) often collaborate with other IDs, sponsors, clients, learners, subject matter experts (SMEs) and others. All of this collaboration and co-ordination requires organizations to manage their projects. Figure 2.1 depicts the role of project management in relation to other ID systems in the LeaPS ID model. Project management resides within the larger system of the organization. And organizations and the projects they manage exist within the larger systems of government, economy, culture, and society.

By itself, the management of instructional design is a big topic. By the end of this chapter, you will be able to:

- Describe a few common elements of project management that typically involve instructional designers and their projects.
- Describe the roles typically involved in ID projects, including their responsibilities and the project management tools they often use.
- Apply ID project management approaches that are culturally relevant and inclusive.

ID PROJECT MANAGEMENT

The creation of learning and performance support materials is no simple task. Each situation demands its own ID project. Ideally, each of these projects begins with:

- The realization that there is a performance gap, or discrepancy, between the actual system performance and the desired system performance.
- A decision that the performance gap is worth closing.
- A conclusion that the solutions to the root causes of the gap include adequate guidance describing how to perform the job or skill along with necessary knowledge development.

DOI: 10.4324/9781003360612-2

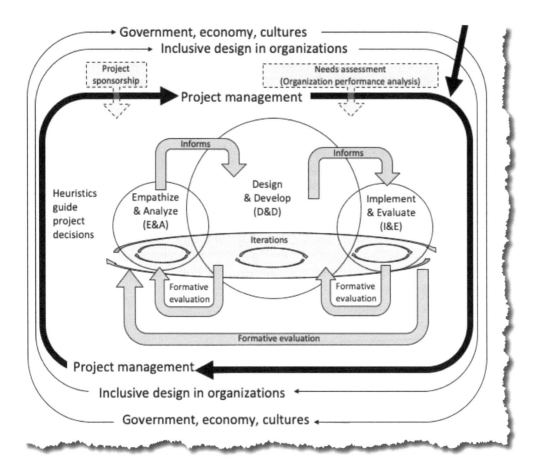

FIGURE 2.1 Project management in the LeaPS ID model.

Based on these considerations, an organization decides to invest its resources (e.g., time, money, effort) to create instructional and non-instructional interventions (i.e., learning experiences, training, and performance support materials). ID project management responsibilities include managing relationships with team members and stakeholders. In addition, IDs often contribute project management documentation and updates for larger project scopes, which they may create themselves, collaboratively, or cooperatively with others.

How to Center an Anti-Deficit Human Perspective in Performance Improvement

Diverse people and learners are assets in organizations. They bring different identities, experiences, approaches, perspectives, etc. to the table, which enable creativity and innovation. However, the organizational system and its subsystems may not provide adequate support (e.g., training, feedback, guidance) for specific desired performances either at the environmental level or individual work level. That's when you notice opportunities for better interventions to address some system or subsystem deficits.

Here's why: Organizations are actually systems made up of many different subsystems. Performance gaps are found in the system or subsystems of organizations. A performance gap can describe a deficit in an existing capacity or an opportunity to build new capacity. The root cause may be found at the environmental and/or work levels in the larger system or components of its subsystem(s).

The learning and development (L&D) function is one subsystem of a larger organizational system. Hence, better L&D [subsystem] interventions can help improve organizational system performance gaps at the environmental or worker levels. Therefore, be sure to focus your performance gap root cause analysis on the organization's system and subsystems' performance at both the environmental and individual level. After all, we are trying to change the organization's system and subsystems to better support diverse learners.

The Business Case

Owing to their complexity, L&D groups typically build business cases for ID projects to create the learning and performance interventions. Typically, senior personnel are responsible for creating these cases.

To determine if a given performance gap is worth closing, a business case will typically argue that the benefits that the organization will receive from creating, implementing, and maintaining the intervention are greater than the associated costs of letting the gap exist. To determine the return on this investment, they may use a calculation like this (Phillips & Phillips, 2007):

ROI (%) = ($value of the benefits/total program costs) × 100

Seen this way, the value of the benefits the organization gets from training should exceed the cost of creating the training. And the difference between the two can shape the total budget for completing the project (i.e., the money that the organization is willing to spend).

The Project Plan

Organizational sponsors pay for the work IDs complete. Sometimes, a project's sponsor and client are different people. Clients have approval power. Other times, a project's sponsor and client can be the same person. This means that IDs have a professional responsibility to deliver what clients and sponsors expect, when they expect it, at the price they expect. Most sponsors will have some sort of overall cost in mind associated with a given ID project. This overall cost could be the product of a preliminary needs assessment, a detailed estimation activity, or a given amount of money they have in mind. Sponsors also typically have a sense of when they need the project completed and the resources they can make available to the ID team. In most organizations, more experienced IDs begin using these parameters to create a plan for a given project. While these project plans can vary from one organization to the next, and with the complexity of a given project, they typically include a detailed:

- *Project scope.* Also sometimes called a "scope of work," this includes a master list of what needs to be done to complete the project. Specifically, the project scope specifies all the tasks that the ID team will undertake to complete the project, generally in the order in which they will complete them. A project scope can also specify potentially related tasks that the project team will not complete because the client and sponsor have agreed that they shouldn't be part of the project (Wiley et al., 2022). Some of these tasks involve creating ID "project deliverables"—plans, reports, draft materials, or other tangible things (either print or electronic), given to clients at various points during the project. Other tasks involve managing the ID project itself. For each task, the project scope specifies the ID responsible for completing it. The project scope may also specify when sponsors, clients, SMEs, learners, and other stakeholders will review and test ID project deliverables.
- *Budget.* Each line in the budget corresponds to the cost of completing a task in the project scope. The budget specifies the time allotted to each ID to complete a given task. Multiplying the time by the ID's rate produces a value for the given task. The total values for all of the items in the project scope should be equal to the budget for the project.
- *Schedule.* To coordinate the work of the ID team, clients, sponsors, SMEs, and learners, a schedule lists the days for starting and completing each item in the project scope. IDs know when they will begin working to create a given project deliverable. SMEs know when they will need to review it. Sponsors, clients, and learners know when they will then need to review it.

In many organizations, more experienced IDs create project plans. If you have to create one, you'll want to keep the overall project budget in mind. It can be difficult to plan projects around the resources that will be available. You'll gain expertise in this area the longer you work on ID projects and learn that each organization handles this differently. When doing this for the first time, or in a new-to-you organization, it's a good idea to network with other IDs and find out how they plan projects around budgets. Check with managers and leaders in your organization, too. Ask them for copies of similar project plans that you can use as models for the project plan you need to create.

Table 2.1 displays part of a project scope for the Empathize & Analyze component deliverables for a hypothetical project involving a single ID paid $36/hour. Of course, the tasks appearing in a project scope, along with the assigned personnel, their rates, and hours will vary from one organization and one project to the next. All the same, a project scope will typically contain this type of information and show a total cost for the project based on the accumulated cost of completing each task.

Throughout the duration of the project, ID project managers, sponsors, and clients will monitor the team's actual progress completing the project. IDs and project team members typically report the time they spend on the project each week, and these reports will indicate where the project is on schedule and within budget—and where

TABLE 2.1 Sample project scope

Task	Staff	Rate	Hours	Cost
Phase 1: Empathize & Analyze				
1.1 Conduct a training requirements analysis	ID	$36	8	$288
1.2 Revise learning requirements analysis based on client feedback	ID	$36	4	$144
1.3 Conduct a task analysis	ID	$36	16	$576
1.4 Revise the task analysis based on results of a learner tryout	ID	$36	4	$144
1.5 Conduct a learner and environmental analysis	ID	$36	16	$576
1.6 Revise the learner and environmental analysis based on client and subject matter expert review	ID	$36	4	$144
Subtotal				$1,872

Note: Median US salary for instructional designers in September 2022 was USD $78,130/year according to Glassdoor.com (e.g., ~$36/hr for 40 hours a week for 52 weeks a year).

it isn't. This situation is common. And, as more information becomes available in the project, its project plan will likely have to change as well.

Scope Creep

To be successful, an ID team will need to deliver quality deliverables specified in the project scope, both on time and within budget. While this project management goal appears straightforward, achieving it can be wickedly difficult. For instance, IDs trying to be relevant to their clients and sponsors may:

- Overpromise what they can deliver, producing deliverables of poor quality and behind schedule.
- Create interventions that learners don't need or overly fancy multimedia that clients may not want to pay for. Producing higher quality than necessary can quickly break the project budget and the project schedule.
- Experience client-caused delays in being able to obtain data or input required to create project deliverables. Such delays can break the project schedule, and starting and stopping work repeatedly can increase the project budget.
- Agree to all client requests, leading to a situation where IDs have added new tasks to their project scope without adding the additional budget or lengthened schedule to support them.

These situations, where the number of tasks in the project scope or the time in the schedule have increased without corresponding increases to the budget, are called "scope creep." To be successful, most ID projects must employ project management approaches. In some organizations, project managers are more experienced IDs who manage project teams. In other organizations, a team of IDs may report to a dedicated project manager who isn't an ID.

To keep your project management on track, you may at times need to make business decisions. These can include when the new information will result in a change order to your statement of work and when it should inform the next generation of deliverables, or a new project scope. As you gain experience, you will determine how to know when to do a change order and when to leave it for a new project.

Consider the Impact of Working New Information into Your Project After Deliverable Sign-Off

IDs should do right by their clients and stakeholders. However, sometimes new information will require IDs to pause and consider whether or not they can go forwards with a new iteration. If you can still meet deadlines and keep within the budget, then it's something to consider within the current project scope. If it would drastically change your ability to meet deadlines or work within the budget, then it's time to talk with the client or project manager about a potential change order.

Project Scale

The scope of different ID projects can vary widely in scale. The types of deliverables that IDs will create affect the scale of the project. It's likely that a single ID wouldn't always be able to create, implement, and maintain a large-scale learning program composed of multiple interacting components. Furthermore, an ID team, SMEs, learners, supervisors, and managers would also need adequate organizational sponsorship to harness their efforts to create such programs. In a similar manner, a single ID couldn't bring forth a larger-scale learning and performance ecosystem, either. Instead, multiple IDs would probably need to partner with others throughout the organization, including people in the Information Technology group, to create, implement, and maintain such an ecosystem.

A small piece of "microlearning" (i.e., a very short, concise learning unit) might involve the work of a single ID and a small budget of a few hundred or thousand US dollars. A medium-sized project might involve the work of several ID team members who produce one or a few longer lessons or modules for a few thousand or tens of thousands of dollars. A large project might involve multiple ID teams creating one or more curricula consisting of multiple modules for hundreds of thousands or millions of dollars. And the larger the scale and budget of the project, the more complex its management will be. ID projects typically involve these project management activities, which will vary across project scale:

- *Monitoring, assessing, and mitigating risks to project completion.* Any project worth completing faces risks that threaten its successful completion. Depending on the organization's culture and project complexity, project managers may use different techniques to identify and manage risks as they arise. In smaller projects, these risks may not even arise—or require less sophisticated techniques to manage them.
- *Communicating with different project players.* The bigger the project, the more people will be involved. And the more people, the more communication will be needed to

coordinate their efforts. Smaller projects typically require less communication with fewer people.

- *Scheduling and coordinating the completion of different project deliverables.* Larger projects involve multiple parts in movement at any given time. IDs may be creating some deliverables at the same time other IDs are conducting reviews of other deliverables and still other IDs are testing other deliverables. The larger the project, the more scheduling will be needed to coordinate the completion of the project scope.
- *Reporting about project status.* The bigger the project, the more people will be involved in reporting the status of their efforts to other people involved in the project. Sponsors, clients, project managers, and IDs use regular status reports, the weekly time reports that IDs submit, and other reports to determine the overall status of the project and whether the project manager needs to address any issues involving scope creep. The larger the project, the more people will be involved in creating and using this reporting.

CAST OF CHARACTERS

Because ID is a team sport, IDs can work with a wide-ranging cast of characters. Table 2.2 depicts some of them.

Instructional Designers

As an instructional designer working on an ID project, you will probably work as part of a team. The team may include just you, a client, and a SME. Or the team may include multiple IDs, graphic artists, a client, a sponsor, multiple SMEs, learners, or other ID team roles (e.g., see below). You will be in charge of completing specific tasks in the project scope and creating deliverables. In smaller projects and organizations, you may be involved in completing all or most of the project tasks and creating all or most of the project deliverables. In larger projects and organizations, you may be involved in only those tasks and deliverables that a project manager assigns. As a contributing [or the only] ID, you will need to lead yourself. Part of this will involve defining your own professional and personal values and making decisions that align with them. No matter how you look at it, ID is usually a team sport. It would be prudent to assume good intentions, act transparently, be diplomatic, and act ethically. The following organizations provide additional guidance in their own professional standards and ethical codes that you can find on their websites:

- International Society for Performance Improvement (ISPI).
- Association for Educational Communications & Technology (AECT).
- Association for Talent Development (ATD).

Be equitable. Be kind. Be inclusive. Be collaborative. Focus on solutions and customer service. Make reasonable assumptions, and then collect the necessary data to either validate or jettison them. Respect other people's expertise, and listen to others for understanding.

TABLE 2.2 ID project roles, responsibilities, and tools

Roles	Responsibilities	Tools
Instructional Designers	• Contribute to an ID team • Work in a way that is professional, equitable, kind, and responsive • Organize assigned project tasks • Create assigned project deliverables • Collect and analyze data to complete LeaPS ID model components • Facilitate ID project processes (e.g., learner, client, and stakeholder reviews; tests of project deliverables)	• ID project templates • eLearning authoring tools • Project scope • Schedule • Budget • ID project templates • Team charters • Project status reviews
ID Project Managers	• Coordinate with sponsors and clients on a regular basis • Manage ID teams • Ensure ID teams complete the tasks in the project scope • Ensure ID teams submit quality deliverables on time and within budget • Avoid scope creep	• Project scope • Schedule • Budget • Project status reviews
ID Team members	• Coordinate with ID project managers • Coordinate with sponsors and clients • Collect and analyze data to complete LeaPS phases • Create project deliverables	• Project scope • Schedule • Budget • Project templates • Team charters • Project status reviews
Sponsor	• Owns the project budget • Coordinates with the client and ID project manager as needed • Expects to see learners perform their jobs better • Ensures project deliverables align with the organization's strategic business objectives • Exercises final approval authority; makes final decisions when SMEs, clients, or IDs disagree	• Project scope • Schedule • Budget • Project status reviews
Client	• Coordinates with the sponsor and ID project manager on a regular basis • Expects to see learners perform their jobs better • Provides access to data sources the ID team needs to create project deliverables • Reviews and approves project deliverables, ensuring they fit the organizational culture, across the organization's multiple sites • Provides release time for learners, SMEs, and other stakeholders to participate in reviews and tests of project deliverables	• Project scope • Schedule • Budget • Project status reviews
Learners	• Provide data to IDs via surveys and interviews • Review ID project deliverables • Test ID project deliverables • Use the learning and performance support materials to build new skills and knowledge • Apply what they've learned back on the job	• Not applicable
Subject Matter Experts (SMEs)	• Work with ID teams to create a representation of their work setting performance • Review project deliverables to ensure their technical accuracy, completeness, and authenticity	• Schedule • Project templates

(Continued)

TABLE 2.2 (Continued)

Roles	Responsibilities	Tools
Evaluators	• Work with ID team, client, and stakeholders to specify measures that describe successful work setting performance • Create an evaluation plan • Implement the evaluation plan • Report evaluation results	• Measures • Evaluation plan • Evaluation report
Stakeholders	• Review ID project deliverables • Participate in tests of ID project deliverables	• Not applicable

As an ID, you will probably be creating or using a set of templates to complete projects. Well-designed templates can help IDs create more effective project deliverables more efficiently. And most IDs will modify these templates as needed. In other words, the templates themselves are often flexible. IDs typically use, modify, and improve them as they need.

Towards Inclusive Design in ID Practice: Culturally Relevant and Equitable Results

To create organizationally just interventions, address these diversity, equity, and inclusion (DEI) considerations in your own ID practice. Gamrat, Tiwari, and Bekiroglu (2022) contend that IDs should begin with introspection. They suggest that IDs should reflect on:

- Their professional identities—which describe how they see themselves in the workforce, as well as their personal identities beyond the workforce.
- The cultural influences (worldview) that guide them. These influences can come from communities, education, religion, geography, socioeconomic status, gender, ethnicity, etc.
- The organizational cultures that IDs influence and attend to power dynamics, which are informed by their formal and informal social and organizational positions. Instructional designers who create performance-based interventions are disruptive influencers. The very training they create often changes people's roles or how they perform their job tasks.

Adefela (2022) recommends that IDs look outward to the organization and their role in supporting DEI and organizational justice. She suggests that IDs:

- *Review what their organization says about DEI both internally and externally.* This would include web pages containing the organization's mission, vision, and values, along with presentations and articles that the organization's executives have delivered. IDs may also want to review existing materials that the organization's Human Resources (HR) department or employee resource groups have created.
- *Conduct a review of the professional literature.* IDs should identify relevant articles and evidence-based practices they can apply to their organization's learning and development programs. IDs can also review what organizations similar to theirs are doing (and not doing) in ways that help them identify trends and best practices.

- *Help your organizations build inclusive structures.* If an organization already has a DEI or resource group, IDs can start attending their meetings. IDs can participate in company-wide open forums and raise DEI concerns to HR and business partners. IDs could even establish an email mailbox to share DEI concerns and provide a safe place to discuss DEI experiences and concerns.

ID Project Managers

ID teams often report to project managers. In some organizations, project managers may also be experienced IDs responsible for completing different tasks in the project scope. In other organizations, project managers may focus on managing several ID teams and their projects, rather than completing any ID work themselves. Regardless, ID project managers communicate and coordinate with sponsors, clients, and ID teams for the duration of the project. They are responsible for ensuring that ID teams complete tasks, meet quality standards, stay within the budget, and keep on schedule. They hold formal accountability for preventing scope creep. They monitor project completion and review project status. They work with clients and the ID team to adjust project scope, schedule, and budget as needed.

Exceptional project managers also meet their leadership responsibilities. They create trusting spaces for their teams to complete their work, and they keep the team safe from organizational politics. They listen, innovate, inspire, develop, and nurture their people. They communicate continuously and transparently. They hold themselves and others accountable. They are authentic and professional. Articulating shared values and building consensus on decisions is a PM responsibility.

Towards Design Justice in ID Project Management Practice

A recent survey from the Project Management Institute (2020) reported that 88 percent of project leaders agreed that culturally diverse and gender diverse teams increase project value. ID project managers can work with their clients and ID teams to ensure organizational justice and DEI, in the team that undertakes a given ID project.

Booker (2021) notes that organizations and their project managers may use a variety of different project management methodologies, such as Agile, Lean, Kanban, or Waterfall. They may use a variety of techniques to visualize the work, including Gantt Charts, Burndown Charts, or Critical Path Charts. These methods and techniques enable project managers and teams "to eliminate confusion, define decision-making, strengthen communication, and improve outcomes." Organizational justice and DEI are neither a project management methodology nor a visualization technique. However, ID project managers can apply these principles to early stages of project planning by identifying the people who will be involved in the project and the roles they will play. Applying these principles can help project managers ensure:

- The roles that people will play in the project are as diverse as they need be to adequately represent the organization.
- Project personnel can make the decisions they need to deliver a success story.

ID project managers often decide who will play what roles on the project. By creating a RASCI matrix of project personnel, ID project managers can determine who is:

- *Responsible* for creating given deliverables.
- *Accountable* for task completion, approving deliverables, and making final decisions.
- *Supportive* by providing resources, information, or generally helping to get the work done.
- *Consulted* to provide insight and opinions before a decision or action.
- *Informed* to keep them up to date after decisions or actions.

Having created the matrix, project managers can review it to determine if there is a diverse set of people working on the project and whether inclusion of diverse identities has been overlooked, including women, members of minoritized racial or ethnic groups, LGBTQA+, abilities, and so on. For ID project managers, these roles can include both SMEs and learners who will review deliverables and participate in tests of draft deliverables, instructional materials, and performance support materials. ID project managers often ask their teams to review matrices like these. In these situations, IDs and project managers can reach a consensus making sure that they aren't missing any potential team members or stakeholders.

ID Team

ID is a team sport, and most IDs work as part of a team. Much like a sports team, some members may play similar roles from one project to the next, while others play different roles. While the workload for a given project might not be exactly equally distributed, the project will likely involve all team members along the way. Depending on the nature of a project, an ID team may involve, but is not limited to:

- Project managers.
- Instructional designers of different experience levels.
- SMEs.
- Graphic designers, who create artwork that will appear in printed and online instructional and performance support materials.
- Web and multimedia developers, who create instructional videos and eLearning materials.
- Videographers and audio technicians who record digital video for use in video and eLearning materials.
- Voice artists who narrate digital video and eLearning.
- Actors who may appear in digital materials.
- Application developers who may program online software and mobile apps for learners to use.
- Copy editors, who review printed and online materials to ensure they don't contain spelling and grammatical errors.

Sometimes team members will use a "divide and conquer" approach to work cooperatively. For example, IDs may create storyboards, and then web and multimedia developers may create eLearning materials. At other times, team members will work in parallel. For example, IDs could use Google Docs to create an eLearning storyboard. As they write the script, graphic artists create the artwork. In another example from a larger project, different ID teams could begin working on different parts of a project at the same time, with each team responsible for creating a different module.

Effective and inclusive ID teams *believe every member is needed*; they learn to build on others' ideas and negotiate how to complete assigned tasks. They make space for each other to build relationships. IDs work best when they develop supportive, healthy, professional relationships quickly. In your meetings, you'll need time for introductions when working with new people. Also, you'll need time for sharing personal interests and experiences that relate to your work throughout a project.

The best team experiences happen when each person on the team values others' perspectives and input, is able to build on others' ideas, agrees on workflow and expectations, negotiates with transparency, assumes good intentions, follows through, and is fair and respectful. If team members don't perform well in these areas, the team experience will likely be affected.

ID Team Tools

ID teams use a variety of tools to complete their work. The project scope, schedule, and budget should guide their efforts. If a team feels they are beginning to experience scope creep, or their client is unhappy with their work, or contributors are missing deadlines, they should escalate the issue to their project manager immediately. Like IDs, teams often use project templates (e.g., team charters, status reports).

Team charters. Savvy teams often employ charters to map out their shared ID project journey. A team charter specifies how a team of people will work together successfully. Often these charters consist of three major sections that work together to provide guidance that ID teams can use to coordinate their efforts. Answering "yes" to each of these questions can indicate a useful team charter.

- Project success specification

    - Is the team's stated mission reasonable and useful?
    - Are the stated critical success factors (CSFs) reasonable and useful?
    - Do the team's lessons learned in other projects lead to reasonable lessons learned that appear useful for this project?

- Project management

    - Does the charter provide complete, reasonable, and useful methods for:
        - Managing team roles and responsibilities?
        - Coordinating the team's efforts?
        - Managing team communications?

- Project teaming

    - Does the charter provide complete, reasonable, and useful methods for:
        - Establishing team accountabilities?
        - Recognizing and resolving team conflict?
        - Continuously improving how the team performs?

Team Project Status Reports. ID teams typically provide status reports to project managers, sponsors, or clients. These reports vary across different organizations and projects. This said, it's fairly common for status reports to include:

- A summary of the project status to date that describes the extent to which the project is producing quality deliverables on time and within budget.
- Answers to questions like this: What parts of the project:
  - Have the team completed?
  - Are in progress?
  - Will the team work on next?

Status reports may also contain information about actual or potential roadblocks that the team wants to communicate and what the team plans to do to work through them. To this end, status reports can contain answers to questions such as:

- What obstacles has the team run into so far and how did it work through or around them?
- What potential obstacles does the team see related to what it will be working on next?
- What, if any, help will the team need to overcome the obstacle(s)?

Towards Design Justice in ID Team Practice

Let the goal of design justice guide your work. At every step of the way, your ID team should be asking the following questions: Would all SMEs and learners involved in reviewing and testing project deliverables be equally burdened by the:

- L&D intervention design; both affordances and disaffordances?
- Processes your team uses to complete the ID project? The resources you include or leave out from the instructional and performance support materials?
- Materials or products your team creates, modifies, or selects?

Some reflection question to ask yourself, and act on, might include, but are not limited to:

- Is the team working with diverse identities in all roles (e.g., SMEs, learners, team members)?
- Does participating in the project pose an undue burden on any particular group?
- Are the processes accessible and inclusive for individuals with diverse identities?
- Are the inputs from contributors appropriately recognized?
- Are the contributors appropriately compensated?

Sponsors and Clients

IDs complete projects on behalf of their sponsors and clients. In some organizations, sponsors own ID project budgets. They are responsible for ensuring the alignment of the project with the organization's strategic business objectives. Because they own the budget, they exercise final approval authority as they accept ID project deliverables. While they're typically not involved in managing the project when everything is going well, they often have the final voice in settling any disputes when IDs, clients, and SMEs disagree.

Clients are involved in managing the "organization's side" of the ID project. They are often most concerned with operational performance. To this end, they regularly coordinate with project managers to ensure the project is delivering quality deliverables, on time, and within budget. Much of this coordination involves scheduling release time for people in the organization to review deliverables and test them. It also involves providing release time for successful performers to act as SMEs and for them to be available when the ID team needs them. Clients may also work with project managers to arrange for learners to complete surveys or interviews related to the ID project. Clients also provide access to relevant extant data the organization already possesses that may be useful to the ID team. Clients often review all project deliverables, ensuring that they align with business objectives, fit the organization's culture, and will work across multiple sites.

In many organizations, the project's sponsor and client are the same person. Moving forwards, this text will use the term "client" to refer to a single person performing both the sponsor and client roles.

Ideally, the client will be your ally in cases where you need access to resources or people. Hopefully, they can also fill you in on what keeps executive and senior leaders (and the clients themselves) up at night. In a general sense, they worry about whether the organization is bringing in sufficient revenue and controlling costs in ways that keep the organization financially viable. They worry about meeting the terms of their performance goals or bonuses. They also worry about timely issues that can affect the organization's strategic objectives. These concerns can include (Cerius Executives, n.d.):

- *Innovation*. Keeping the organization relevant and offering products customers want.
- *People*. Finding and cultivating high-performing talent that shares the organization's vision.
- *Money*. Sustaining monetary stability in a rapidly changing world. Adjusting budgets for multiple years.
- *Growing healthy relationships*. Taking the time to understand and communicate with business partners to maintain and grow inclusive, flexible, solution-focused, professional relationships, both in-house and externally.
- *Customers*. Ensuring that customers are happy to spend money for the products and services they purchase.

Regardless of the size of the project, it's wise for clients and ID project managers to share regular and honest communication about the status of the project, including work completed, work underway, and work planned. The two should also work together to identify and mitigate sources of risk that threaten project quality, schedule, and budget. This includes access to timely and relevant data, reviews of project deliverables, and potential changes to the project scope. Should a change to the scope of the project arise, the client and the ID project manager should employ an agreed-upon process to define the change and estimate its impact on the project budget and schedule. Ultimately, the client either approves or rejects the proposed change to the project's scope. And not having such a project/scope change process in place is a recipe for scope creep!

Learners

Because ID is a team sport, the ID team should be collaborating with learners throughout a given project. The LeaPS ID model itself is based on the practice of collaborative analysis and design, which originated at IBM in the late 1970s (August, 1991). With this approach end users (i.e., learners in this case) provide timely input on the ID project deliverables that will affect them and their performance on the job. In this collaboration, learners, clients, SMEs, and other stakeholder representatives work together to specify performance requirements, review instructional and performance support materials, and test them. Learners also provide input in the form of interviews and surveys, and IDs use these data to determine what learners already know, what they need to learn, and how the learning and performance environments will affect them.

In contrast, other project management approaches minimize learner involvement. In some management approaches, learners are involved only late in the project. For example, IDs could create drafts of all of the instructional and performance support materials and then test them (also known as a "pilot test") using a representative set of learners. This minimal learner involvement runs the risk of finding out too late that learners don't like their instructional and performance support materials—or find them useful. At this late time, it's likely that there is no remaining schedule or budget in the project to address these issues. Collaborating with a diverse team of learners in the creation of their training simply leads to better training that learners are more likely to complete and apply in the work setting.

Subject Matter Experts (a.k.a. "SMEs")

In some organizations, IDs act as their own subject matter experts (SMEs). However, IDs in many organizations don't possess, working on their own, the expertise required to ensure the technical accuracy, completeness, and authenticity of the learning and performance support materials that they create. These IDs simply can't support the desired performance outcomes of any given project. Instead, IDs commonly collaborate with SMEs who are often high performers. Clients and learners typically value them highly. They may even be opinion leaders in their organizations. The larger the scale of the project, the more likely that IDs will need to collaborate with SMEs.

Unfortunately, SMEs cannot always tell IDs what they know or are thinking about (Villachica & Stone, 2010). SMEs don't always know what makes them experts, and they can have a hard time talking about it. They may be willing to help, but what they articulate about how they do things is often incomplete. This is because experts often work automatically, without conscious attention or thought. People who are really good at doing something don't always think or talk a lot about what they are doing.

For example, have you ever tried to get a recipe out of an experienced cook? The cook could say, "Add a bit more garlic, and that sauce would sing!" Someone who isn't an experienced cook, or even one who is but also from a different culture, would have a hard time knowing how much garlic to add and when to add it, or even what a "singing" sauce tastes like. That's why IDs will need to use careful questioning to tease out details that have become invisible to their SMEs—as well as the details they have forgotten they too, once had to learn. At this point, an ID might ask, "Ok, can you tell me more about that?"

Further, just as every human you meet in your ID work is unique, SMEs are no exception. Their expertise is highly idiosyncratic. They will see the world through their unique perspectives, which are products of their own knowledge, skills, and experiences. Each SME will have different ways of speaking about their expertise and different experiences. Each SME will have different motivations, values, and approaches to their work. Odds are that you will need to find a different way to work with each SME you encounter.

Tips for Working with SMEs

- Work with more than one SME (e.g., two or three) whenever you can. This helps you build a better idea of what is possible.
- Find out how each SME likes to work. Adapt your approach to accommodate their preferences, abilities, and availability.
- Meet with SMEs regularly.
- Agree in advance on a process for reviewing materials.
- Find out what matters to a SME (e.g., recognition, sharing knowledge, helping others) and be intentional about connecting their work to what they value.
- Relate any information they give you back to desired performance outcomes.

Given a big enough budget and adequate organizational sponsorship, IDs can get input from multiple SMEs. In addition to steering away from idiosyncrasies of any one SME, using multiple SMEs will help avoid building on one person's bias. In some situations, an ID can work with multiple SMEs at the same time. In other situations, IDs may work with one SME and submit the work to another SME for their review. SMEs will note their differences and resolve them so the ID can produce a "reconciled consensus" version of their expertise. If you don't have enough resources, do what you can to include multiple perspectives at key points, such as the beginning of the project and/or each phase. Note that you will then have work to do to reconcile differences in SMEs' input.

Working with a SME can involve some improvisation. Don't be afraid to change approaches with a SME if something doesn't work. Many SMEs find it best to respond to initial drafts of deliverables that IDs create—knowing that they will work with the ID to correct any errors or omissions they contain. Some SMEs do well with working on assignments independently and then bringing products to meetings for discussion. Some can input into documents and prefer your written feedback. Others will do best if you meet with them and create a document or draw on a whiteboard together while you ask questions, and you both add ideas to the document or whiteboard together.

Sometimes, IDs may interview clients and SMEs at the same time. At other times, clients may give IDs resources from which they had to pull content, start drafting out a representation of the SMEs expert performance, and then have the SME take it from there. The SME and ID could then meet again to revise it together.

Stakeholders

Stakeholders include all people in the organization who have a say in determining whether the learning and performance support materials that IDs create are successful or not. In one sense, project stakeholders include all the roles that have appeared thus far in this chapter. In a larger sense, stakeholders also include other people who have a voice in determining overall project success. If they have a voice, the project should somehow include them in creating, reviewing, or testing ID project deliverables.

CASE STUDY

The People's FoodBank (pseudonym) is a non-profit organization that delivers 1 million meals to beneficiaries who are food insecure in a large urban area. The organization has multiple sites across a city with over 4 million residents and wants to grow a state-wide presence. They have identified an opportunity to create standardized training materials and programs, which have never existed before. In the past, volunteers would on-board and train new volunteers as best they could.

The warehouse manager was referred to you by a colleague in the organization who has worked with you, a learning and development consultant, in the past. They want you to create training on food safety policies and practices.

- How would you decide if you wanted to work with this potential client? What information would you need to gather? How would you gather this information?

REFLECTION QUESTIONS

- Have you ever observed a situation where some learners or employees were overburdened by learning and development interventions? What could have been done better in planning and scoping the ID project, so as to avoid a similar situation?
- How have you collaborated with project partners in the past? With clients? What have you learned about them? What worked well? What didn't work well? What have you learned from these experiences? What have you learned about how you prefer to work with clients?
- How have you scoped projects in the past? What did you learn from this experience? What would you do differently in the future?
- Have you ever experienced scope creep? How did you manage it? What advice would you give others?
- Have you ever had to adjust a project scope? How did you resolve the change in scope? What did you learn from this experience?

REFERENCES

Adefela, A. A. (2022). The intersection of L&D and diversity, equity, and inclusion. *Training Industry Magazine* (Winter), 38–39. https://www.nxtbook.com/nxtbooks/trainingindustry/tiq_winter2022/index.php#/p/38

August, J. H. (1991). *Joint application design: The group session approach to system design.* Yourdon.

Booker, C. (2021, September 28). How to use a popular project management framework to improve DEI. *Forbes.* https://www.forbes.com/sites/chakabooker/2021/09/28/how-to-use-a-popular-project-management-framework-to-improve-dei/?sh=73d662243525

Cerius Executives. (n.d.). The five business challenges that keep a CEO up at night. *Thought Leadership.* https://ceriusexecutives.com/business-challenges-five-keep-ceo-night/

Gamrat, C., Tiwari, S., & Bekiroglu, S. O. (2022, March 10). Inclusive ADDIE: Initial considerations for DEI pedagogy. *Educause Review.* https://er.educause.edu/articles/2022/3/inclusive-addie-initial-considerations-for-dei-pedagogy

Glassdoor. (2022, September). Instructional designer salaries US. Retrieved from https://www.glassdoor.com/Salaries/instructional-designer-salary-SRCH_KO0,22.htm

Phillips, J. J., & Phillips, P. P. (2007). *Show me the money: How to determine ROI in people, projects, and programs.* Berrett-Koehler.

Project Management Institute. (2020). *A Case for diversity: The ROI of inclusion on project teams.* https://www.pmi.org/-/media/pmi/documents/public/pdf/learning/thought-leadership/pulse/a-case-for-diversity.pdf?rev=331e1034c28948d8a7b5edc241e63bb5

Villachica, S. W., & Stone, D. L. (2010). Cognitive task analysis. In K. H. Silber & W. R. Foshay (Eds), *Handbook of improving workplace performance* (Vol. 1: Instructional design and training delivery, pp. 227–258). Jossey-Bass/Pfeiffer.

Wiley, D. et al. (2022). *Project management for instructional designers* (3rd ed.). EdTech Books. https://edtechbooks.org/pm4id

CHAPTER 3

How to Set Up an Iterative Instructional Design (ID) Process

INTRODUCTION

The LeaPS ID model depicts instructional design as a systematic, systemic, and iterative process. The process is systematic because the work of earlier phases informs the work of later ones. For example, deliverables that instructional designers (IDs) create in the Empathize & Analyze (E&A) component act as inputs for creating deliverables in the Design & Develop (D&D) component. The model is systemic because it depicts ID as a process that occurs within larger systems:

- Government, economy, cultures, and society.
- The organizational culture and inclusive design.
- Project management and inclusive design.

As depicted in Figure 3.1, the LeaPS ID model depicts ID as largely an iterative process. It shows that the components of the ID process can overlap. For example, experienced IDs create learning and performance support materials with the performance goal in mind. Early in a project, they can envision the deliverables that will comprise the learning experience. When they are working on the Empathize & Analyze component, they are already thinking about implications for the Design & Develop component, and also the Implement & Evaluate component of projects. And as experienced IDs create deliverables, they are continuously looping back to collect feedback (a.k.a. "formative evaluation") about the deliverables they are creating. As they receive this feedback, they will review and revise their work. For example, IDs could create a mock-up (a.k.a. "prototype") of a lesson. IDs may then ask clients and subject matter experts (SMEs) to review the prototype. IDs would then revise the prototype based on their feedback. IDs may then ask a representative set of diverse learners to complete the lesson. IDs would then revise this prototype based on the learners' feedback. This process of creating, reviewing, trying, revising is what makes ID iterative. In short, the LeaPS ID model represents a systematic and systemic process as IDs gather feedback from various stakeholders and iterate better prototype designs to provide more support and function more effectively within organizational systems.

DOI: 10.4324/9781003360612-3

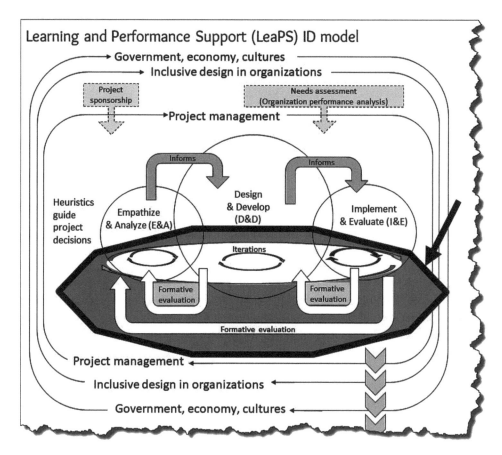

FIGURE 3.1 Formative evaluation and iterations in the LeaPS ID model.

These systematic, systemic, and iterative properties of the LeaPS ID model are all well and good. But what do they mean for IDs who are completing projects? After reading this chapter, you will be able to:

- Build an argument for collaborative ID practice that is just, inclusive, and equitable.
- Describe how to manage iterative workflows in ID projects that use feedback from continuous formative evaluation.

Using these techniques can help ensure IDs work in ways that lead to creating culturally relevant and inclusive interventions. They can also ensure that the culturally relevant and inclusive interventions IDs create work as expected for all learners and produce work setting results that stakeholders expect.

WHY USE A COLLABORATIVE ID APPROACH?

Chapters 1 and 2 of this book mentioned that the LeaPS ID model employs an ID framework (e.g., performance-based learning and development (L&D), Inclusive Design,

Organizational Justice, diversity, equity, and inclusion (DEI)) and advocates for including people in ways instructional systems design (ISD) textbooks haven't traditionally invited, with the goal to produce culturally relevant, equitable, and performance-based interventions. Collaborating with others can involve more work than completing ID tasks without the input of others in the organization. Why go through this extra work at all?

Contextualized and Culturally Relevant Learning Is Effective Learning

In general, organizations create interventions to meet regulatory requirements, to improve work setting performance in ways that meet strategic business objectives, or both. To meet compliance requirements and improve performance in the work setting, learners need to build job skills. The most effective approach for building these skills is to ensure that what people do in the learning environment matches what they do in job settings as closely as possible (Thorndike & Woodworth, 1901). Stated simply, any learning that transfers to the work setting is well designed and contextualized.

As mentioned in Chapter 2, IDs usually collaborate with other people in the organization to represent what successful performers do. Alone, IDs stand at risk of creating learning materials that may not work for classroom trainers, eLearning users, or workers on the job. They also risk building materials that don't earn the support of the work setting supervisors and managers who will monitor learners when they apply their learning on the job.

Learners May Resist Change that Is Forced Upon Them

Learning experiences ask learners to adopt new ways of doing things. Seen this way, learners may resist changes that they feel are forced upon them (Rogers, 2003; Dormant, 2011). To help ensure that learners will be willing to adopt new roles and new ways of performing their job tasks, organizations can involve IDs and other personnel in change management efforts (Creasy, 2023). Some of these efforts involve helping learners work through phases of adoption, and these techniques lie beyond the scope of this book. Other efforts involve IDs using collaborative approaches to ensure that the learning and performance support materials they create possess these characteristics that influence the adoption of new ways of doing things:

- *Relative advantage*: Learners believe what they learn offers them new advantages they value.
- *Simplicity*: Learners believe they can easily build their skills and apply them in the work setting.
- *Compatibility*: Learners believe what they are learning aligns with how they will do things in the work setting.
- *Observable*: Learners can watch others who successfully apply the skills in the learning environment and the work setting.
- *Trialable*: Learners can build and try out new skills without risk.

Towards E³⁺ with Culturally Relevant and Equitable Learning Designs

Giving people a voice in the creation of their learning and performance support materials is a self-evident, ethical imperative deeply entrenched in notions of democracy. Further,

Svihla (2017) reminds IDs to focus on understanding human needs, and on inclusivity, diversity, and participant safety. A more collaborative ID approach, which involves diverse stakeholders, can also produce highly contextualized training that learners across the organization will be more willing to complete and apply in the work setting. In effect, this transforms Merrill's (2008) e^3-learning design challenge for effective, engaging, and efficient to the desired state of *effective, engaging, and equitable*, or E^{3+} in all interventions. Chapters 1 and 2 have noted that using these approaches can increase the likelihood that the learning materials will produce the expected performance results. Figure 3.2 depicts these relationships. Incorporating an inclusive design framework into the ID process may initially increase the costs to create, implement, and maintain. But in the longer run, these costs will be far less than those of creating learning experiences that are ineffective or that learners and their bosses reject.

MANAGING ITERATIVE WORKFLOWS IN ID PROJECTS

A collaborative and inclusive approach to instructional design is also important in the continuous formative evaluation that will help create performance support materials that are just and effective. These formative evaluation loops provide the information IDs use to iterate the creation of increasingly refined project deliverables. This means that IDs will need to manage input and feedback from a larger number of people for the duration of the project. Because ID is scalable to the size of the project, some projects will include all components of the LeaPS ID model. Other projects may include only one or two components. Some larger

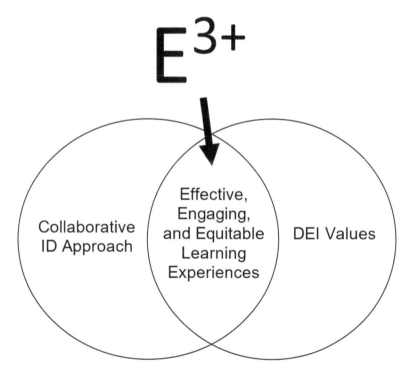

FIGURE 3.2 Combining a collaborative approach to ID with DEI values to produce E^{3+}.

projects may even call for multiple ID teams working on different deliverables, from different components of the LeaPS ID model at one time in a staggered project plan.

Regardless of the scale of a given project, the LeaPS ID model includes formative evaluation that looks to inform:

- *Future project work.* For example, IDs who have completed a task analysis may collect feedback by asking a client to review it and then asking a representative learner to try using it to complete the task it describes. IDs would revise the task analysis after the review and again after the tryout. IDs could later use the revised task analysis to draft objectives in the Design & Develop component of the LeaPS ID model.
- *Previous project work.* IDs often complete task, learner, and environmental analyses early in a project, as part of the Empathize & Analyze component. As they switch their efforts to focus more on design, they may begin creating and testing prototypes. As they begin observing representative learners trying out the prototypes, they may learn more about the learning and performance environment. Feedback from a design activity can inform and refine IDs' understanding of earlier ID activities.

To ensure that resulting learning and performance support materials are just and inclusive, Costanza-Chock (2020) recommends a co-design approach. Inclusive co-design means that IDs work in collaboration with end users or learners with diverse identities in the design process as members of the design team to meet community members' goals in a context where community members retain some level of ownership of a project. Thus, IDs should involve more stakeholders than in the past, in different ways and at multiple points in the process. As we mentioned previously, at the very least, stakeholders such as clients, learners, SMEs, novices, supervisors, managers, and others should partner with IDs to *participate* in helping define the learning and performance problem, identify their needs, and ideate towards potential solutions.

Inclusive design also means including stakeholders from all parts of the organization: from headquarters to satellite offices; from managers to line personnel and supervisors in the shop or on the warehouse floor; from central office staff to people working in the field; from people producing a product and service to the customers using it. Creating learning experiences that are effective as well as just and inclusive often requires IDs to manage feedback loops. Specifically, IDs, project managers, and their clients need to work together to:

- Scale feedback mechanisms.
- Find, pay, and recognize collaborators (e.g., co-designers, participatory designer, feedback participants).
- Place feedback loops.
- Communicate and coordinate.
- Use and adapt templates.

Scale Feedback Mechanisms

Clients, project managers, and IDs will need to determine the formative evaluation mechanisms they'll use during the project to obtain the feedback they need to guide their efforts. Because ID itself is scalable, formative evaluation is scalable as well.

Large Scale. Big projects involving large budgets and multiple components can employ both a project steering committee and technical review teams. Members of the steering committee are drawn from the organization's executive suite, key line managers, the client, the ID project manager, and leadership from the ID team. The primary duty of the steering committee is to provide strategic direction for the project to ensure that it aligns with strategic business objectives and addresses performance gaps that are worth closing. The steering committee resolves any disputes arising from the technical review teams. The steering committee also ensures that the project is adequately funded and resourced. It is responsible for change management. And membership in the steering committee can vary. For example, Villachica and Stone (2010) describe the use of a steering committee to represent the expertise that police detectives use when they conduct criminal investigations. The steering committee consisted of the two clients (one of whom was a Bureau chief), the ID team, and 11 experienced investigators with over 200 years of hard-won experience.

Technical review teams support each of the project's major components. In addition to representatives from the ID team (e.g., graphic artists, developers, programmers, etc.) and the ID project manager, these teams can include SMEs, classroom instructors, and novice performers from the organization. These teams are responsible for providing access to subject matter expertise and for reviewing project deliverables to ensure their technical accuracy, completeness, and authenticity. They are also responsible for helping the ID team recruit participants (e.g., learners, supervisors, instructors) to participate in tryouts of project deliverables. IDs can also present the results of tryouts to technical review teams so that they can prioritize the subsequent revisions that IDs will make.

> *Medium Scale.* A medium-sized project with a mid-range budget and a few components might employ a smaller panel of people who fill the responsibilities of both the steering committee and technical review teams. This review team might include a project sponsor, the client, several SMEs, and the ID project manager. This team might also recommend representative learners with diverse identities from the organization to be involved in ideating and tryouts of the project deliverables.
>
> *Small Scale.* A small project with one or two components and a small budget might use just a client and a SME or two to review ID project deliverables. There might be a few learners involved in tryouts.

Regardless of scale, IDs and their project managers will also need to weigh the trade-offs involved in striving for diverse, inclusive participation in collaborative ID efforts. On one hand, the more IDs involve diverse learners in each phase of the process, the more potentially just, culturally relevant, equitable, and inclusive the resulting intervention will be. On the other hand, the more people participating, the more time-consuming and difficult it will be to manage the project. Many people will tend to offer more contradictory suggestions that may need to be reconciled. Ultimately, right-sizing the number of feedback loops and participants will depend on project size, budget, the diversity of the organization, and the complexity of the ID project.

FIND, RECOGNIZE, AND PAY FEEDBACK COLLABORATORS

A collaborative approach to ID that produces organizationally just and culturally relevant training will require the participation of a larger number of diverse people from throughout the organization—and perhaps beyond. Where do IDs find them? It's important to include willing learners, supervisors, managers, trainers, and any other stakeholders. It's also important to pay particular attention to groups of people who have routinely been underrepresented in past projects and who feel comfortable sharing their input.

To this end, IDs can approach leaders of affinity groups (e.g., lesbian, gay, bisexual, transgender, queer, questioning, intersex, asexual/aromantic, pansexual, and others not represented in the acronym LGBTQIAP+; Black, indigenous, and other people of color; women; veterans; aging people; people with different physical or cognitive abilities; parents). Such groups often consist of individuals who come together for support. They may also help educate others regarding how to best support their members in larger organizations. In addition, Chapter 14 of this text provides recommendations for growing sources of organizational intelligence. By expanding their own networks to include these affinity groups, IDs can expand the number and diversity of the people who can serve different roles on ID projects.

Participation in interviews, design thinking activities, co-design, tryouts, and other feedback loops can become a burden for already busy employees. At the minimum, all participants in the design process should be recognized in ways they value and compensated for their time and expertise. No matter what, contributors inside of organizations should be granted release time to contribute during their regular hours. With sufficient project sponsorship, managers should adjust their workloads accordingly. People external to the organization should be paid at the same rate as an equivalent full-time employee, with additional compensation for their short-term contract work. Ideally, and especially when working on community-driven projects, contributors should be recognized and the community should retain ownership of the outputs and products.

PLACE FORMATIVE EVALUATION LOOPS

ID should be data-driven. IDs collect data from clients, organizational leadership, learners, SMEs, supervisors, trainers, and other stakeholders to guide their creation of learning and performance support materials. Other times, IDs collect data to make decisions about revising the things they've created. This process of using collected data to make evidence-based decisions about creating and revising is iterative and occurs throughout the ID process. IDs should also collect feedback data to make evidence-based revisions to, or iterate, ID deliverables.

There are a few general ways to obtain feedback in ID projects. One way is to ask people to review ID project deliverables. Such reviews typically ensure the technical accuracy, completeness, and authenticity of project deliverables. IDs then use their comments and suggestions to determine revisions for the next iteration of the deliverables. However, reviewing something that IDs created isn't the same thing as actually using it. So the other way to obtain feedback is to ask people to try out the deliverables by using them. IDs will typically observe the users, note what they have difficulty with, and ask for their comments and suggested revisions. These tryouts indicate the extent to which the project deliverables are ready for implementation and what IDs can do to improve them. IDs then use these data to determine the revisions to the deliverable.

Because project budgets and schedules are finite, project managers and IDs will need to determine where to place these loops. Savvy IDs and their project managers often want to use enough reviews and tryouts to ensure that the deliverables are on target. When IDs, their managers, clients, SMEs, and others have a track record of success completing similar projects on time, on budget, and within schedule, they may choose to use fewer feedback loops. As depicted in Figure 3.3, they could opt to use a SME review for each deliverable and use the resulting feedback to revise them. After they have drafted all of the learning and performance support materials, they might opt to conduct a single tryout. (This type of feedback loop is often called a "pilot test.") Or they may choose to conduct one tryout of the draft materials, revise them, and then conduct a second tryout on the revised materials. (These two feedback loops are often called an "alpha test" and a "beta test.")

In contrast, ID teams, ID project managers, and their clients can also face situations where they are attempting new types of projects, or different personas, or new ways of completing ID processes. Because they haven't experienced success yet, they may opt to conduct tryouts of project deliverables earlier in the project. This practice can help reduce the overall risk to the project scope, budget, and schedule. For example, IDs may choose to engage in some early co-designs of a prototype and conduct a tryout of the task analysis during the Empathize & Analyze component work. This could involve asking a small group to help frame needs and requirements of intervention support systems, task analyses, and prototypes. One or two representative learners might then use a task analysis as a prototype guide to actually perform the task. Early tryout helps

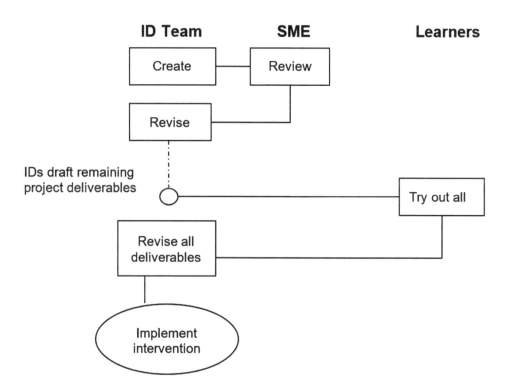

FIGURE 3.3 Simple feedback loop consisting of deliverable SME reviews and a single tryout.

the team avoid unplanned revisions later in the project resulting from errors in the initial task analysis.

Likewise, IDs may choose to spend more time at the beginning of the project understanding their learners and their performance environment on the job. They might create personas and journey maps—and ask learner representatives to review them (e.g., Malamed, 2009; Gibbons, 2018). They may then use the revised personas and journey maps to create mock-ups (a.k.a. "prototypes") of key components. They might then conduct one or more reviews and tryouts of the prototypes.

How many feedback loops with their reviews and tryouts will be enough? As many as:

- *Clients, project managers, and IDs feel they need.* The more unknowns the project faces, the more feedback loops and iterations they may want.
- *The budget can afford and the schedule will allow.* Budgets are limited, and the project will ultimately need to produce completed deliverables. Schedules have set start and stop times. Ultimately, the ID project will need to implement the learning and performance support materials that IDs have created. Seen this way, project budgets and schedules place a cap on feedback loops and iterations.
- *Clients can arrange.* Clients have finite time and resources to sponsor feedback loops. They can only identify so many participants, obtain approval from their supervisors and managers to participate, and provide them with release time.

As much as possible, the goal is to involve an adequate number of diverse participants reviewing an adequate number of project deliverables to be able to generalize the results their reviews and tryouts provide to the larger project and the organization itself.

COMMUNICATE AND COORDINATE

ID projects typically involve multiple people and moving parts. Planning feedback loops is largely about coordinating activities and communicating with clients, the ID team, and other project stakeholders. Within an ID team, members may need to determine who starts drafting a given deliverable, who will revise it, and who will submit it to the client. Clients, SMEs, learners, and other project stakeholders involved in feedback loops will need to know when they can expect to receive a deliverable, what they will need to do to review it, and when they need to submit their comments and revisions. The project management goal is to ensure that deliverables keep moving from one person to the next—losing as little time as possible. IDs need to coordinate all of these activities in ways that meet the deadlines in the schedule. As IDs get to know their project team and client organization better, they begin to get a sense of how long feedback loops may take. IDs may consider giving someone at least three business days if they have already agreed to a project schedule. Without this prior agreement, a reviewer might need at least five business days.

There's an old saying attributed to German military strategist Helmuth von Moltke that "No plan, no matter how brilliantly it is conceived, will survive its first encounter with the enemy." ID does not involve enemies but, similar to military strategists, IDs and project managers need to coordinate their responses and address new demands when the unexpected occurs. This means continuously working to:

- Clarify and shape client expectations.
- Monitor client satisfaction with the ID team and the work they have completed.
- Clarify values of the client and each team member (along with any similarities and differences in those values).
- Develop standards and procedures for dealing with problems and unexpected changes to project scope that affect the budget and schedule.
- Deal with problems as soon as possible.
- Revisit past decisions when new, relevant information becomes available.
- Negotiate and resolve conflicts.
- Develop trust with others.
- Foster good project culture with a strong shared vision and consistent values to guide decisions.

To foster effective coordination and minimize unexpected work, project managers and IDs can strive to communicate continuously and effectively. To this end, they can:

- Hold a project kickoff meeting early in the project to:
  - Clarify expectations for project deliverables.
  - Review project deadlines.
  - Review meeting timelines. Set specific dates for regular meetings. Set broader time frames (e.g., "on or about the first week . . .") for as-needed meetings.
  - Review the process clients, project managers, and IDs will use to identify issues, explore potential changes to project scope, schedule, and budget, and approve them.
- Send meeting and review reminders as the deadlines draw near.
- Provide weekly (or at least frequent and regular) project status updates to share new and relevant information to the client and project team.
- Schedule regular in-person or virtual meetings among clients, the project manager, and the ID team to review project status, identify and address issues, and specify next steps.
- Schedule as-needed in-person or virtual meetings with other specialized professionals (e.g., videographers, audio technicians, web developers, graphic designers, software developers). Schedule these meetings to coincide with project workflows in the schedule.
- Create meeting agendas and use a timekeeper to keep the meeting on track.
- Use an action item log to record meeting decisions and actions that participants should complete after the meeting is over.
- Use formal and informal meetings with the client, learners, SMEs, supervisors, managers, and other stakeholders to ask how the project is going.
- Adjust the rhythm of project deadlines, update distributions, and meeting times as the client, project manager, and ID team adjust to working with each other and stakeholders in the organization.

- If possible, add additional time to the schedule for reflection. Ideally, this would include time to let a deliverable rest unattended for a while. After a little time off, IDs can return to the deliverable to revise it and catch any errors. Savvy IDs also tend to let a project rest any time they become frustrated with it. They might let a draft deliverable rest up to a day before they make their final revisions.
- Whenever an ID project scope requires work across cultures (e.g., organizational, geospatial, community), especially those that are unfamiliar or at a distance, IDs will need to plan more time to responsibly and ethically do their work (Asino & Giacumo, 2017, 2019; Breman & Giacumo, 2020; Giacumo & Asino, 2022; Giacumo, MacDonald, & Peters, 2021; Peters & Giacumo, 2020).

Iterative ID Processes

- ID should be an evidence-based practice.
- ID work can start and finish anywhere in the LeaPS ID model components or processes.
- IDs sometimes skip steps or combine components.
- Formative evaluation can include reviews, usability tests (tryouts), and other feedback loops that can occur throughout a project.

Use and Adapt Templates

Much of the work that is involved in feedback loops will include the use of templates that IDs often use to create project deliverables. For example, IDs may use one template to complete a learner and environmental analysis, another template to complete a task analysis, and yet other templates to create instructor guides and learner guides. These templates help save time from doing repetitive formatting work while creating consistent materials that meet organizational standards.

In other situations, IDs may not have a ready template available to use. They may then turn to a similar document that they or someone else has created. They begin by modifying a copy of the old template to contain new information relevant to the current project. They may choose to keep the main headings, delete old information, and add new headings or information for the new project. In cases like this, older documents can become templates for newer ones. An Internet search will result in many different examples of ID templates. The search can be made easier by searching for templates for specific ID project deliverables (e.g., task analysis, project status report).

IDs use templates because they save time and help ensure consistency across different project deliverables. They help guide information sharing so that it is standardized across individuals when multiple individuals need to share similar information from different perspectives and sources. They are also used to help ensure that the information collected meets organizational standards and performance expectations. In this way, templates are similar to the worksheets you might have used in school. These templates make reviewing others' inputs far easier because reviewers soon know where to look for specific information. In fact, in many situations, IDs create templates for others on the project team (e.g., junior IDs, instructional developers, SMEs) to use and are actually the ones who review others' work and provide feedback.

Savvy IDs don't use templates blindly. They make wise decisions about the parts of the template they will use without modification and the other parts of the template that they will modify to better meet the needs of their learners and organization. They will also seek any necessary approvals to modify the templates. As with any new learning and performance support materials, a new template prototype should be tried out, piloted, revised, and finalized over time, based on results from formative evaluation.

CASE STUDY

EnergyToday (pseudonym) is a national organization that delivers power to over 10 million businesses and homes. Through federal and state government regulations, they are required to provide safety training to all employee lineworkers. The Learning & Development Manager has selected an ID to work on updating an out-of-date course and communicated a clear deadline for the completion of the course revision. A SME has been identified by her manager to partner with the ID. The ID has proposed a project schedule for SME reviews and iterations, to which the SME agreed. The ID has also made all of the necessary file formatting updates, created a list of questions, and identified the files, pages, and areas where the SME expertise is required. The SME has been busy on two other projects and has not had a chance to meet or work with the ID yet.

- Think back to Chapter 2. What could this ID do to facilitate working with this busy SME? How could the ID change their process to ensure the updated course materials are just, culturally relevant, equitable, and inclusive?
- What should the ID do about the missing SME input? Whose responsibility is it to manage a project timeline?

REFLECTION QUESTIONS

- Whose responsibility is it to ensure project workflows result in materials, products, and services that are just, culturally relevant, equitable, and inclusive?
- How can you select representative learners to provide input that would help you ensure materials, products, and services are just, culturally relevant, equitable, and inclusive?
- How can you select representative stakeholders to provide input that would help you ensure materials, products, and services are just, culturally relevant, equitable, and inclusive?
- What are some strategies you've used to negotiate shared values on a project? How has this influenced your project outcomes?

REFERENCES

Asino, T., & Giacumo, L. A. (2017). Culture as a design "next": Theoretical frameworks to guide new design, development, and research of learning environments. *The Design Journal, 20*(sup1), S875–S885. doi:10.1080/14606925.2017.1353033

Asino, T., & Giacumo, L. A. (2019). Culture and global workplace learning: Foundations of cross-cultural design theories and models. In Kenon, V., Palsole, S., Ong, R., & Duff, N. (Eds), *Wiley handbook of global workplace learning* (pp. 395–412). John Wiley & Sons. doi:10.1002/9781119227793.ch22

Breman, J., & Giacumo, L. A. (2020). A cross-cultural instructional design case situated in a global workplace learning context. *Handbook of research in educational communications and technology.* Springer. doi:10.1007/978-3-030-36119-8

Costanza-Chock, S. (2020). *Design justice: Community-led practices to build the worlds we need.* MIT Press. https://library.oapen.org/bitstream/handle/20.500.12657/43542/external_content.pdf?sequence=1&isAllowed=y

Creasy, T. (2023). Definition of change management. Prosci.com. https://www.prosci.com/blog/definition-of-change-management#:~:text=Prosci%20defines%20change%20management%20as%20the%20application%20of,related%20concepts%3A%20the%20change%20itself%20and%20project%20management

Dormant, D. (2011). *The chocolate model of change.* Diane Dormant.

Giacumo, L. A., & Asino, T. (2022). Preparing instructional designers to apply human performance technology in global context. In Stefaniak, J. (Ed.), *The instructional design trainer's guide.* Routledge.

Giacumo, L. A., MacDonald, M., & Peters, D. T. (2021). Promoting organizational justice in cross-cultural data collection, analysis, and interpretation: Towards an emerging conceptual model. *The Journal of Applied Instructional Design, 10*(4). doi:10.51869/104/lgi

Gibbons, S. (2018, December 9). Journey mapping 101. Nielsen Norman Group. https://www.nngroup.com/articles/journey-mapping-101/

Malamed, C. (2009). Learner personas for instructional design: How to develop a learner persona in three steps. *The eLearning Coach.* https://theelearningcoach.com/elearning_design/audience/learner-personas-for-elearning/

Merrill, D. (2008). Converting e_3-learning to e^3-learning: An alternative instructional design method. In Shank, P., & Carliner, S. (Eds), *The e-learning handbook: Past promises, present challenges* (pp. 359–400). Pfeiffer/Jossey-Bass.

Peters, D. T., & Giacumo, L. A. (2020). Ethical and responsible cross-cultural interviewing: Theory to practice guidance for human performance and workplace learning professionals. *Performance Improvement, 59*(1), 26–34. doi:10.1002/pfi.21906

Rogers, E. M. (2003). *Diffusion of innovations* (5th ed.). Free Press.

Svihla, V. (2017). *Design thinking and agile design: New trends or just good designs. Foundations of learning and instructional design technology.* EdTech Books. https://edtechbooks.org/lidtfoundations/design_thinking_and_agile_design

Thorndike, E. L., & Woodworth, R. S. (1901). The influence of improvement in one mental function upon the efficiency of other functions. *Psychological Review, 8*, 247–261. http://psychclassics.yorku.ca/Thorndike/Transfer/transfer1.htm

Villachica, S. W., & Stone, D. L. (2010). Cognitive task analysis. In Silber, K. H., & Foshay, W. R. (Eds), *Handbook of improving workplace performance* (Vol. 1: Instructional design and training delivery, pp. 227–258). Jossey-Bass/Pfeiffer.

CHAPTER 4

Why Should We Empathize and Analyze?

INTRODUCTION

In Chapter 3, we considered how to set up an ID process that is iterative and collaborative, one with repeated feedback loops including information from a diverse set of learners, SMEs, stakeholders, and clients. We also introduced the concept of "affinity groups;" individuals who feel discriminated against, underrepresented, marginalized, or who desire more connections or support within the workforce often get involved with these groups. The groups can be based on gender, race, ethnicity, nationality, sexual orientation, socioeconomic status, religion, (dis)ability, parental status, veteran status, political affiliation, and so on. In this chapter, we highlight empathy with and analysis of the learners as an essential beginning point for the LeaPS ID model.

It's difficult to create culturally relevant, inclusive, and effective interventions without a clear understanding of the learners and the larger organization in which they work. Gaining this understanding involves more than analyzing data into a few aggregated data points for interpretation; it also requires developing an awareness of and sensitivity to the diverse experiences those learners represent and how they think and feel about those experiences. This will help ensure that the ID's understanding of the learners incorporates the full range of their experiences. After reading this chapter, you will be able to:

- Build an argument for developing a clear and complete understanding of the learners and the organization.
- Articulate two important assumptions made at the beginning of the LeaPS ID model.
- Explain "Learner and Environmental Analysis" (LEA), "Task Analysis" (TA), and "Learning Requirements Analysis" (LRA), and why they are an important part of the Empathize & Analyze (E&A) component of the LeaPS ID model.

LEAPS ID MODEL: EMPATHIZE & ANALYZE

We know it's near impossible to work well when one is not feeling good about leaders' decisions, policies, procedures, and colleagues. In this chapter we'll make the case that we need to empathize with our learners as much as possible, although we'll never

DOI: 10.4324/9781003360612-4

absolutely know how others experience life (Heylighen & Dong, 2019). We will then identify a few ways to approach empathy and analysis. In the next chapter we will explore how to apply this empathy/analysis when creating ID project deliverables.

The information IDs collect and create in empathizing and analyzing should help them understand who their learners are, what they already know, what motivates them, and what factors in the learning and transfer environments will affect their performance. This is the place where savvy IDs focus on empathizing with their learners by collecting data to understand what they already know and do, what they will be learning, and the contextual factors in the learning and transfer environments that can affect how learners orient themselves to the training, complete the training itself, and transfer their learned skills to the workplace.

One way to gain empathy is to employ multiple perspectives, which can better guide a design project. IDs are responsible for knowing their own perspectives. Experienced IDs will also be aware of some other perspectives, too. However, no ID can have all they need to create culturally relevant and inclusive interventions on their own. To achieve better performance outcomes, IDs need to become more familiar with the different types and groups of learners they serve. To do this, experienced IDs may have to get out of their own comfort zone. After all, we can't expect different results moving forwards if we use the same inputs and approaches as we have in the past. In this chapter, we'll show you why this is the case.

As depicted in Figure 4.1, the LeaPS ID model begins with the Empathize & Analyze (E&A) component. In this component of the LeaPS ID model, IDs begin by

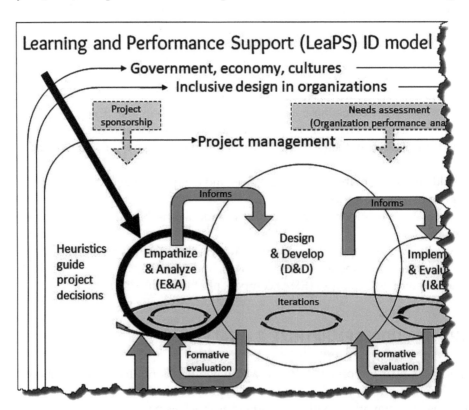

FIGURE 4.1 The Empathize & Analyze component in the LeaPS ID model process.

understanding the learners, the organizational culture, the job tasks the intervention will support, the overall complexity of the tasks, and the different configurations of learning and performance support solutions. On the whole, the information, as well as the deliverables, that IDs create will inform what they do in the Design & Develop (D&D) component of the LeaPS ID model. In some projects, IDs may complete the Empathize & Analyze component before they begin the Design & Develop component. In other projects, they will approach these components in parallel, working on collecting data and creating project deliverables for both.

E&A Deliverables

Typical E&A deliverables include empathy maps, personas, a learner and environmental analysis, a task analysis, and an LRA. Figure 4.2 illustrates the relationships among them, showing how these inputs inform the creation of other ID project deliverables.

Why this Component Is Important

A robust approach to Empathize & Analyze can often provide most, if not all, of the information an ID team will need to complete the design component of the intervention—without having to return to clients, SMEs, project stakeholders, and learners to backfill missing data. However, new information that the team could use to inform this

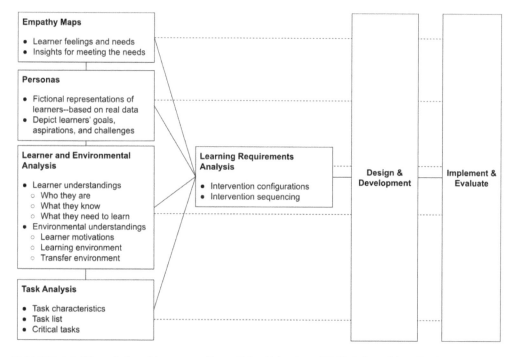

FIGURE 4.2 The relationship among Empathize & Analyze (E&A) deliverables, Design & Develop (D&D), and Implement & Evaluate (I&E). Solid lines indicate how earlier E&A variables inform the LRA. Dotted lines indicate how these deliverables inform later D&D and I&E deliverables.

component of the LeaPS ID model sometimes becomes available at a later date. It's fine to view your empathizing and analyzing work as somewhat fluid and iterative.

LEAPS ID MODEL ASSUMPTIONS

Any model is based on assumptions, and the LeaPS ID model is no exception. The LeaPS ID model makes two important assumptions. Both act as inputs to the model itself. Violating these assumptions altogether can put ID teams at risk of either:

- Creating learning and performance support materials that are inappropriate and waste the organization's time and money.
- Trying to create learning and performance support materials without adequate organizational sponsorship.

Assumption 1: A Learning and Development (L&D) System Gap Worth Closing Exists

The LeaPS ID model doesn't use learning and performance support solutions as a panacea for all of the organization's problems or opportunities. Instead, the LeaPS ID model assumes that someone in the organization has already conducted an adequate needs assessment. This needs assessment has already:

- Specified a performance gap, or discrepancy, between the actual system performance and the desired system performance.
- Built an argument that the performance gap is worth closing.
- Concluded that the solutions to the root causes of the gap include providing adequate guidance describing how to perform the job or a need for skill and knowledge intervention.

In addition, the organization should have used the needs assessment to inform other groups in the organization about any causes of gaps that lie outside of the L&D system. In some cases, other groups in the organization, such as information technology or quality assurance, may address these causes. In other cases, the L&D group may partner with these groups to address these causes. In either situation, the L&D group doesn't merely ignore or walk away from these causes of system gaps.

What Indicates a Lack of Adequate Guidance or Skill and Knowledge Intervention?

Conducting a credible needs assessment is more than just asking learners and other stakeholders if they know how to perform a task, if the task is new, or if they feel they need more feedback, support, or training. A case for engaging and effective intervention centers on the nature of the tasks that learners perform in the workplace and whether learners have had adequate support to perform them (e.g., equitable access to resources, equitable processes and procedures, inclusive learning and development designs, guidance that's respectful and dignified). If the only way to come up to speed on a task is to practice it in a safe environment while receiving extended real-time coaching and delayed feedback, then the situation may be ideal for a performance-based learning and development (PBL&D) intervention. If learners can come up to speed with minimal practice, coaching, and feedback, then it's probably a lack of guidance (data) in the environment. The L&D group in organizations typically addresses both of these causes of performance gaps.

Further, an L&D system gap means that in the past learners have never been supported in performing the task in ways that are respectful, or are accessible, or meet specified standards. Hence, barring evidence of skill decay, learners who've already demonstrated that they can perform work setting tasks to standards don't need more learning solutions.

To What Extent Do Organizations Actually Conduct Needs Assessments?

The extent to which organizations conduct needs assessments before they create learning interventions varies. In some organizations, needs assessment begins with project qualification, where savvy IDs turn clients' often well-intentioned but ill-informed requests for learning intervention to improve performance. In other organizations, senior leaders conduct versions of needs assessments whenever there's a gap between existing and desired performance that keeps the executive suite and senior managers up at night. In other organizations, there may be a group of senior IDs who conduct needs assessments, high-level design activities, and evaluations. In some organizations, every L&D project includes a needs assessment phase.

Workarounds: When There Isn't a Previous Needs Assessment

Some organizations don't typically conduct formal needs assessments before undertaking L&D intervention projects. In these situations, IDs adapt. Needs assessments are highly scalable. Larger, more formal, needs assessments may involve lengthy schedules, bigger budgets, collecting and analyzing different types of data from multiple sources, and numerous project personnel. Smaller, less formal, needs assessments can be conducted on the back of a napkin or in interviews with selected personnel. In these workarounds, IDs work with the limited data available to them, the needs assessment models and tools they've internalized, and the application of structured interviews, surveys, focus groups, observations, etc.

IDs might even conduct a more consolidated or integrated version of a needs assessment by including it in other ID project tasks. IDs can conduct the needs assessment as they work on other parts of the project. It's important to do one's best to conduct either a formal or some sort of informal needs assessment. Without any needs assessment at all, IDs can proceed at risk of creating interventions that don't address a skill gap and don't produce valued behavior change in workplace settings.

Assumption 2: Adequate Sponsorship Exists

The LeaPS ID model also assumes that clients and other organizational stakeholders collaborate with the ID team throughout the ID project. Ideally, this means that clients have ownership and vested interest, or "skin in the game," to meet sponsorship responsibilities that support the work of their ID teams. This sort of sponsorship aligns with established professional standards about working in partnership with clients and stakeholders (International Society for Performance Improvement, 2013; AECT, 2012; IBSTPI, 2012). These responsibilities include:

- Being a trustworthy source of organizational intelligence about how the organization works.
- Providing release time for:
  - Organizational stakeholders to review key ID deliverables.
  - Successful performers/SMEs to participate in task analysis.
  - Learners and job incumbents to participate in reviews and tryouts of ID project deliverables, including job aids or developed drafts of intervention materials.
- Providing access to data sources.
- Arranging for management and supervisor support for skill transfer to the work setting after a learning intervention has been implemented.
- Supporting formative and summative evaluation efforts.
- Providing overall project oversight to ensure that the intervention meets the organization's strategic business objectives and that an adequate change management effort will support the adoption of new or changed performances in the workplace.

Workarounds: When Sponsorship Is Lacking

IDs may find themselves in situations where client sponsorship is lacking. In some cases, the lack of sponsorship is part of the organizational culture. In other cases, the lack of sponsorship may be associated with a particular client or organizational stakeholder. Again, IDs must adapt. In these situations, savvy IDs often employ the "consultant's back-step shuffle," moving from one alternative to the next best. Some of these alternatives include:

- *Create topic-based training.* Without access to SMEs and participants for interviews, surveys, observations, and formative evaluation, IDs may create topic-based training based on information they can find online or from other sources. This training approach often creates "information dumps" that fail to improve performance in workplace settings.
- *Find substitutes for SMEs and potential learners.* When SMEs and representative learners are scarce, IDs might find substitutes outside the organization.
- *Build sources of organizational intelligence.* Savvy IDs often find potential allies and get information about how the organization works. Chapter 13 provides more guidance on organizational intelligence.

LEARNER AND ENVIRONMENTAL ANALYSIS

Savvy IDs tend to avoid decisions about interventions based solely on habit, guesses, or assumptions. Instead, they often begin their work by understanding learners and the organizational environment where they learn and perform their job tasks. This means that ID teams should have adequate, data-informed answers to these questions:

- Who are the learners?
- What do they already know?
- What do they need to learn?
- What's hard about that?
- What environmental factors influence learning and skill transfer to the workplace?
- How do learners feel about the above considerations?

Answers to these questions will later inform specific and defensible ideas about the components of a proposed intervention and how they will work together.

IDs often need to collect and analyze data about learners so that they can later make sound decisions during the Design & Develop component of the LeaPS ID model. In some situations, IDs already have good answers to the preceding questions. In other situations, IDs will have to collect data from learners, clients, SMEs, existing sources, and other stakeholders in the organization. They will collect these data using observations, interviews, and by using extant (known) data. In other words, savvy IDs don't like to rely solely on things that subject matter experts, clients, or other extant data tell them. Instead, they prefer to base their decisions on data collected from the field.

Why Conduct a Learner and Environmental Analysis (LEA)?

ID is like engineering in that the designer works to create an intervention that will work within a given context and situation. One essential element of any situation is the intended audience (e.g., "learners"). Some IDs mistakenly overlook learner analysis. But it's an important aspect of ID because it allows you to maximize the value of the intervention by helping you make good, data-informed decisions about things such as:

- Introducing new job tasks.
- Demonstrations and examples.
- Kinds of assessments and practice activities.
- Coaching (e.g., real-time error detection and correction) and feedback.
- Instructional pacing.
- Minimal content.
- Amount of autonomy and control the learners will have.
- Delivery methods.

The idea is to tailor the L&D intervention or L&D strategy to the intended audience rather than the other way around. Even an "off-the-shelf" training program can typically benefit from some tailoring to make sure that it "fits" the intended audience and helps them learn the skills they're supposed to master and transfer to the work setting.

Further, the intervention that IDs create affects how learners will perform their jobs in the work setting. Without understanding the skills learners need to build and the contextual factors in the work setting that can affect their acceptance of the intervention, IDs can spend a lot of time, effort, and client dollars building interventions that don't work. An LEA can ensure interventions are culturally relevant and inclusive, adequately support all learners' performance, and are accepted by managers.

TASK ANALYSIS

Performance-based learning and development (PBL&D) interventions may contain demonstrations, practice exercises with coaching and feedback, and mastery tests. How do IDs know what these different interventions should contain? Sometimes projects are so small that IDs who have a lot of experience with a given task and the learner population can conduct their own task analyses, using themselves as a SME.

The larger the ID project, the greater the chance that a given ID won't possess the requisite experience to conduct their task analyses alone. When this happens, IDs don't just "make this stuff up." Instead, they work with SMEs and other stakeholders to conduct a task analysis to represent what exemplary performance looks like on the job. Stated simply, a task analysis decomposes what exemplary performers do in the work setting when they perform their job tasks.

Crandall, Klein, and Hoffmann (2006) discuss the traditional notion of a task as "people engaged in discrete activities or sequences of activities aimed at achieving some particular goal" (p. 3). Given that the tasks some people perform require them to make decisions and solve problems, their activities may not be readily observable. This is why Crandall et al. (2006) extend their notion of a task to include "the outcomes people are trying to achieve" (p. 3).

A completed task analysis represents the workflow and "thoughtflow" of successful task performance. For less complex tasks, flowcharts may suffice. For more complex tasks, IDs often create a task list, as depicted in Figure 4.3. In addition to providing a hierarchical organization depicting the steps, substeps, and tasks comprising the job, the task list also:

- Uses *if/then tables* to describe how successful performers *make decisions* associated with a given step.
- Uses icons to call *hot tips* that provide hints about successful performance and *cautions* about things to avoid or be careful about while completing a given step.

A useful task analysis is:

- *Accurate*—it describes what successful performers do in the work setting.
- *Complete*—it provides a representation of both the actions and the thought processes that produce exemplary performance. It also describes what is critical, difficult, and complex about task performance.

1. Major task 1
    1.1. First subtask
        1.1.1. First step of the subtask
        1.1.2. Second step of the subtask

        > Sample graphic
        > illustrating this step.

        1.1.3. Third step of the subtask (with a sample of a simple decision table)

If Today is	Then
Tuesday	Pay for the hamburger.
Other days of the week	Ask for a hamburger.

    1.2. Second subtask
        1.2.1. First step of the subtask

         Caution: Sample caution about the first step

        1.2.2. Second step of the subtask
    1.3. Third subtask
2. Second major task

FIGURE 4.3 Sample task list formatting.

- *Authentic*—it uses the language of the workplace setting in ways that exemplary performers, clients, learners, and other project stakeholders use them.
- *Accessible, inclusive, and respectful*—it demonstrates dignity for learners; presents skills and concepts in respectful ways that all intended learners can decode, relate to, and performances that all intended learners can do.

How to Determine the Level of Detail in a Task Analysis

Task analyses differ from standard operating performance specifications (SOPs) in that they are created with the intended learners in mind. Unlike SOPs, a task analysis contains only the information required to support the desired performance *of the intended learners.*

Why Conduct a Task Analysis?

In work settings, IDs conduct a task analysis to decompose critical tasks into their component parts. IDs will later mine the contents of the task analysis throughout the rest of the project. For example, IDs will use the completed task analysis to:

- Conduct a learning requirements analysis.
- Ensure that the performance requirements and assessment instruments they write match the tasks people perform on the job.

- Write demonstrations that depict both the *visible steps* comprising successful performance as well as *hidden decisions*.
- Write coaching sequences that can focus on *common errors* (i.e., cautions) and how to *correct them* (i.e., hot tips).
- Write job aids that supervisors and managers can use on the job to provide coaching and feedback to learners who have returned to the job.

Seen this way, a task analysis is the basis for the design work that comprises the next phase of the LeaPS ID model. A good task analysis makes it easy to create job aids, assessments, and practice exercises. A poor task analysis can lead to schedule slips and busted project budgets as IDs try to "backfill" information that should have appeared in the task analysis.

What Is a Task?

So how do you determine what a task is? Harless (in Hardin, 2009) provides a series of characteristics to make this decision in Table 4.1.

Types of Tasks

There are three broad ways to categorize job tasks that IDs encounter in work settings. Table 4.2 depicts them. Tasks comprising job duties and responsibilities may include combinations of procedural, conceptual, and process tasks that are required to make valued decisions. For example, an automobile worker completes a given procedure to add a component to cars on an assembly line. This same worker also can decide to stop the line if there is a significant quality problem. And the same worker may serve on their unit's quality committee, where they implement procedures, concepts, and processes to improve the assembly of the automobile.

In a similar manner, a single process often consists of different types of tasks (e.g., concept decisions, procedure decisions). For instance, police detectives investigating a crime complete an investigative process that varies with each incident. They have to make decisions about seizing evidence in ways that meet legal standards (e.g., concept decisions, what is and what is not). They follow a procedure to advise a suspect of their legal rights.

TABLE 4.1 Task qualification checklist

	Check One:	
Characteristic	Yes	No*
This completes a work assignment.		
This results in a meaningful product or service.		
This is a job the learner does or should support.		
Add up checks: *Any "no" disqualifies this as a task.		

TABLE 4.2 Types of tasks in workplace settings

If the Task Involves	Then the Task Is About	Examples
Performing a set of steps largely the same way every time.	Completing a procedure.	• Using psychomotor skills to assemble something.
		• Assembling a wire harness for a car's electrical system. • Making a pizza for a restaurant chain store.
		• Training a dog to recognize its name. • Cleaning food assembly areas in a food bank. • Completing profile information for an online account.
Making one or more discrete decisions.	Applying concepts to make the decisions.	• Identifying task-relevant cues and their meaning, • determining when to do something. • Determining if one thing is like another. • Applying definitions, standards, or regulations determining compliance. • Determining if the use of copyrighted material meets fair use regulations. • Determining the alignment of a business owner's beliefs, values, and attitudes. • Determining whether a given behavior meets ethical standards.
Completing a similar set of related steps somewhat differently each time.	Completing a process.	• Auditing a firm's accounts. • Using the LeaPS ID model to create workplace training. • Diagnosing a patient. • Reconciling an accounting error. • Troubleshooting a problem. • Conducting a cause analysis in a needs assessment.

Being able to recognize these different types of tasks is important. Why? IDs will use different variations when they conduct their task analyses for each of these types of tasks. Chapter 7 will describe them in greater detail.

LEARNING REQUIREMENTS ANALYSIS

Having gained an understanding of the tasks comprising successful performance and their overall complexity, IDs can conduct a learning requirements analysis (LRA) to make initial decisions about the configuration of interventions. More specifically, an LRA

- Further refines learning and performance support system needs after a needs assessment has already identified them.
- Specifies appropriate training system configurations to close guidance, skill, and motivation gaps specified in the needs assessment.

Why Conduct a Learning Requirements Analysis?

We advocate for the term "learning requirements analysis" (LRA) for a few reasons. First, we are looking at both instructional and non-instructional interventions design in this book. Second, with conducting an LRA, IDs can create a focus that leads to data-informed decisions about learning intervention configurations that are feasible for the context in specific systems. In other words, if you have people coming to you asking for "training," an LRA can help you determine the components that any "training" (learning and performance support materials) might include.

To conduct an LRA, use language that clients and learners understand and identify how to deliver what they need (Hardin, 2009). Determining what clients and organizations need can be complicated. For example, you don't want to recommend eLearning if the client doesn't have the resources to track completion or the learners don't have the prerequisite skills or tools to access it. The LEA findings should support your decisions. If there's no rationale for the training configuration in the LEA, it's time to collect more LEA data or determine an alternative configuration.

Additionally, to clients, the term "training" or "L&D" can mean just about any sort of performance solution addressing any environmental or individual cause of a performance gap (Villachica & Stepich, 2010). In this view, these terms can even include non-instructional performance improvement solutions. Further complicating this terminology problem is the common use of the term "training needs analysis" (TNA). While many IDs use this term, Watkins and Kaufman (1996) note that the term itself is an oxymoron. "If you know that training is the solution, why do a needs assessment?" (p. 13). Therefore, it's important to go over potential intervention configurations and concrete deliverable expectations with clients early in a project.

Types of Learning Intervention Configurations

Given the sources of system gaps and the results of a task analysis, IDs can configure different types of interventions, which can act as modular "building blocks." Chapter 5 will provide more guidance about this configuration process, which can include:

- Job aids.
- Performance support.
- Personal learning networks.
- Organizational communities of practice/affinity groups.
- Training.
- Job aids + introductory training.
- Job aids + extensive practice/coaching/feedback.
- Coaching.
- Mentoring.
- Online learning.
- Self-paced eLearning.
- Instructor-led training.
- On-the-job training.

As building blocks, these interventions are scalable. For example, a smaller ID project might consist of job aids alone to address a simple procedure that requires step-by-step guidance in workplace settings. In contrast, a larger ID project might consist of job aids and training combined with mentoring to address a more complex process that requires guidance, extended practice with coaching and feedback, and support for skill transfer from training to the workplace setting.

TOWARDS DESIGN JUSTICE DURING EMPATHIZE & ANALYZE

Data Collection Considerations

Conducting an LEA will probably involve collecting data from learners and other stake-holders. Conducting a TA will probably involve working with SMEs, clients, learners, and other stakeholders to collect data. Likewise, conducting an LRA will probably involve working with people filling similar roles. Practicing inclusive design could require the ongoing collaboration of a lot of people and roles. Likewise, it is important to use non-extractive design to create value for learners, center their needs, build on existing solutions, recognize their contributions, provide economic rewards, build their capacity, incorporate concrete mechanisms for community accountability, and produce outputs that are effective and maintainable (Costanza-Chock, 2020). In a similar manner, ID teams will need to choreograph ways of avoiding bias when working with different groups and intersectional subgroups of learners.

Empathizing Techniques

IDs can use different techniques coming from design thinking (Rodgers, 2013; Svihla, 2017) to collaborate with learners to better understand them and their needs. Building empathy for learners can be used to create motivation to do something, which can in turn also lead to action by instructional designers (Baaki et al., 2021). Two useful techniques from Stanford's Design School (d.school, 2013) are empathy maps and personas.

Empathy Maps

Empathy maps can help design teams build and articulate insights into learners' experiences, motivations, and wishes (Boller, 2022, p. 22). IDs can use empathy maps to:

- *Identify learner needs.* These needs appear when learners describe their activities and desires.
- *Form insights.* These insights take the form of realizations where learning and performance support materials can address learner needs.

There's no one correct way to build an empathy map. Stanford's d.school (2013) uses four quadrants to indicate what learners say, do, think, and feel about a given job task or situation. Baaki et al. (2021) share an empathy map with six components (thoughts and feelings, influences, tasks and questions, actions and responses, pain points, goals). Schmidt and Tawfik (2022) describe an empathy map with six slightly different components (say, do, think, feel, pain, gain). These components of an empathy map should align with the project goals and can guide the organization of data, which is then used to inform design decisions (Melo et al., 2020; Schmidt & Tawfik, 2022).

Kouprie and Visser (2009) describe a framework for empathy building with four phases: discovery, immersion, connection, and detachment. During discovery, designers enter into their first contact with learners, either in person or through previous documentation, and they embrace curiosity to learn more about learners' situations and experiences. During immersion, designers enter into learners' worlds with an open mind, and willing to absorb their experiences, ideally through observation. During connection, the designer recalls similar feelings and makes meaningful understanding of the learners' emotions, thereby connecting with them in heart and mind. During detachment, the designer steps back, reflects on their new insights, and begins imagining multiple solutions.

While IDs may find it useful to build empathy, there are also risks by not attending to power dynamics appropriately. Ahmed (2013) shares that "empathy sustains the very difference that it may seek to overcome: empathy remains a 'wish feeling', in which subjects 'feel' something other than what another feels in the very moment of imagining they could feel what another feels" (p. 30). Empathy can lead to more defined "others," denial of expertise of the "others" by obscuring individuals' contributions and failing to compensate contributors, as well as treating individuals or groups as something on display (Bennett & Rosner, 2019).

More Socially Responsible Design Integrates Empathy with Elements of Co-design

Leaning in to the lived experiences of learners and integrating some co-design approaches can avoid unintended consequences of "othering," failing to adequately address diverse learners' identities and lived experiences, and attending to these implications in design. Designers should not assume they can understand others completely through their own actions alone. Those with lived experiences should either participate in empathize, analyze, design, and develop processes or exchange critical dialogue to unpack limitations of design decisions (Vink & Oertzen, 2018).

Personas

Using insights gained from empathy mapping and other LEA data, IDs can build thematic personas (Wertz et al., 2020). Personas are fictional representations of different types of learners, based on data that the ID team has collected. Personas depict learner knowledge, skills, attitudes about a given job task, and any associated learning and performance support materials. Personas can also reflect any concerns users may have about learning and performance support materials that may change their role in the organization and their job tasks.

Personas are qualitative fictional characters that represent characteristics of learners, which are used to guide design, prototyping, and development decisions. They can be a great starting point and reference for design work, they are well defined and clear, unlike authentic learners who are beautifully complex (Johansson & Messeter, 2005). Personas can help design team members to switch between their own and a learner's perspective, thereby keeping the learner present in design and development (Johansson & Messeter, 2005). Also similar to empathy maps, the same risks of superficial understanding and inappropriate power dynamics exist and can undermine potential benefits.

There are many different ways of constructing learner personas (Oganetse, 2022). They can help designers and stakeholders recognize learners' knowledge, skills, needs, goals, and characteristics that are relevant to a specific intervention and context (Maier & Thalmann, 2010). Schmidt and Tawfik (2022) share an example persona with a name, role, quote, demographic information, goals, attitudes, behaviors, motivations, and barriers. These data can be collected during interviews, observations, focus groups, workshops, and a wide variety of extant data sources. It can be good ID practice to use footnotes to cite the data sources that ID teams use to create personas. Using this convention can help ID teams avoid simply "making stuff up" without an empirical basis.

Co-designing Personas in Workshops with Select Participants Can Offer Advantages

- Include more diverse identities.
- Foster empathy, sympathy, and memory of process.
- Increase design confidence of participants.
- Facilitate communication and critique by using persona as proxy (Neate et al., 2019).

CASE STUDY

The corporate university of the multinational Energy World (pseudonym) is proud of offering interventions for managers to learn how to demonstrate the principles of organizational justice in their work. An ID team from Energy World produced the course. They have selected a book that was wildly popular in the United States, written by an American. The learning designers integrate a short survey at the end of each module to track learners' time on task and their reactions to the instruction. After running a new course design for two semesters, they notice learners who identify as women, or who are Black, Indigenous, Latine, Asian American, or Pacific Islander, or who speak English as a second language, are tracking twice as much time in responding to discussion prompts as those who identify as white men from the United States, who speak English as a first language. The retention rates of learners who are women and Black, Indigenous, Latine, Asian American, or Pacific Islander, are living in countries outside of the

United States, or who speak English as a second language, are three times lower than those of white cisgender (a person whose sense of personal identity and gender corresponds with their birth sex) men from the United States, who speak English as a first language. The retention rates of learners who are women who are Black, Indigenous, Latine, Asian American, or Pacific Islander, living in countries outside of the United States, and who speak English as a second, third, or fourth language, are five times lower than those of white cis men from the United States, who speak English as a first language. The L&D program manager has decided to assign you as the lead instructional designer to remedy this situation.

- What are the questions you would ask yourself to critically interrogate the ID practices and decisions that were made to help re-envision this course?

REFLECTION QUESTIONS

- Can you create organizational justice or practice inclusive design without engaging the learners, users, and stakeholders at multiple times in the process? What kinds of questions do you need to ask to build empathy for the learners, users, and stakeholders? How do you handle competing priorities?
- What are some strategies you've used to grow empathy for others who have values or lived mind and body experiences that are different from your own?
- What do you do when your values conflict with those of an organization? When your values conflict with those of your leaders?
- How have you scoped design projects? Who were the people affected by the problems or opportunities? How were they involved in scoping and framing the project?
- What is at risk when, or if, you don't create a design that's non-extractive?

REFERENCES

Ahmed, S. (2013). *The cultural politics of emotion.* Routledge.

Association for Educational Communications and Technology (AECT). (2012). *AECT standards.* https://www.aect.org/docs/AECTstandards2012.pdf

Baaki, J., Tracey, M. W., Bailey, E., & Shah, S. (2021). Graduate instructional design students using empathy as a means to an end. *Journal of Design Research, 19*(4–6), 290–307.

Bennett, C. L., & Rosner, D. K. (2019, May). The promise of empathy: Design, disability, and knowing the "other." In *Proceedings of the 2019 CHI conference on human factors in computing systems* (pp. 1–13). CHI.

Boller, S. (2022). *Design thinking for TD professionals.* ATD Press.

Costanza-Chock, S. (2020). *Design justice: Community-led practices to build the worlds we need.* MIT Press. https://library.oapen.org/bitstream/handle/20.500.12657/43542/external_content.pdf?sequence=1&isAllowed=y

Crandall, B., Klein, G., & Hoffman, R. R. (2006). *Working minds: A practitioner's guide to cognitive task analysis.* MIT Press.

d.school. (2013). *Bootcamp bootleg.* http://dschool.stanford.edu/wp-content/uploads/2011/03/METHODCARDS2010v6.pdf

Hardin, D. (2009, September). *Dealing with information: Training solutions vs. data in the environment.* Boise State University's IPT 537 Instructional Design course, Boise, ID.

Heylighen, A., & Dong, A. (2019). To empathise or not to empathise? Empathy and its limits in design. *Design Studies, 65,* 107–124. doi:10.1016/j.destud.2019.10.007

International Board of Standards for Training, Performance and Instruction (IBSTPI). (2012). *Instructional designer standards: Competencies & performance statements.* https://ibstpi.org/instructional-design-competencies/

International Society for Performance Improvement (2013). *CPT performance standards.* https://www.ispi.org/ISPI/Credentials/CPT_Certification/CPT_Standards.aspx

Johansson, M., & Messeter, J. (2005). Presenting the user: Constructing the persona. *Digital Creativity, 16*(4), 231–243.

Kouprie, M., & Visser, F. S. (2009). A framework for empathy in design: Stepping into and out of the user's life. *Journal of Engineering Design, 20*(5), 437–448. doi:10.1080/09544820902875033

Maier, R., & Thalmann, S. (2010). Using personas for designing knowledge and learning services: Results of an ethnographically informed study. *International Journal of Technology Enhanced Learning, 2*(1–2), 58–74.

Melo, Á. H. D. S., Rivero, L., Santos, J. S. D., & Barreto, R. D. S. (2020, October). EmpathyAut: An empathy map for people with autism. In *Proceedings of the 19th Brazilian Symposium on Human Factors in Computing Systems* (pp. 1–6). ACM.

Neate, T., Bourazeri, K., Roper, A., Stumpf, S., & Wilson, S. (2019). Co-created personas: Engaging and empowering users with diverse needs within the design process. In *CHI '19 Proceedings of the 2019 CHI Conference on Human Factors in Computing Systems.* ACM. doi:10.1145/3290605.3300880

Oganetse, D. K. (2022). Putting empathy at the center of instructional design process in early childhood: Dismantling and re-constructing personas. *Journal of Asian and African Social Science and Humanities, 8*(1), 21–31.

Rodgers, P. A. (2013). Articulating design thinking. *Design Studies, 34*(4), 433–437. doi:10.1016/j.destud.2013.01.003

Schmidt, M., & Tawfik, A. (2022). Activity theory as a lens for developing and applying personas and scenarios in learning experience design. *Journal of Applied Instructional Design, 11*(1). https://edtechbooks.org/jaid_11_1/activity_theory_as_a

Svihla, V. (2017). Design thinking and agile design: New trends or just good designs? In West, R. E. (Ed.), *Foundations of learning and instructional design technology.* EdTech Books. https://edtechbooks.org/lidtfoundations/design_thinking_and_agile_design

Villachica, S. W., & Stepich, D. A. (2010). Surviving troubled times: Five best practices for training professionals. *Performance Improvement Quarterly, 23*(2), 93–115. doi:10.1002/piq.20083

Vink, J., & Oertzen, A. S. (2018, July). Integrating empathy and lived experience through co-creation in service design. In *ServDes2018. Service Design Proof of Concept, Proceedings of the ServDes. 2018 Conference* (pp. 18–20). Milan: Linköping University Electronic Press.

Watkins, R., & Kaufman, R. (1996). An update on relating needs assessment and needs analysis. *Performance & Instruction, 35*(10), 10–13. doi:10.1002/pfi.4170351005

Wertz, R. E., Fila, N. D., Smith, K. A., & Streveler, R. A. (2020, October). How do I understand them? Integrating empathy into course design through personas. In *2020 IEEE Frontiers in Education Conference* (FIE) (pp. 1–3). IEEE.

CHAPTER 5

Strategies to Empathize and Analyze

INTRODUCTION

In Chapter 4, we addressed why it's important to empathize and analyze in ID projects. In this chapter, we will introduce you to ways you can actually do this work. After reading this chapter, you should be able to describe how to:

- Use empathy mapping and personas to empathize with learners.
- Conduct a learner and environmental analysis (LEA).
- Conduct a task analysis (TA).
- Complete a learner requirements analysis (LRA).

TOWARDS DESIGN JUSTICE IN EMPATHIZING WITH LEARNERS

In Chapter 1 we defined culture focusing not on geolocations or ethnicity, but on *identities*. Each organization has a unique set of cultures and identities. The individuals who IDs support also have unique cultures and identities. To engage with culture as an asset, we first need to be able to identify the cultures involved. Cultural identity refers to an individual's sense of belonging to a social group. This is often related to abilities, gender, religion, generation, social class, race or ethnicity, nationality, political affiliations, or any other group with a distinct set of values, norms, practices, and language. Understanding these cultural identities will enable IDs to use their rich, varied perspectives as assets in the ID process.

There will be many ways to approach the work associated with the Empathize & Analyze (E&A) component of the LeaPS ID model. Thus, our goal is not to prescribe any single method, but rather to consider each project through the lens of inclusive design. Costanza-Chock (2020) notes it is commonplace to encounter or create interventions that don't support the needs of each subgroup they are intended to serve. When beginning their E&A efforts, IDs should work with their clients to explicitly identify who a learning and development (L&D) intervention will burden more heavily. Whenever possible, they should then make alternative plans to support those it will burden.

For example, an all-day training at a location with little to no breaks will overburden many diverse learners who have been excluded in the past (e.g., individuals with

DOI: 10.4324/9781003360612-5

specific healthcare needs, individuals with specific learning needs). Finding ways to offer additional support to those who are more burdened is one solution. An even better solution is to consider organizational justice theory in decision-making, to ensure the intervention design creates a learning environment that's more fairly distributed, accessible, dignified, and respectful of everyone who would use it.

Costanza-Chock (2020) also states that there are many existing tools and materials that aren't just or inclusive, so you might not be able to start from scratch on a given project. You might need to focus on making improvements on existing systems, programs, tools, and materials so that they become more culturally relevant and inclusive. This would all likely call for different levels of collaboration on each project, different approaches to facilitate the collaboration, and a multifaceted, flexible support system to equitably meet the needs of diverse learners.

When selecting a representative set of stakeholders from across the organization to work on an ID project, include learners and other upstream and downstream stakeholders who are willing, culturally diverse, and from underrepresented groups. Under the right circumstances, along with appropriate input and good design processes, diverse design team members can help guide the project so that it is culturally relevant and equitable.

How to Create Fair Decision-Making Processes

- Use clear, transparent processes that reduce the impact of implicit bias.
- Design systems that serve the needs of all employees, especially those who identify with historically marginalized and intersectional populations.
- Make decisions that are informed by disaggregated data representing diverse, intersectional identities.
- To create buy-in, involve leaders and managers in efforts to improve organizational justice.

(Equitable Data Working Group, 2022; Rusinowitz, 2022)

LEARNER AND ENVIRONMENTAL ANALYSIS (LEA)

What LEA Data Do You Need?

As mentioned in Chapter 4, IDs can use empathy maps and personas as inputs to inform their LEAs. A completed LEA will provide multifaceted descriptions of:

- Who the learners are, their identities, their prior knowledge, and the critical tasks they will need to learn.
- The learning and performance environment, including learners' motivations, the learning environment, and the transfer environment—the learning and work settings where learners will apply what they have learned.

Savvy IDs often use empathy maps to gather the wide variety of data points from numerous learners from an intended audience for specific interventions. They can help the ID identify what learners might think, feel, hear, see, say, do, their pain points, and their potential to gain from an intervention. A visual representation of an empathy map template is shown in Figure 5.1.

Savvy IDs often use these visual examples to keep the learners and their experiences centered in design decisions. The images and attributes of personas are compelling to display during relevant design decision-making exercises. A visual representation of a persona template is shown in Figure 5.2.

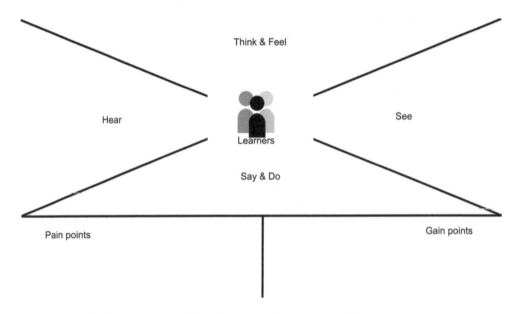

FIGURE 5.1 A visual representation of an empathy map template.

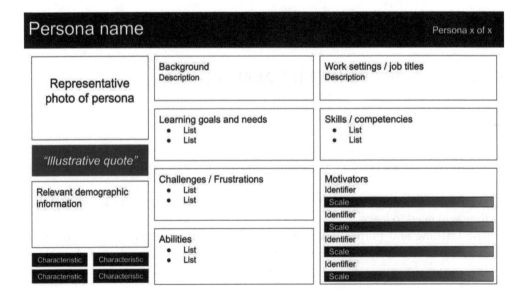

FIGURE 5.2 A visual representation of a personal template.

The following steps describe how to conduct the learner and environmental analyses comprising the LEA.

Step 1. Prepare to Conduct Your Learner Analysis

One way to begin an LEA is learner analysis. Like other analyses, this begins with some planning to determine the data needed. As with other ID tasks, it's helpful to keep the ends in mind. The goal of learner analysis is to provide an understanding of the learners. This can be done through a variety of methods, including but not limited to using empathy maps, personas, and the LEA deliverable itself.

As shown in Table 5.1, ID teams will need to plan how to collect and analyze data from different sources that can provide different types of useful information. Be sure to plan to collect data across different sites and groups (e.g., clients, managers, task performers, experience levels), so that you can identify potential risks to mitigate.

As part of your planning, coordinate with clients to:

- Arrange for the distribution of any extant data to the ID team.
- Schedule any observations, interviews, or surveys the ID team will conduct.
- Provide adequate release time or compensation to all people who will be providing data to the ID team.
- Review key findings from the LEA. Clients, SMEs, representative learners, and other stakeholders should participate in this review.

Step 2. Collect and Analyze Data about Learners

Collect and Analyze Data about Learner Characteristics

Your learner analysis should employ extant data and collect new data regarding the relevant cognitive, physical, affective, and social/cultural characteristics that affect learning, memory, and performance. In Table 5.2, Morrison et al. (2013) list some of the characteristics (e.g., cognitive, physical, affective, social) that could apply in a given ID project. Not all will apply in every case. You should select the learner characteristics relevant to your project.

Trying to collect useful data about all of these factors in each and every ID project would be time- and cost-prohibitive, as well as unnecessary. That's the main reason that most L&D organizations leverage what they already know about their learners. Not every ID project will include its own extensive, dedicated learner analysis effort.

TABLE 5.1 Ends of learner analysis, sources of data, and types of data

By the end of this analysis, you will need to describe	So you'll need to make plans to collect these sources of data	Using these methods
• Who the learners are (learner characteristics) • What they already know (prior knowledge) • What they will need to learn at a high level (critical tasks)	• Extant (known) data • Learners themselves • Learners' bosses • Learners' customers • SMEs	• Extant data analysis • Observations • Interviews (individual or group) • Surveys

TABLE 5.2 Example learner characteristics

Cognitive	Physical	Affective	Social/Cultural*
• Education or training completed • General aptitudes • Developmental level • Language ability • Reading ability • Visual literacy • General knowledge • Specific subject knowledge • Learning preferences or strategies • Attention span	• Age • Gender • Sensory capacities • General health • Motor skills • Physical dexterity	• Motivation to learn • Goals and interests • Attitude towards the subject or the delivery system • Attitude towards the organization providing the training • Academic self-concept • Anxiety level • Expectations of the training	• Work experience and job status • Socioeconomic background • Relationships with peers in communities • Level of moral development • Feelings about authority and power • Acceptance and prioritization of traditional gendered traits • Level of desired structure vs. flexibility • Preference for short-term vs. long-term gains • Strict vs. flexible social norms • Focus on optimism vs. pessimism • Language, symbols, heroes, rituals, and values • Race/ethnicity

Note: This table shows example learner characteristics and is not an exhaustive list. Cultural* traits are informed by Hofstede, Hofstede, and Minkov (2010).

Given the large number of potential measures, it's important to focus on those measures that will be useful for a particular project. Prior knowledge of the task and motivations to learn are almost always relevant measures in ID projects, as are the cultural identities. When possible, learners who have diverse identities should be included as full participants on the design team.

However, other characteristics may not be relevant in a particular situation. As an example, motor development will be more relevant in some jobs (those that involve strength or fine motor control) than in others. Thus, it's important to focus on characteristics that are relevant in the particular situation—those that are likely to influence the design and delivery of the intervention.

Regardless of the data source and types you use, it's important to check your assumptions and stereotypes. For example, not all high school graduates can read at a 12th-grade level. Not all men understand sports examples. Not all older people are computer-phobic. Not all accountants are _____ (fill in your own stereotype). Sometimes assumptions are unavoidable. Whenever you do make assumptions, clearly identify them so that you and your stakeholders can discuss and validate or reject them.

Further, any group of learners will vary in their existing knowledge, motivation to learn, and the cultures they represent. This is what makes data analysis important and challenging. It's also where personas can be useful. A number of personas will allow you to segment and better represent the wide variety of themes you will likely find in your data sources.

In general, it's important that learners feel welcome, have a sense of belonging and inclusion, and receive the support they need to succeed. Completing this part of the learner analysis requires an awareness of the ranges of learners' diverse identities, cultural backgrounds, accessibility needs, and relevant demographic information. Relevant demographic data may be available through organizational databases. If ranges of demographics or identities and abilities are unknown, IDs can invite learners to describe what helps them be successful, and what helps them feel a sense of being welcome and belonging.

Collect Data about Prior Knowledge

"Prior knowledge" is the single greatest predictor of future learning, memory, cognition, and performance (Ormrod, 1995). This broad term incorporates prior education, training, experience, knowledge, skills, and abilities. Stated briefly, IDs need to know what learners already know so they can create interventions that:

- Don't try to teach what learners already know.
- Use terms, concepts, and practices that are already familiar to users.
- State prerequisite skills and any abilities learners should already possess before they begin completing new learning experiences.
- Link what learners already know to what they will be learning.

Table 5.3 suggests potential data collection questions for collecting and analyzing data about prior knowledge.

Learner Motivations

This factor is about learners' attitudes towards the L&D intervention itself. Table 5.4 describes the components of the motivational factor and provides suggested questions for collecting data about each. As ID teams investigate environmental factors, they will collect and analyze data regarding the potential use of job aids. These "cheat sheets" provide the information learners need to perform job tasks. Savvy IDs use job aids wherever possible because they can eliminate the need for formal learning activities or shorten them. Both of these options save organizations the cost of otherwise creating formal learning interventions.

TABLE 5.3 Prior knowledge component and suggested questions for collecting data

Prior Knowledge Component	Suggested Data Collection Questions
Knowledge	• Learners' education level? • Learners' reading level? • Relevant formal and informal training completed about the tasks the intervention will address?
Experience	• What relevant job tasks are learners already performing? • How long have learners held this job? • What other related jobs have they typically held?

TABLE 5.4 Learner motivation component and suggested questions for collecting data

Learner Motivation Component	Suggested Data Collection Questions
Learners' goals for completing the intervention	• How will completing the intervention personally benefit learners?
Perceived utility of the intervention	• To what extent would learners find the intervention useful in performing their jobs?
Perceptions of accountability for mastering the intervention objectives and applying them in the work setting	• To what extent do learners believe it's important to master the intervention? • To what extent do learners believe they are responsible for applying new skills they've learned in intervention to the work setting?
Attitudes towards job aids	• Do learners think that using job aids in training and in the work setting will help or hurt them? • To what extent do learners think job aids may be useful?

Step 3. Report Learner Analysis Results

Having collected and analyzed the data, report your conclusions based on the data that you've collected.

Tips for Reporting Findings

Use the information you've gathered to describe learner characteristics in a clear and coherent way. You'll want to provide detailed, precise descriptions of what you've found out about the learners. Reporting the data with precision will help your readers understand the relevant characteristics of the learners. Watch out for phrases such as: "Some (or many or a few or most) of the learners . . . " Also, reporting that most users feel their previous training hasn't prepared them to perform their jobs is too general. More precise findings would report that:

- 4 out of 7 learners report that . . .
- 25% of 50 learners state that . . .
- Over two-thirds of learners reported . . .

Your findings about the learners should include multifaceted descriptions of the:

- *Learner roles, responsibilities, and identities.* In a few sentences, describe the intended audience for the intervention, focusing on their job title(s) and major job responsibilities. Include any relevant and useful demographic data. Mention any relevant group identities or subgroup intersectionalities. Mention key characteristics of any relevant personas.
- *Learners' prior knowledge and abilities.* Describe what learners already know, mentioning relevant education levels, completed formal and informal training, and the job tasks that the intervention will address. Mention the range of learner abilities.

- *A description of learner motivations.* Describe the attitudes of different learner groups towards the intervention. Describe their perceived goals, the perceived utility of the intervention, their perceptions of accountability, and their attitudes towards job aids. Mention any relevant results of empathy mapping.

Step 4. Prepare to Conduct Your Environmental Analysis

The other part of LEA is investigating the situational factors that can affect learners' motivation, learning, and performance in work settings. Table 5.5 depicts the sources and types of data to collect and analyze.

Step 5. Collect and Analyze Data about Environmental Factors

Specify three broad sets of relevant environmental factors, including motivational, learning environment, and the transfer environment (Morrison et al., 2013).

Learning Environment

The learning environment includes any factors in the learning environment that may affect what, where, and how learners learn. People can complete interventions in classrooms, online, in the workplace, at home, or in other locations. Each of these learning environments could introduce factors that could either promote or interfere with learning. Table 5.6 describes the components of the learning environment and provides suggested questions for collecting data about each.

Transfer Environment

It's a dirty industry secret that most interventions fail to transfer to the job. This means that the organization's investment in creating, implementing, and maintaining the interventions doesn't produce any valued behavior change in the work setting. For example, Brinkerhoff (in Weinbauer-Heidel, 2018) contends that about 15 percent of learners successfully transfer what they've learned in training. About 70 percent make

TABLE 5.5 Ends of environmental analysis, sources of data, and types of data.

Describe How Learners Will	Plan to Collect these Sources of Data	Using these Types of Data
• Orient to their L&D intervention (motivations). • Interact with their learning environment. • Receive support in the work setting to transfer and apply what they've learned.	• Extant data. • Learners and job incumbents (asking about their motivations related to interventions and the extent to which, and how their bosses support skill transfer). • Relevant L&D personnel and supervisors and managers about learning environments. • Supervisors and managers about their support for skill transfer.	• Extant data analysis • Observations • Interviews (individual or group) • Surveys

TABLE 5.6 Learning environment components and selected questions for collecting data

Learning Environment Component	Data Collection Question Examples
Learning facilities, equipment, or supplies	• To what extent do the physical lighting, noise, temperature, seating capacity, space, supplies, and equipment in the learning environment lend themselves to learning? • To what extent can any physical barriers be mitigated?
Scheduling	• What are clients' and other organizational stakeholders' plans for scheduling when the L&D intervention will be offered? • Who will facilitate the L&D intervention? Who else will support the implementation of the L&D intervention? • How many learners would be served during the implementation at one time? • Who will coordinate the scheduling of the learners, facilitators, and support staff? • To what extent can any scheduling barriers be mitigated?
Job aids or technology	• To what extent will learners be able to use any job aids during the time they complete the intervention? • To what extent will facilitators or learners have access to or be expected to use any technology during the intervention?

TABLE 5.7 Transfer components and suggested questions for collecting data

Transfer Component	Suggested Data Collection Questions
Access	• To what extent do learners have access to the tools and resources they need to apply what they've learned in the work setting? • To what extent can any access barriers be mitigated?
Support	• To what extent does the organizational culture actively support learners transferring skills they learned to the workplace setting? • To what extent do supervisors and managers give learners adequate release time to apply what they learned to the work setting? • To what extent do supervisors and managers provide coaching and feedback to help their teams apply what they've learned? • To what extent do learners have access to peers and other experts who can help them apply what they've learned? • To what extent can learners use the job aids they received during the intervention in the work setting? • To what extent can any barriers to transfer be mitigated?

some attempts to transfer what they've learned and then give up. About 15 percent don't even try. In other words, about 85 percent of all learners don't experience any success transferring what they learn in training to the work setting.

To counter this sad situation, savvy IDs often begin conversations about transfer when clients first request interventions. IDs later revisit transfer support when they collect and analyze data as part of their environmental analysis. Table 5.7 describes the components of the transfer factor and provides suggested questions for collecting data about each.

Job aids can play an important role in supporting skill transfer to the work setting. This said, it's not always possible to use job aids. A useful LEA will investigate if there could be:

- *Environmental or physical barriers to using a job aid in the work setting.* Jobs that require quick or smooth performance may preclude the use of job aids. Jobs that require performance in cramped locations may preclude the use of job aids.
- *Social barriers that make it undesirable to use a job aid in the work setting.* Learners using job aids back in the work setting need to feel comfortable about using them. They won't use job aids if they feel doing so makes them "look bad" in front of others or if their managers and supervisors don't support their use on the job.

Step 6. Report Learner and Environmental Analysis Findings

Having collected and analyzed the environmental analysis data, report your findings about the learning environment. Your LEA deliverable should include:

- *A description of the learning environment.* Describe any relevance affordances or physical barriers in the learning environment, any relevant facilities, supplies, scheduling, or facilitation details, and any opportunities or potential problems with learners using job aids or technology during the L&D intervention.
- *A description of the transfer environment.* Describe any issues related to learners' ability to access the tools and resources they will need to apply their learning in the work setting. Describe the extent to which learners will receive the transfer support they will need, noting any issues involving organizational culture, release time to apply learned skills, manager coaching and feedback, access to peer support, and ability to use job aids in the work setting.

Be sure to note inconsistencies between findings across different sites and groups (e.g., clients, managers, task performers, experience levels), as they exist. And note any issues that will need to be mitigated for the intervention to be successful.

TASK ANALYSIS

Useful task analyses represent successful work performances and are used to complete a learning requirements analysis (LRA) as well as the Design & Develop (D&D) component of the LeaPS ID Model. Given their key role in informing later deliverables in an ID project, task analyses should meet these three criteria:

- *Accurate.* They specify what successful performers do and think as they perform the task.
- *Complete.* They contain all relevant steps and decisions involved in performing the task (both the workflow and the "thoughtflow").
- *Authentic.* They use the terms and language of successful performers.

Task Analyses—When to Conduct Them and When to Skip Them

Depending on the size of the project and your expertise, you may not conduct a task analysis at all. In a smaller-scale project where you already possess considerable expertise with the critical tasks, you might choose to omit a task analysis. Instead, for these situations, you might build a rapid prototype—a quickly produced mock-up depicting key aspects of the L&D intervention.

In a larger and more complex project, you may opt to complete some sort of an initial task analysis, even if you are already an expert. This TA will help you organize the materials required to build a prototype, communicate potential designs, and explore potential development activities—especially if you need to obtain client buy-in or will be handing the project off to someone else to develop after the design is finalized.

However, if the critical tasks lie outside of your area of expertise, then you will typically need to collaborate with SMEs. We choose to collaborate with SMEs when it's not cost effective to try to acquire this expertise on our own. This kind of work is usually iterative and refined over a short period of time until it is complete enough to move on to LRA and subsequent D&D efforts.

Task analyses that meet these criteria can help ensure smoother sailing in later parts of an ID project. Not meeting these criteria can result in unplanned revisions throughout the rest of a project.

Depending on the ID project and culture of the organization's L&D group, some IDs will conduct an LEA before conducting a task analysis (TA). Other IDs will conduct a TA first. Still other IDs will create these LEA deliverables in parallel. In Chapter 4, you learned about common types of tasks that appear in work settings: completing procedures, applying concepts to make decisions, completing processes. Savvy IDs match the types of job tasks learners are completing to the approach they'll use to conduct a task analysis. IDs often combine different task analysis approaches when analyzing more complex tasks.

Collect and Analyze Data about Critical Tasks

An ID team will also need to collect and analyze data about the critical tasks learners don't know how to perform. These critical tasks could be specific job responsibilities, duties, tasks, subtasks, steps, and/or key complex decisions. To collect these data, IDs often ask clients and other relevant stakeholders about the critical tasks learners are unfamiliar with or find difficult to learn. The L&D intervention(s) the ID team creates will then address these tasks. Table 5.8 suggests potential data collection questions about critical tasks.

TABLE 5.8 Critical tasks and suggested questions for collecting data

Critical Tasks	Suggested Data Collection Questions
Critical, difficult, and complex aspects of tasks that learners will need to learn	• What should learners be able to do on the job after completing this L&D intervention that they couldn't do before? • What makes this particular task critical? Why is it important to perform it correctly? • What, if anything, is difficult about performing this critical task? Why is it hard? • What, if anything, is complex about performing this critical task? What makes it complex?

Analyze Procedures

The term "task analysis" usually refers to what Jonassen, Tessmer, and Hannum (1999) call "procedural analysis." However, it's important to understand that this is only one of many task analysis techniques. Knowing how to conduct a procedural analysis is useful because:

- It's the most familiar and widely used task analysis method.
- IDs can easily adapt this technique to fit a wide range of instructional design situations, including interventions for both physical and cognitive tasks.
- IDs can easily adapt this technique to conduct task analyses for concepts and processes.

Clark (1986) describes a procedure as a "series of steps whereby an individual completes a task" (p. 13). Performers complete procedural tasks by completing the same set of steps the same way every time. Analyzing procedural tasks involves decomposing them into their component parts. The level of detail that IDs pursue when they conduct a task analysis varies depending on the intended learners, complexity of the project, and the tasks. This usually includes:

- A job (typically a collection of responsibilities and tasks), which is made up of . . .
- Broad responsibilities, which are made up of . . .
- Duties, which are made up of . . .
- Tasks, which are made up of . . .
- Subtasks, which are made up of . . .
- Steps (discrete, observable actions).

A procedural analysis might also include any necessary additional information about individual steps, which may include:

- Graphics (screen shots, pictures, diagrams, etc.).
- If/then decision tables describing how to determine something.
- Hot tips that provide hints to efficiently perform a step.
- Cautions that point out errors to avoid when performing a step.

This hierarchy is intended to be a guide. Depending on the specific project, you might add or subtract one or more levels of detail.

Step 1. Prepare to Conduct the Task Analysis

1. Coordinate with the client and SME to arrange day and time for the task analysis. Ask for two to four hours to begin with.
2. Ask the SME to bring samples of things that they use or complete when they perform their jobs. If this is problematic, try to conduct the task analysis in their workplace as they perform the task.
3. Review the needs assessment results and any other relevant extant data the client or SME can provide before your first meeting.
4. Use the needs assessment and extant data to create initial, draft versions of the task characteristics and initial details—either a task list or information about key concepts.

TA Preparation Tips

Try to be better organized than your SME. Try to get everything you need to create a complete, accurate, and authentic task analysis in the time you have. This eliminates later trips back to the SME to collect additional information and clarifications during D&D. Besides, getting access to SMEs can be dicey, and a SME who's available at one time may not be available at another.

Tell the SME that what you've drafted is likely wrong and incomplete, but that it's easier to revise something wrong than to build from scratch.

If possible, avoid a situation in which you rely solely on manufacturers' manuals, standard operating procedures (SOPs), or other extant data. These sources don't always accurately describe the way real experts actually perform a particular task on the job. Experts are likely to know shortcuts, workarounds, "tricks-of-the-trade," and other variations that aren't in the manual. Experts' knowledge is more likely to be current than other extant sources.

Step 2. Refine the Task Characteristics

During your SME interview(s), refine the draft you created in step 1. The task characteristics provide an overview of the major tasks that your intervention will address. In addition to helping ID teams "get the lay of the land" before they start creating task lists, specifying task characteristics now will save time later during the D&D effort trying to "backfill" this information. Think about these characteristics as "background information" about the jobs and the major tasks that successful performers complete in work settings. Table 5.9 provides additional information about each task characteristic.

TABLE 5.9 Task characteristics and suggested descriptions appearing in your task analysis

Task Characteristic	Suggested Descriptions Appearing in Your Task Analysis
Critical tasks	List the job responsibility, duty, or critical task (or parts of them) that the L&D intervention will address.
Goals for each major task	Specify organizational and individual goals for each critical task.
Cues	List all cues that initiate task performance ("when do you do this?").
Resources	List all resources that exemplary performers use when they perform the task.
Task frequency	How often a competent performer typically performs the task.
Task duration	How long it typically takes a competent performer to perform the task. If duration is variable, include both an average time and a range (minimum and maximum time).
Standards that the completed task should meet	List standards that the completed task should meet ("how do you know you've done the task correctly?")
Prerequisite skills	List things learners should already know and do on the job before they can attempt to complete the task. These are skills learners will already need to possess before they begin the intervention that your team will design.
What is critical, difficult, and complex about the critical tasks	You asked clients, learners, job incumbents, managers, supervisors, and other stakeholders this question during the LEA. You will now ask the SME so you can further refine this information.

Tips for Facilitating Your Task Analysis

To set the stage, tell SMEs that you're hoping to work with them to represent their expertise in ways that will help others in the organization perform more like them. To this end, you'll be asking them to perform their real-world job tasks—or as close to that as possible. Ask them to think aloud as they perform. Ask them a lot of questions about what they're doing, how they're doing it, and why. At the end of your time together, you should have a representation of what the SME does in the workplace—thereby "capturing lightning in a bottle."

During your time together, always appreciate the SME's expertise! When your interview is over, thank them for their insights and spending time with you. Ask them if you can follow up with them with any additional questions.

Step 3. Refine the Task List

During your SME interview(s), iteratively refine the initial task list you prepared. Make a special effort to note nuanced aspects of performance that are otherwise invisible using pictures, if/then decision tables, hot tips (hints), and cautions (how to avoid errors).

Tips for Refining the Task Analysis

1. Work in layers, revising, refining, and adding additional detail as you work along.

   • For tasks that involve procedures and processes, you may detail duties, then subtasks, and then the steps comprising each subtask. This collection of duties, tasks, subtasks, and steps is called a "task list."
   • For tasks involving concepts you might move from a definition of the concept to key features of the concept to a prototypical "best" example to a collection of examples and non-examples of the concept.

2. Add additional information to describe aspects of key steps that are otherwise invisible. (If you're sure that learners already know this missing information, you may choose to omit it.)

   • Graphics/illustrations/pictures/photos.
   • Decision tables.
   • Hot tips.
   • Cautions.

3. Stop detailing when your SME tells you that novices already know how to perform a given task, subtask, or step.

Step 4. Highlight What the Intervention Will Address

Use highlighting, boldfacing, listing, or some other convention to mark the critical tasks your intervention will address.

Step 5. Add Any Footnotes

As you conduct the task analysis, you and your SMEs may find yourselves making guesses and other working assumptions as you go along. Doing so helps you complete the task analysis. This said, it's good practice to footnote those items that you'll need to verify with other SMEs, the client, or other organizational stakeholders.

Step 6. Complete the Task Analysis Deliverable

A procedural task analysis is often a word-processed document that consists of:

• A table containing the sources and types of data the ID team used to conduct the task analysis.
• A table specifying task characteristics.
• A hierarchically organized task list (often numbered) that decomposes tasks into their component subtasks, steps, and corresponding information.

- A specification of the critical tasks that the intervention will address (highlighted portions of the task list).
- A refined description of what is critical, difficult, and complex about the critical tasks.

Task Analysis Variations for Concepts and Processes

Analyze Concepts

To complete many work tasks, performers often make decisions that involve using concepts. Clark (1986) defines a concept as "a category of items that share common features" (p. 13). Concepts are associated with characteristics ("key features") that distinguish a given concept from others. For example, the key features of an editor are:

- A person.
- Responsible for articles written by others.
- Revises articles to reflect publication standards.

Performers could be making decisions about whether a given thing or situation is legal, compliant, or ethical. For instance, a university instructor determining whether to include an image copied from the Internet in their classroom lecture slides must decide if it would meet fair use regulations (Giacumo, Savenye, & Smith 2013; Giacumo & Savenye, 2020).

Conversely, performers could be applying or using concepts to create something. For example, an entrepreneur creating a business plan could be applying concepts about key partners, cost structures, key resources, value propositions, etc. These and other related concepts would be used in combination to create a coherent business plan. The entrepreneur will then make decisions about how to apply each of these concepts in a way that should lead to a successful business.

After completing the task characteristics for their task analyses, IDs typically work with SMEs to either:

- Apply the concepts to complete a job task. For example, to determine fair use of an image copied from the Internet, IDs might work with a SME as they review images online, or
- Review a completed work sample to reverse engineer the concepts they applied. For example, to determine the concepts involved in creating a business plan, IDs might work with a SME to review "good" and "bad" examples of completed plans.

IDs might also review extant data to analyze concepts. They might review organizational data that a client or other key stakeholders provide. Or they might conduct a review of the relevant professional literature. IDs analyze concepts by collecting information that can later appear in the learning and performance support materials. For every relevant concept comprising a task, they may collect data about:

- Definitions.
- Characteristics or key features of the concept that distinguish it from other concepts.

- Work settings in which performers typically recognize or use the concept.
- A "best," "easy," or "prototypical" example of the concept.
- Other increasingly difficult examples of the concept.
- Non-examples of the concept.
- Analogies or similes describing the concept and what distinguishes it from others.
- Mnemonics describing concept characteristics.
- Graphic depictions of the concept.

Analyze Processes

Clark (1986) defines a process as a "series of steps whereby several individuals, departments, or objects accomplish a task." Processes are more complex than procedures. Most processes require complex cognition. They require performers to recognize situations, make complex decisions, solve problems, and weigh results. Processes typically involve some sort of novelty, and people don't complete them exactly the same way each time. People in work settings complete processes when they:

- Audit a firm's accounts.
- Diagnose a patient.
- Use the LeaPS ID model to create an L&D intervention.
- Troubleshoot a complex problem.

Processes are typically timebound. While there's variation, performers typically do some things before others. This said, the specific order of steps in a process can change each time.

To analyze processes, use the approach for conducting a procedural task analysis. Either work with the SME as they complete the process in real time or review completed work samples with them to reverse engineer the process. To complete the task list, work with the SME to specify what they do to:

- Prepare to complete the process.
- Complete the process. Specify the major tasks and subtasks first, then the steps that comprise them.
- Finish the process, including any associated follow-up activities.

Write Your Task Analysis Deliverable

Specify the task characteristics first. Then create the task list. Use the same hierarchical numbering and indenting scheme as a procedural analysis. Tell the SME, clients, and other organizational stakeholders that the numbers are merely unique identifiers for each activity. They do not represent a strict linear sequence of activity. Create graphics to depict non-linear aspects of the process.

Once you've decomposed the tasks, use graphics, decision tables, hot tips, and cautions to provide additional relevant information about a given step.

Your completed task analysis should include:

- A brief description of the learners.
- A description of any data sources used to conduct the task analysis.

- An overview of major tasks and their characteristics.
- A completed task list or concept analysis.
- Highlighting to identify the critical tasks that the intervention will address.
- A short description of what is critical, difficult, or complex about the tasks you've highlighted.

Review and Try Out Your Task Analysis

To ensure your task analysis is accurate, complete, and authentic, it's good practice to:

- Ask clients, representative learners, and other stakeholders to review and approve the TA.
- Ask representative job incumbents to try out the TA by using it to perform their job tasks in the work setting.

LEARNING REQUIREMENTS ANALYSIS

Let's recap. An LEA describes who the learners are, what they need to learn, and what factors in the environment can affect their learning and performance. A TA describes the characteristics of the critical tasks the intervention will address, provides a task list that represents successful performance in the work setting, and specifies what is critical, difficult, and complex about these tasks.

An LRA can rely upon these analysis results to make initial decisions about how to configure the interventions to be created, implemented, and maintained. It's wise for organizations to minimize the cost of creating, implementing, and maintaining interventions over time. The goal is to close a performance gap at the lowest reasonable cost (e.g., time, effort) to meet the desired results in ways that are culturally relevant and inclusive. After all, in some form or another, clients and organizations always pay for interventions, whether the budget is for an internal L&D group or an external vendor.

Step 1. Prepare to Conduct the LRA

To conduct an LRA, you will want to mine the contents of these ID deliverables. They will inform your ID decisions about the configurations the L&D intervention will use.

- *Needs assessment*. Review the contents of any existing needs assessment noting, in particular, the system gap to close and the causes of the gap.
- *LEA*. Review the descriptions of learner characteristics, their prior knowledge, and the critical tasks they need to learn.
- *TA*. Review the task characteristics, task list, and what's critical, difficult, and complex about the critical tasks.

Step 2. Chunk the Critical Tasks

Organize ("chunk") the critical tasks (and parts of them) that the intervention will address.

- Break down larger bits of instruction into smaller ones that are easier for learners to complete and apply in work settings. Start by grouping one or more subordinate critical tasks (or parts of them) under one overarching major critical task (Giacumo & MacDonald, 2022).
- Organize the chunks into a logical order for learners to complete them.

The sizes of the "chunks" that IDs use will vary with the scale of the ID project. A larger ID project may consist of several courses corresponding to critical tasks. Each course may consist of several modules. Each module may consist of several lessons. A smaller ID project may consist of a single lesson corresponding to a single critical task.

Step 3. Specify Initial Configurations for Each Critical Task

A review of the needs assessment, learning requirements analysis, and task analysis will identify all of the critical tasks that are associated with either a lack of adequate:

- *Guidance in the workplace setting.* This refers to job aids, information sources, and access to coaches or mentors.
- *Skill arising from a failure of the L&D system.* This refers to the critical tasks that the learners don't know how to perform. This will require access to learning interventions.

Use Table 5.10 to make a configuration decision about each of these tasks.

CASE STUDY

The Professional Society of Socially Just IDs (pseudonym) is proud of offering a competitively priced, high-quality annual conference as a professional development opportunity for its members and the public. After receiving feedback requesting support from members who have different mobility and care-giving needs, the organizers decided to try to address these individuals' needs. However, many of the voting executive board members don't feel it's appropriate to spend money on creating a more inclusive and accessible conference for these individuals. They feel the scarce resources should be spent on the majority of the attendees and won't vote to spend money to make the conference more accessible.

You are on the executive conference planning committee this year. As part of the committee, you will work in concert with the executive leader and board members of the organization to secure resources required to design, plan, and implement the conference.

- How would you begin a learner and environment analysis (LEA) in this situation? What affinity groups would you want represented in your data collection?
- What strategies can you use to influence a more just, inclusive, and equitable, event?

TABLE 5.10 Critical task LRA configuration table

If the Critical Task Is	Then	So Select this Configuration for the Intervention
Not associated with any stated mission or strategic organizational objective from the needs assessment or a client request	Don't use the organization's IDs to create formal job aids or learning interventions. Learners and learner communities can create their own informal learning resources.	Use informal learning instead.
Associated only with a lack of guidance	Provide job aids learners can use in the work setting. Learners don't need other learning interventions.	Job aids alone.
Associated with a lack of guidance and the LEA notes that learners aren't willing to use job aids without some sort of initial learning event	Provide minimal demonstrations, practice, and coaching to introduce the job aids.	Job aids with introductory learning.
Associated with a lack of guidance and skill that will require practice, coaching, and feedback to master	Learners will need to learn how to perform critical tasks by actually performing them in a safe and authentic learning environment. Learners will need to complete an authentic assessment to show their mastery.	Job aids with extensive learning.
Associated with a lack of skill that will require practice, coaching, and feedback to master AND it's not feasible for learners to use job aids	Learners will need to learn how to perform critical tasks by actually performing them in a safe and authentic learning environment— without using job aids.	Extensive training to memory.
Associated with a lack of guidance, feedback, and incentives AND learners don't feel a sense of belonging AND the organization is looking to promote from within or reduce attrition of skilled personnel	Learners need a safe, interactive environment where they can receive guidance and feedback while feeling a sense of belonging.	Coaching.
Associated with a lack of guidance, feedback, knowledge, skills, abilities, or motives AND learners don't feel a sense of belonging AND the organization is looking to promote from within or reduce attrition of skilled personnel	Learners need a safe, interactive environment where they can receive guidance and feedback to build knowledge, skills, and abilities while feeling a sense of belonging.	Mentoring.
Associated with a lack of guidance, feedback, knowledge, skills, abilities, or motives AND formal organizational resources are not adequate	Learners need safe, informal access to trusted career-based feedback, advice, ideas, emotional support, and/or mentoring to meet their own interests and career development goals (Trust, Carpenter, & Krutka, n.d.).	Personal learning networks. Affinity groups.

Note: We will take a deeper dive into job aids in Chapter 9. We will take a closer look at non-instructional interventions (e.g., organizational communities of practice, affinity groups, mentoring, job shadowing, and curated content repositories) in Chapter 8.

- Referring to Table 5.2, what learner characteristics would you be most interested in? What methods would you use to collect data about those learner characteristics?
- Referring to Table 5.6, what environmental characteristics would you be most interested in? What methods would you use to collect data about those environmental characteristics?

REFLECTION QUESTIONS

- How do you include, as design team members, individuals who belong to under-represented groups; who represent people (e.g., managers, IDs, SMEs, learners) who have diverse identities? How would you encourage them to join the team? How would you help them feel valued as fully participating members of the team?
- What might you do to work towards "co-design" (refer to Chapter 1) when conducting an LEA and TA? How might you move towards a level of "community ownership, or assigning incentive/rewards, or credit, or visibility" (Costanza-Chock, 2020), with SMEs, and/or managers? What would you do to counter resistance from those who think the work is inconvenient for whatever reason?
- What other processes or inputs have you used to analyze and empathize with intended learners?
- Think specifically about task analysis. The purpose of a TA is to break down critical tasks in their procedures, concepts, and processes. How would you apply the principle of "expanded collaboration" to help accomplish that goal?

REFERENCES

Clark, R. C. (1986). Defining the "D" in ISD: Part 2: Task-specific instructional methods. *Performance + Instruction, 25*(3), 12–17. doi:10.1002/pfi.4150250306

Costanza-Chock, S. (2020). *Design justice: Community-led practices to build the worlds we need.* The MIT Press. https://library.oapen.org/bitstream/handle/20.500.12657/43542/external_content.pdf

Equitable Data Working Group. (2022). A vision for equitable data: Recommendations from the Equitable Data Working Group. Retrieved March 9, 2023, from https://uidl.naswa.org/bitstream/handle/20.500.11941/4716/eo13985-vision-for-equitable-data.pdf?sequence=1

Giacumo, L. A., & MacDonald, M. (2022, May 12). How to get started with chunking & sequencing elearning design. https://www.learningguild.com/articles/how-to-get-started-with-chunking-sequencing-elearning-design/

Giacumo, L. A., & Savenye, W. (2020). Asynchronous discussion forum design to support cognition: Effects of rubrics and instructor prompts on learners' critical thinking, achievement, and satisfaction. *Educational Technology Research and Development, 68*, 37–66.

Giacumo, L. A., Savenye, W., & Smith, N. (2013). Facilitation prompts and rubrics on higher-order thinking skill performance found in undergraduate asynchronous discussion boards. *British Journal of Educational Technology, 44*(5), 774–794.

Hofstede, G., Hofstede, G. J., & Minkov, M. (2010). *Cultures and organizations: Software of the mind* (3rd ed.). McGraw Hill.

Jonassen, D. H., Tessmer, M., & Hannum, W. H. (1999). *Task analysis methods for instructional design.* Lawrence Erlbaum Associates.

Morrison, G. R., Ross, S. M., Kalman, H. K., & Kemp, J. E. (2013). *Designing effective instruction* (7th ed.). Wiley.

Ormrod, J. E. (1995). *Human learning* (2nd ed.). Prentice-Hall.

Rusinowitz, S. (February 22, 2022). Organizational Justice 101: How to foster fairness in the workplace. Retrieved March 9, 2023, from https://www.charthop.com/resources/blog/dei/organizational-justice-fairness-workplace/

Trust, T., Carpenter, J. P., & Krutka, D. G. (Eds.). (n.d.). Professional learning networks. https://edtechbooks.org/encyclopedia/professional_learning_networks?book_nav=true

Weinbauer-Heidel, I. (2018). *What makes training really work: 12 levers of transfer effectiveness*. Institute for Transfer Effectiveness.

CHAPTER 6

Iterative Design and Development

INTRODUCTION

ID teams often mine the contents of the Empathize & Analyze (E&A) deliverables, or related findings, to create Design & Develop (D&D) deliverables. As ID teams undertake the E&A component of the LeaPS ID model, they may also begin to create components of learning and performance support materials. As depicted in Figure 6.1, these activities occur in the Design & Develop component of the LeaPS ID model.

Clearly, the Design & Develop component in the LeaPS ID model covers a lot of ground—more than a single chapter in a single book can address. This chapter will focus on some of the design activities of this component. Other chapters will focus on other design activities. And still other chapters will focus on development activities. By the end of this chapter, you should be able to:

* Describe the purpose of the Design & Develop component deliverables.
* Explain the use of feedback loops in creating output iterations.
* Explain the benefits of a backwards design approach.
* List common design document headings.
* Create performance requirements (PR).

COMBINING DESIGN AND DEVELOPMENT INTO A SINGLE COMPONENT

Instructional design models often consist of five common but separate components in an instructional systems design (ISD) process: Analyze, Design, Develop, Implement, Evaluate (ADDIE) (Branch & Dousay, 2015). In actuality, however, design and development have always co-existed in an interactive and messy process. This allows IDs to get some feedback early in a project. Working iteratively, IDs will then make revisions to refine the deliverables. IDs may use several iterations to begin laying out high-level designs or prototypes and refine them to depict additional levels of detail.

Design and development activities are iterative and synergistic. Because this work typically overlaps, the LeaPS ID model combines them into one component: Design & Develop. The work IDs complete in design and early prototype development gives

DOI: 10.4324/9781003360612-6

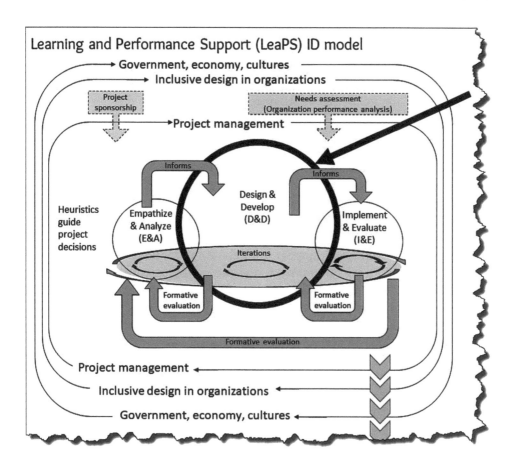

FIGURE 6.1 Design & Develop components of the LeaPS ID model.

them more data to clarify their design decisions and advance towards developing better prototypes and eventually working products.

In the design portion of the D&D component, ID teams work to determine the outputs that will comprise the instructional and performance support materials and how they will work together. To describe this work to clients, stakeholders, and all members of the ID team, IDs commonly create design documents. Another part of the work in this component involves development. ID teams may start creating early versions of some of the materials they've envisioned. For example, an ID team may use personas and empathy maps they've already created to inform mock-ups (a.k.a. "prototypes") of one or more key instructional components. These prototypes would show what these components could look like and how they could work. IDs may then use feedback loops to conduct reviews and tryouts of these prototypes to ensure they work as planned before ramping up larger-scale development efforts. In using this prototyping-based approach, IDs can:

- Create and try out key components of the learning and performance support materials before developing all of them.

- Apply what they learn creating the prototypes to define the processes they will use for larger-scale development.
- Continuously improve their development processes.

New IDs often ask the following questions regarding design and development.

Do I Really Have to Design *Everything* Before I Start Development Activities?

No. The LeaPS ID model includes both "design" and "develop" in order to better depict the various tasks that IDs carry out during this part of the ID process. Some deliverables are more related to "design" (e.g., performance requirements, design documents, storyboards). Some are more related to "development" (e.g., assessment instruments, eLearning objects, job aids, participant guides, instructor guides). And similar overlaps within and between components appear throughout the LeaPS ID model. In this vein, the work associated with the Empathize & Analyze component often overlaps with the work associated with the Design & Develop component. And, this work can overlap with the work associated with the Implement & Evaluate component.

How Much Overlap and Iteration Does a Project Need?

This answer depends on several factors.

- *Experience with similar projects.* The more the ID team, the client, and the sponsoring organization have experience successfully completing similar types of projects, the less overlapping and iteration the project may need.
- *Task complexity.* The more straightforward the tasks are that learners complete on the job, the less IDs will need to iterate and separate project components. Job tasks requiring learners to remember facts aren't as complex as job tasks requiring learners to perform a task the same way each time. And tasks that require lots of decision-making in novel situations that are never the same are even more complex. The more complex the task, the more overlapping and iteration the project may need.
- *ID familiarity with tasks.* If the ID is also a subject matter expert (SME), they will likely spend less time working through D&D. If they are new to the tasks, they will likely need more time. The work associated with any given LeaPS ID model component eventually ends as specified in the project timeline.
- *Project complexity.* The larger the project and the more components it has, the greater the need to make sure that all of the project parts integrate seamlessly. This means more overlapping and iteration.

All of these factors are associated with risk to the project scope, budget, and schedule. The greater the risk to project scope, schedule, and budget, the more IDs may overlap and iterate their efforts across the model components. Conversely, the more work that's been done to frame a problem or need, articulate potential solutions, create design documents, blueprints, and/or prototypes, the faster and easier it can be to finish development-related work.

In all projects, IDs reach a point where they stop empathizing and analyzing work and some point where they stop designing and developing work. The upper limits of overlap and iteration are always set by risk. The work associated with any given LeaPS ID component eventually ends as specified in the project timeline.

What Should I Do If I Don't Have All the Inputs the LeaPS ID Model Says I Should Have?

You should simply do your best to look to other sources that can provide the information you need. IDs don't always enjoy such a happy state of affairs! Sponsorship issues may have precluded IDs from conducting adequate work during the Empathize & Analyze component. When these inputs are not available, IDs put on their detective hats to find other relevant information from other sources they can use. There are many practical ways to access this information and obtain input from a wide array of diverse stakeholder perspectives. Many times, IDs can find creative ways to obtain this kind of information by asking questions at the water cooler, joining colleagues in an informal lunch, networking at events, walking around the floor where the work is done, looking into the business intelligence (BI) system, internal websites, connecting with folks who could share perspectives on internal or external social media groups, or other internal communications tools and systems.

BACKWARDS DESIGN

In some circles, ID teams create learning and performance support materials by working only with SMEs and/or conducting their own research. ID teams then specify the topics the intervention will address. After building the content associated with the topics, ID teams may create learning objectives, which are largely about "knowing," "understanding," "describing," or "being aware of." The teams may then even create multiple-choice knowledge tests. The focus of these materials is "covering the topic." Unfortunately, this approach to instructional design tends to produce "information dumps" that are less focused on decision-making skills. Further, the content tends to be neither socially just nor culturally relevant. In this chapter you'll learn how to lay the foundation for performance-based learning and development (L&D) intervention design through a backwards design process. Subsequent chapters continue to build this process.

As shown in Figure 6.2, the LeaPS ID model uses a backwards design approach that allows IDs to design "with the end in mind" (Wulfeck et al., 1978). Why? For learning

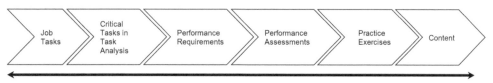

FIGURE 6.2 Backwards design in creating interventions.

experiences to produce valued behavior change on the job, all interventions need to align with critical job tasks. This avoids creating content that learners don't need. IDs creating performance-based L&D often work on deliverables in roughly this sequence:

1. Performance Requirements to specify what learners should be able to do upon completing their learning experiences and returning to the workplace. IDs base these requirements on the critical tasks they identify in the task analysis, which are part of the larger set of tasks learners complete in the workplace.
2. Performance Assessments to show that learners can meet the performance requirements.
3. Practice Exercises that learners complete to build the skills they need to pass the assessments.
4. Content (including information and demonstrations) that learners need to begin the practice exercises.

This alignment of ID components ensures that performances, conditions, and criteria remain consistent throughout the ID project. Input from diverse stakeholder perspectives can help to ensure more culturally relevant and inclusive outputs by specifying:

- The *performances* that people complete, including tasks, subtasks, and steps.
- One or more *conditions* that need to be in place before people perform the task. These conditions include cues that tell someone to start performing the task and resources they use to complete the task.
- *Criteria* that the task should meet.

A systematic approach to instructional design means that the conditions, performances, and criteria in the critical job tasks that a diverse ID team identified earlier in the project remain consistent throughout the creation of the design deliverables. Should there be any misalignments among these components, people won't be able to learn how to perform their jobs in ways that meet specified standards for their job tasks. Across all of these ID components, these attributes should remain consistent. This approach has been described as a "backwards design" systematic process (McTighe & Wiggins, 2012).

1. *Identify desired results.* In backwards design, these "desired results "are also called "learning outcomes" or "performance requirements."
2. *Determine acceptable evidence.* This evidence consists of assessments that indicate learners can meet specified criteria at acceptable levels of performance.
3. *Plan learning experiences and instruction.* Finally, create practice exercises and relevant content.

DESIGN DOCUMENTS

To communicate internally among members of the ID team and externally with clients, SMEs, learners, supervisors, managers, and other project stakeholders, IDs often summarize their project plans in design documents. The contents of design documents can vary widely across client organizations and ID teams. The purpose is to build off of the design implications from Empathize & Analyze (E&A) deliverables by specifying more detailed plans for intervention development. They also often outline relevant theories, frameworks, and approaches. Additionally, IDs may include a plan for conducting a summative evaluation after the organization has implemented the intervention. Such an evaluation can determine the overall worth of the intervention and the organization's return on its investment. Figure 6.3 shows common components that can appear in a design document, along with corresponding definitions and locations in this textbook.

In other words, design documents can include decisions representing agreements between an ID team, clients, and SMEs. Sometimes they serve as a mechanism to solicit feedback. In addition to what's noted in Figure 6.3, they can include:

- Outlines of modules/lessons and eLearning storyboards.
- Final iterations of personas, journey maps, or prototypes.

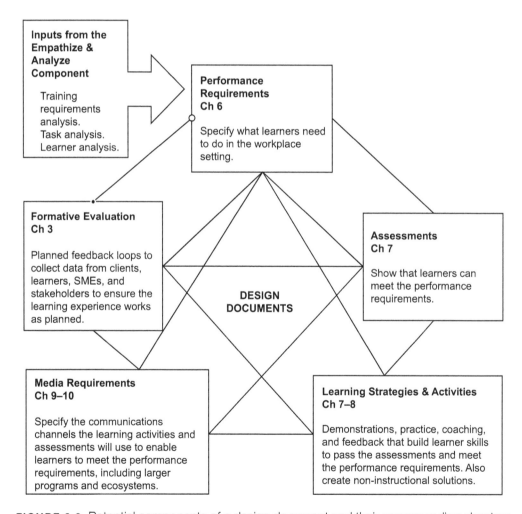

FIGURE 6.3 Potential components of a design document and their corresponding chapters in this text.

- Potential learning paths, or the ways in which learners could progress through an intervention or series of interventions.

These deliverables can specify:

- Descriptions of the performance requirements, assessments, interventions, and practice opportunities.
- Alignment between the performance requirements, assessments, interventions, and practice opportunities.
- The purpose of practice and assessments (e.g., certification, reflection, feedback, acceptable vs. mastery).
- Positions of assessments (e.g., preassessments, paced self-checks, post-assessments).
- Quality specifications of assessments (e.g., coverage, validity, reliability, practicality) and trade-offs among these four aspects of quality.
- Format(s) for assessments (e.g., observations, simulations, ratings, closed-ended, open-ended, portfolio).
- Development specifications.
- Time on task estimates.

Design documents for eLearning projects may also include blueprints or wireframes, scripts, and storyboards. IDs generally create blueprints or wireframes first. These documents often become inputs for creating, later, higher fidelity prototypes. Once these later prototypes are reviewed and approved, IDs work with all key stakeholders to make sure they agree with the vision and objectives of the eLearning course.

Document-based (e.g., slides, word-processed, spreadsheet) eLearning prototypes (e.g., scripts, storyboards, course templates) tend to include both text and graphics, although the graphic indications can range widely. They might include anything from descriptive text to stick figures, to draft images or early prototype examples. More advanced storyboards can have all of the information that developers would need to build prototypes such as the function of buttons, scripts, and some might even simulate actual potential onscreen navigation options. Functional or interactive eLearning

How Would Creating and Refining these Documents Vary Based on Organizational Culture?

Every organization does things differently. IDs in some organizations work on prototypes from the start before they speak with any learners. Others prototype after they have spoken with learners. In fact, the LeaPS ID model allows the three inner circles (i.e., Empathize & Analyze, Design & Development, Implement & Evaluate) to move so they are on top of each other, or they get larger, or smaller, or more spread out, or closer together. They are meant to be dynamic and scalable rather than static. Also, co-design would require a different approach from that of participatory design.

prototypes (e.g., games, video, tutorials) may be partially or fully working. These kinds of prototypes can include mechanisms for collecting reviewer feedback.

Do I Really Need to Create Design Documents?

It's often up to the ID. It depends on the size of a given project, the client, and the ID team. The larger a project, the more useful a design document might be. This said, clients, SMEs, learners, supervisors, managers, and other organizational stakeholders can be largely unfamiliar with these documents and how to interpret them. In spite of the good faith work that IDs can put in to create a design document which they think is clear and concise, these documents can still be abstract and overwhelming to people who aren't used to them. While it's common practice to require client review and approval of design documents in some organizations, clients and IDs can still find themselves in situations where they've interpreted the document differently. Further, clients may balk at paying for the creation of a document they don't find particularly useful.

Some IDs find design documents so useful that they create them even when clients don't require them. Design documents can help them organize their ideas about the design of the instruction in a single place, ensure that they've figured out how to develop the project, and verify they have the information in hand they need to move forwards with development.

PERFORMANCE REQUIREMENTS (PR)

The task analyses that ID teams complete during the Empathize & Analyze component represent how successful performers complete their job tasks. Early in their Design & Develop efforts, ID teams mine the contents of these task analyses to create performance requirements. And these performance requirements help IDs "design with the

Include Learners with Diverse Identities to Build Design Document and PRs

It's no secret that inclusive design approaches are like universal design approaches; they help all learners. Therefore, including learners with diverse identities in your design and development process helps to improve organizational performance. It's easier to build accessible and inclusive designs when they are planned from the start, and there are many different approaches to achieve this goal (Lowenthal et al., 2020). Therefore, we recommend that you include learners with diverse identities as much as possible in your ID process to ideate, provide input, review, and approve for both the design document and the performance requirements. As mentioned previously, you can use participatory (Rodriguez et al., 2020) or co-design approaches (Dennerlein et al., 2020; Geraldes et al., 2021) to include their input.

end in mind" by specifying what learners should be able to do upon completing their learning experiences—and in the workplace when they apply what they've learned.

From Critical Tasks (a.k.a. Objectives) to Performance Requirements

You may be thinking, "Gee, the critical tasks from Chapter 5 and these performance requirements sound a lot like learning or performance *objectives*." Objectives go by many names: "Learning objectives," "behavioral objectives," "performance objectives," "instructional objectives," and various others. When they speak to higher-level goals, they are often called "performance outcomes," "learning outcomes," "learning goals," or another term.

Regardless of what they're called, critical tasks usually describe the goals of the instruction—what the learners should be able to do in workplace settings upon completing the intervention. Defined in this way, objectives are like the destination for a trip. They describe the endpoint. The intervention, then, becomes the itinerary designed to help the learners reach that destination.

While the term "instructional objectives" may be more common in our area of practice, it's also loaded with baggage. In our consulting practice, we choose to steer clear of this term with clients. Instead, we find clients more readily understand questions about the "critical tasks" and "critical decisions" that people need to make in workplace settings.

Thus, the "critical tasks" provide broader descriptions about what learners should be doing on the job after training; performance requirements add more rigor to specifying exemplary job performance. Performance requirements act as a detailed promise that describes how people should perform their job in the workplace in ways that meet organizational goals. Therefore, each performance requirement specifies an on-the-job performance, as well as all relevant on-the-job conditions and on-the-job criteria.

Writing Performance Requirements

There are different ways IDs can specify relevant on-the-job conditions and on-the-job criteria. One way is to use a variation of the 3-part format that Mager (1997) popularized.

Step 1: Specify On-the-Job Performances

First, use observable, measurable verbs that accurately describe authentic on-the-job performance. Make this easy by using the verbs from the completed task analysis. This will help ensure that the objectives and the task analysis are aligned with one another.

Observable, measurable verbs describe each thing that you can see or hear the learners do. As a result, they provide clear guidance for the design of the instruction and clearly communicate expectations to the learners. In contrast, "fuzzy" verbs (understand, know, be familiar with, appreciate, realize, be responsible for) are ambiguous and open to interpretation. They don't work as well as either guidance or communication tools.

Instead of: Understand (i.e., not observable, not measurable) principles of computer screen design.

Better: Create (e.g., observable, measurable) a set of computer screens to . . .

Second, make sure that you *describe the learner's performance*, not the instructor's performance. Keep in mind that the purpose of the objectives is to identify the *results* of the instruction, *not* the process of the instruction. The focus should be on what the learners will be able to do in the workplace, rather than what the instructor (or instruction) will do. One way to do this is to use the phrase "the learner will be able to" (sometimes abbreviated to LWBAT) to describe the behavior. This may seem contrived, but it will help you focus on the intended results of instruction.

Instead of: The course will teach learners how to write a resumé.

Better: The learners will be able to write a resumé.

Third, include a single performance (verb) in each objective. The problem with including more than one performance in an objective is that different performances often call for different conditions and criteria. Writing a program and debugging a program are different skills that are used under different conditions and are judged against different criteria.

Instead of: Write and debug programs in C++

Better: Write programs in C++

Debug programs in C++

Step 2: Add On-the-Job Conditions to Each Performance Requirement

The conditions describe the circumstances under which the individuals will be expected to perform on the job. The idea here goes back to Thorndike's law of identical elements (Thorndike & Woodworth, 1901). The greater the similarity between the learning environment (your instruction) and the transfer environment (the work setting), the more the learners will be able to transfer what they've learned to performance on the job. Making sure the conditions in the training match those in workplaces helps maximize transfer.

It's important, therefore, to think beyond the boundaries of the instruction and specify the conditions (i.e., cues, resources) that will exist when the performance takes place on the job. This will help you focus on workplace conditions, rather than classroom conditions. Following this convention helps your learners transfer what they learn from the L&D intervention to the real world. A cue is something observable that happens before and signals the start of the performance. A resource (e.g., tool, money, technology) is something that someone needs to use to complete the performance and should be specified precisely.

Any accommodations necessary to support diverse learners in workplace settings should also be noted. Reasonable accommodations are required by federal law to allow those with different abilities to participate in society and larger organizations. It's helpful to articulate any considerations that will be made in the performance environment from the start, so you'll know what's needed when building assessments and instruction later on.

Step 3: Add On-the-Job Criteria to Each Performance Requirement

The criteria describe the standards that will be used to define acceptable performance on the job. They describe how well the learners must perform to be considered successful. You'll find a lot of information relating to the criteria in your project's task analysis.

Carliner (2003) notes that the criteria specify the level of acceptable performance (p. 69). They specify the standards that characterize successful performance. Like conditions, criteria will help clarify the behavior by helping identify what is important about that performance. For example, imagine that you wanted the learners in a sales training class to close a sale. Would you accept any attempt they make? Probably not. You probably have an idea of what constitutes a "correct" or "acceptable" closing strategy. The key, therefore, is to define, in a way that can be measured, the correct or acceptable means for each performance.

An important point to keep in mind is that criteria should describe the *standards* for each performance. The question of "how many times" the learner has to perform the task will be answered later, as part of developing performance assessments.

There are different ways to format performance requirements. You may want to consider using the three-column format that appears in Table 6.1. And Table 6.2 depicts a sample performance requirement.

TABLE 6.1 A three-column table format for performance requirements

#	Performance on the Job	Conditions on the Job	Criteria on the Job
1		Cues • Resources • Accommodations •	•
2		Cues • Resources • Accommodations •	•

TABLE 6.2 Sample performance requirements for construction managers

Performance on the Job	Conditions on the Job	Criteria on the Job
Construction managers will estimate material costs.	Cues • Client request Resources • Blueprint • Estimation spreadsheet Accommodations • None needed	• Within 5% of actual costs • Within project budget

What Happens to Performance Requirements?

During the design and development work of an ID project, performance requirements can act as a "north star" for ID teams, clients, SMEs, supervisors, managers, and other project stakeholders. IDs refer to the conditions and criteria when they create job aids, performance assessment instruments, and instructional plans. SMEs can easily review and revise aspects of performance requirements to ensure they are complete, accurate, and authentic. Clients and other stakeholders can review them to ensure they will meet strategic organizational goals and are culturally relevant and inclusive. Seen this way, performance requirements point the way to desired performance, helping both determine what to include in and exclude from the learning and performance support materials.

As IDs begin developing the instructional materials they've designed, they split apart and repurpose the different parts of the performance requirements that have guided their efforts to date:

- Workplace performances typically appear in module and lesson titles in the training.
- "Conditions" turn into module and lesson headings with names such as "When You Do This" and "Resources You Will Use."
- "Criteria" appear in module and lesson headings such as "Standards to Meet." Criteria also work their way into the checklists that performance assessment instruments use to determine mastery.
- "Accommodations" turn into notifications such as the typical flexibility or options individuals have available while completing tasks.

Final Words about Performance Requirements

Odds are that performance requirements will have multiple conditions and criteria. For example, it's possible to include the following criteria for the performance of composing a letter:

- No more than one error in grammar, spelling, or syntax (accuracy—number of errors).
- Must be at least one full page long (quality—essential characteristics).
- Must use single spacing.
- Must use one-inch margins.
- Must contain a combination of simple and complex sentences (quality—essential characteristics).

Why should IDs ask others to review performance requirements? While it's relatively easy to make any necessary revisions in the detailed tables for performance requirements, it becomes increasingly difficult to make these revisions later on in the project, when each revision affects an increasing number of deliverables.

CASE STUDY

The VP of Sales in charge of a line of cell phones needs training for her sales staff as a new product will be hitting stores in a couple of months. "We should have gotten started on this training earlier. Our sales reps will need to be hitting their sales quotas for this line as the cell phones roll out. I want you to create a detailed stack of slides to help them ramp up their sales."

REFLECTION QUESTIONS

- How might you tell this client about the need to specify performance requirements?
- What would you tell a project stakeholder who suggests that we just don't have time to include intersectional or diverse learners in the design team?
- What would you tell a stakeholder who asks you if you can just create a sample product look and feel first, without any preliminary empathy and analysis work?
- Think about "backwards design" from this chapter and the "expanded collaboration" principle from Chapter 1. Why are these particularly important when designing leadership training?

REFERENCES

Branch, R. M., & Dousay, T. A. (2015). *Survey of instructional design models* (5th ed.). Association for Educational Communications and Technology. https://aect.org/survey_of_instructional_design.php

Carliner, S. (2003). *Training design basics*. American Society for Training and Development.

Dennerlein, S. M., Tomberg, V., Treasure-Jones, T., Theiler, D., Lindstaedt, S., & Ley, T. (2020). Co-designing tools for workplace learning: A method for analysing and tracing the appropriation of affordances in design-based research. *Information and Learning Sciences, 121*(3/4), 175–205.

Geraldes, C. A., Fernandes, F. P., Sakurada, L., Rasmussen, A. L., Bennyson, R., Pellegri, U., & Leitao, P. (2021, October). Co-design process for upskilling the workforce in the factories of the future. In *IECON 2021–47th Annual Conference of the IEEE Industrial Electronics Society* (pp. 1–6). IEEE.

Lowenthal, P. R., Humphrey, M., Conley, Q., Dunlap, J. C., Greear, K., Lowenthal, A., & Giacumo, L. A. (2020). Creating accessible and inclusive online learning: Moving beyond compliance and broadening the discussion. *Quarterly Review of Distance Education, 21*(2).

Mager, R. (1997). *Making Instruction Work: A Step-by-Step Guide to Designing and Developing Instruction That Works*. Atlanta, GA: The Center for Effective Performance.

McTighe, J. & Wiggins, G. (2012). *Understanding by design framework*. ASCD. https://files.ascd.org/staticfiles/ascd/pdf/siteASCD/publications/UbD_WhitePaper0312.pdf

Rodriguez, N. M., Casanova, F., Pages, G., Claure, L., Pedreira, M., Touchton, M., & Knaul, F. (2020). Community-based participatory design of a community health worker breast cancer training intervention for South Florida Latinx farmworkers. *Plos One, 15*(10), e0240827.

Thorndike, E. L. & Woodworth, R. S. (1901). The influence of improvement in one mental function upon the efficiency of other functions. *Psychological Review, 8*, 247–261; 384–395; 553–564.

Wulfeck II, et al. (1978). *The instructional quality inventory: I. Introduction and overview* (ED164870). ERIC. https://files.eric.ed.gov/fulltext/ED164870.pdf

CHAPTER 7

Assessments and Formal Instructional Strategies

INTRODUCTION

In Chapter 6, we described the synergies of design and development and how instructional designers (IDs) iteratively work through this LeaPS ID model component. Using backwards design, you can mine the contents of performance requirements to create assessments. You can mine assessments to select instructional strategies. As you prototype, try out ("test"), and revise, you continue to inform your design, which feeds your development efforts. After reading this chapter, you should be able to:

- Create assessments.
- Select formal instructional strategies.

TOWARDS INCLUSIVE DESIGN IN CREATING ASSESSMENTS AND SPECIFYING INSTRUCTIONAL STRATEGIES

Remember, IDs should create assessment and select instructional strategies that are highly contextualized for both:

- An organization's culture, processes, and practices.
- Learners' own cultural identities, experiences, expectations, and human needs.

There can be tension between learners' backgrounds and expectations and those of managers, organizational processes, and organizational cultures. In these situations, IDs will need to spend additional effort to foster clarity and perceived understanding. To create learning designs that represent learners' own cultural experiences, expectations, and human needs—especially when they may be different from your own—you ideally include learners' input in the design process and the project team.

If you are working in an organization, location(s), culture(s), or situation(s), in which you don't normally live and work, you will need to collaborate with at least one expert of that context who also understands your project purpose and can guide your work. Ideally, you will spend time observing without judgment and learning about the organizational culture and the cultural identities of those who are members of the organization. These

DOI: 10.4324/9781003360612-7

individuals will be able to provide input regarding their experiences in the organization, learning environments, cultural expectations, the barriers they are facing in participating in their learning and development, and what would make it easier to engage in their learning and development. As long as IDs and learning and development (L&D) leaders value this input, are self-aware, carefully monitor their own biases, are motivated to empathize with the learners, find useful ways to integrate it in their work, and effectively manage expectations, learner groups should perceive the products, services, and learner experiences as culturally relevant and inclusive. Further, savvy IDs generally balance these inputs with consideration of evidence-based practices that work well, are within project budgets, and that originate from the specific learning and performance context.

Thus, a lot of reflection (Peters & Giacumo, 2020) is warranted when answering questions such as:

- How does the organization represent itself?
- How do organizational leaders see the organization?
- How do the members see the organization?
- How does everyone identify themselves?

You will also reflect on your own cultural experiences and expectations so that you can identify your own biases, unpack them, and set them aside.

In short, it's important to attend to issues of power in psychologically safe workplaces. When IDs do this appropriately, stakeholders will be able to provide more useful input regarding their experiences in the organization and learning environments. Without attending to issues of power, the barriers learners are facing in participating in their learning and development, and what would make it easier to engage in their learning and development, may remain hidden and derail potential project results.

CREATING ASSESSMENTS

In general, assessments provide feedback about the extent to which learners are building new knowledge, skills, or abilities. This feedback can:

- Indicate the extent to which learners meet the criteria specified in performance requirements.
- Help learners reflect upon their mastery of decision-making knowledge, improve their own understanding, and gain confidence in their skills performance.

Assessments can involve:

- Observing learner performance in actual situations in the workplace setting.
- Observing learner performance in simulated situations.
- Reviewing learner responses to case studies about realistic workplace situations.
- Instructors, eLearning, and others checking learners' responses to quizzes ("knowledge checks" or "knowledge tests").
- Learners checking their own understanding and performance ("self-assessments" or "self-checks").

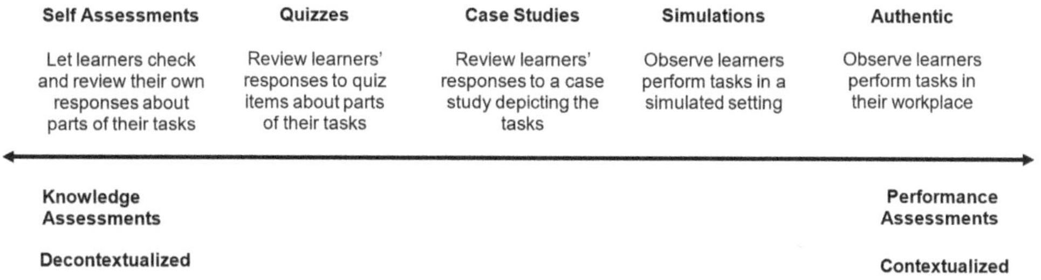

Self Assessments	Quizzes	Case Studies	Simulations	Authentic
Let learners check and review their own responses about parts of their tasks	Review learners' responses to quiz items about parts of their tasks	Review learners' responses to a case study depicting the tasks	Observe learners perform tasks in a simulated setting	Observe learners perform tasks in their workplace

Knowledge Assessments   Performance Assessments

Decontextualized   Contextualized

FIGURE 7.1 A continuum of decontextualized knowledge assessments and contextualized performance assessments.

A given piece of instruction may contain no, one, or multiple assessment approaches.

As depicted in Figure 7.1, assessments exist in a continuum. At one end of the continuum lie knowledge assessments, which focus on what learners *know*. Knowledge assessments are typically somewhat decontextualized, meaning that the items comprising these assessments contain limited information about the task itself. At the other end lie performance assessments, which focus on what learners can *do*. These assessments typically involve having learners actually perform their job tasks—or the closest possible approximation of the tasks. Because they are situated in a workplace situation, or simulated situation, performance assessments are contextualized. The more contextualized an assessment is, the more authentic it is. The more authentic the assessment, the more closely it resembles the actual job context, and the more learned skills and knowledge will transfer to the workplace.

Questions about Assessments

Why Use Assessments?

During an intervention, it's good ID practice to assess the skills and knowledge that learners will use long after the intervention is over. A focus on application to authentic situations will help learners understand the relevance of the instructional content and find value in their efforts to learn. Well-designed feedback from assessments can also enhance learners' motivation.

Well-designed assessments can also support learning by providing feedback to individual learners at key points on key performance indicators. Assessments can also support IDs by providing feedback on the performance patterns of large groups of learners as they interact with any given intervention. This information can help IDs better understand the strengths and weaknesses of their designs and inform future revisions.

How Much Do You Need to Assess?

As a rule of thumb, it's good practice to use performance assessments to determine whether learners have performed well enough to meet the criteria in the corresponding performance requirements. If you are not sure what actually needs to be assessed, start with a "minimal viable product" approach. Build a prototype to assess the authentic desired performance, conduct a tryout, and use the results to inform the design of the next prototype iteration. If learners need additional support, build more instruction and practice opportunities that focus on more basic skills, less nuanced situations, or foundational knowledge. Consider adding additional assessments.

Your ability to make these decisions will grow with your experience as an instructional designer. It will also become more refined for any specific groups of learners and specific organizations as you continue to work with specific clients. You will likely feel more confident by finding out what has worked and hasn't worked for your learners in the past or for learners in other similar situations. Subject matter experts (SMEs), clients, and key project stakeholders can also provide counsel regarding the length and the extent of any assessments they perceive as useful. They can answer questions about what has worked in the past and what learners should be able to *realistically* demonstrate, so they are trusted on the job to perform the job task in ways that meet standards and strategic organizational objectives.

Why Create Assessments Before Content?

It's all about backwards design. Savvy IDs usually create assessments before creating design documents, writing practice exercises, or developing other more detailed instructional content, such as instructor guides and participant guides or storyboards for eLearning content. They build assessments first, so they can avoid creating otherwise unnecessary training "bloatware" that costs clients unnecessary time and money. Knowing the performance requirements that the training will address and how the assessment will measure them provides IDs with the guidance they need to create lean and effective practice exercises and demonstrations in their instructional plans. Consequently, the interventions they produce contain no more guided practice, guided demonstrations, or necessary job aids than learners need to pass the performance assessment and perform their jobs in the workplace in ways that meet strategic organizational objectives.

Assessments measure the learner's ability to do what they need to do in their work setting, as described in the performance requirements. Everything you do after this is done to help the learners pass the assessments that demonstrate their mastery of the performance requirements. You don't want to do anything more and you shouldn't do anything less. Following this philosophy helps you focus on creating "need-to-know" training and avoiding "nice-to-know" information that doesn't relate to specific performance requirements and critical tasks in the workplace.

General Assessment Strategies

The primary strategy that IDs use to design assessments is to match them as closely to the actual job tasks learners perform in the workplace.

- Ideally, this would involve learners completing assessments in the workplace itself.

- When the workplaces themselves are unsafe, confusing, or noisy, or if it would take too much effort to assess large numbers of learners, IDs can use a simulated workplace environment. For example, an assessment might involve watching a learner perform CPR on a manikin, fly a plane on a computer, or work in a student group to complete a class project for a client.
- If a simulated environment isn't feasible, then IDs can use case studies. Provide a description or video of an authentic and representative situation. Then pose questions about what is happening, what learners should do in different situations, what the consequences of different actions might be, how to fix the situation etc.
- If case studies aren't feasible, IDs can use knowledge assessments (quizzes or self-assessments).

In addition to this primary strategy, savvy IDs also "fine tune" their assessment methods based on the types of job tasks that learners are learning. These tasks appear in performance requirements, which act as an input for creating assessments. Table 7.1 describes the relationship among types of job tasks, what learners will need to do in assessments, and specific techniques.

TABLE 7.1 Types of job tasks, what learners will need to do in assessments, and specific techniques

If the Job Task Involves	Then Learners Will Need to Do These Things in Assessments	So Use These Assessment Techniques
Using concepts	Make decisions using declarative knowledge with shared characteristics in a variety of situations that may not have been previously experienced (Smith & Ragan, 2004). Declarative knowledge is verbal information such as labels, names, facts, lists, descriptions, explanations.	• Ask learners to make decisions in authentic or simulated situations (Smith & Ragan, 2004) using the same resources and meeting the same standards as when performing the procedure in the workplace. • If that's not possible, use quizzes or self-assessments asking learners to do one or more of the following activities: 1) Link new knowledge with existing knowledge through review of prerequisite knowledge, advance organizers, or metaphoric devices. 2) Organize new information using mnemonic devices, creating or using images, analogies, clustering or chunking information into categories, recognizing patterns, or using or creating concept maps. 3) Elaborate, make inferences, or imagine examples through writing sentences and identifying rules. 4) Compare examples and non-examples, create concept trees that show hierarchical relationships; use analogies, mnemonics, imagery, visuals, or templates that represent abstract concepts concretely.

(Continued)

TABLE 7.1 (Continued)

If the Job Task Involves	Then Learners Will Need to Do These Things in Assessments	So Use These Assessment Techniques
Completing procedures	Execute a set of specified steps to complete a task the same way each time and make decisions to complete a task, achieve a goal, or use an algorithm (Smith & Ragan, 2004).	Ask learners to complete the procedure in an authentic or simulated setting to demonstrate their ability to follow the correct steps and apply conceptual knowledge to make situated decisions (Smith & Ragan, 2004). Learners should use the same resources and meet the same standards as when performing the procedure in the workplace. If that's not possible, use knowledge assessments to ask learners to make authentic decisions in simulations or case studies.
Completing processes	Execute a set of unspecified steps to achieve a goal or enable completion of processes that contain novel attributes. This broad category includes a few different domains of knowledge (Smith & Ragan, 2004): 1. Principles are the relationship between two or more concepts, or variables, which explains what happens. 2. Metacognitive skills refer to the ability to think about one's own thinking, actions, and learning process. These skills include planning, self-organization, self-regulation, self-monitoring, problem-solving, and self-assessing. 3. Psychomotor skills are the coordinated muscular ability to do something relating to a concept, procedure, or principle in problem-solving situations. 4. Attitudes are the choices to do something relating to a concept, procedure, principle, or psychomotor skill.	Ask learners to make decisions in authentic or simulated situations to demonstrate their ability to correctly use the correct steps and apply conceptual knowledge correctly to make situated decisions (Smith & Ragan, 2004) using the same resources and meeting the same standards as when performing the procedure in the workplace. If that's not possible, then quizzes or knowledge checks and self-assessments might ask learners to demonstrate their ability to do one or more of the following four activities: 1. Demonstrate their ability to state a principle, recognize when to apply a principle, actually apply a principle, and determine if a principle has been correctly applied. 2. Demonstrate their ability to independently plan, access useful resources as needed, and solve novel problems in authentic or simulated contexts. 3. Demonstrate their ability to apply the procedural or conceptual knowledge, as well as adequate physical coordination. 4. Demonstrate their choice in attitude(s), value(s), preference(s), or interest(s), "regarding objects, people, or ideas."

PERFORMANCE ASSESSMENTS

Like other things in instructional design, performance assessments can travel under different names, including "mastery tests," "qualifications," or "accomplishments," or just plain "assessments." Performance assessments provide learners with invaluable feedback that lets them know whether they've mastered the performance requirements and their corresponding job tasks. Assessments tell learners what they're doing well, where they can improve their performance, and how they can make the improvements.

Performance assessments also tell clients, supervisors, and managers in the workplace that learners left the intervention able to perform their job tasks. Supervisors and managers then need to support skill transfer to the workplace to ensure that the intervention produces the promised behavior change.

Questions About Performance Assessments

Why Use Performance Assessments?

Knowledge is an imperfect predictor of future workplace performance. Just because someone knows something about their job tasks, and can talk about them, doesn't mean they can actually perform them. Past performance of job tasks in a learning environment is a much better predictor. Whenever possible, savvy IDs build performance assessments to observe learners in authentic performance situations. In organizations, this often means assessments should reveal learners' competence in conceptual, procedural, and problem-solving skills in authentic situations. It also means ensuring that assessment occurs in a safe learning environment that isolates the consequences of any errors.

Can IDs Skip Performance Assessments?

Some instructional designers skip the creation of a performance assessment. One reason is that learners and clients may not want them. Learners may be afraid of anything called a "quiz" or "mastery test." Clients may want to avoid paying for the cost of creating and administering performance assessments, which can be higher than knowledge assessments. And some forms of introductory training with job aids may not require any assessment at all.

It seems that when budgets or time are limited, one place to cut back is the performance assessment. This practice allows an intervention to focus on teaching rather than testing. But, like many things in ID, this situation may be changing. Increasingly, organizations want to know that the time and money they have invested in training programs has been spent wisely. As part of this, instructional designers are being asked to document the learning gains that have resulted from the instruction they create. Performance assessments (tests)—especially for interventions that teach complex job skills—are the tools that allow them to do this.

Further, use of performance-based interventions helps ensure that all learners are able to pass the assessments. This often requires an intervention to include guided demonstrations and guided practice to required decisions in work settings in ways that meet the criteria in the performance requirements and the mastery level in the assessment. As performance-based interventions are designed to maximize learner success on the job, then learners can rest easier about assessments. Learners can feel confident about passing performance assessments because they've completed the corresponding practice exercises.

There is another reason to skip performance assessments. They may not be necessary. This can happen when IDs find out later in a project that their decisions in a Learning Requirements Analysis (LRA) were off target. IDs complete LRAs early in the life of the project, and often without a deep understanding of job tasks. Later in a project, an ID team could learn that a job task that initially seemed complex during the LRA may not be all that complex. In this case, an intervention based on the use of job aids may be enough and there is no need to create a performance assessment instrument.

Considerations in Creating Performance Assessments

But there's more to creating performance assessments than simply asking learners to perform their job tasks. To produce assessments that measure mastery performance consistently, IDs create "performance assessment instruments" (PAIs). In instructor-led interventions using in-person classrooms, virtual classes, or on-the-job, this means creating the directions and the checklist that a qualified observer will use to assess the learner's performance and determine mastery of the performance requirements. In eLearning, IDs and courseware developers embed the performance assessment instrument into the software itself. Any PAI should be: complete, authentic, and practical.

Complete

The PAI should be clearly written, with directions that will be understood by the learners and instructor or evaluator administering the assessment. The PAI should contain everything that learners and instructors will need to complete the assessment:

- Directions for both learner and instructor/evaluator.
- Answer keys.
- Scoring sheets.
- Rating scales.
- Mastery criteria.
- Any materials needed to complete the assessment (diagrams, role play descriptions, case studies, etc.).

Authentic

A good performance assessment instrument should place learners in realistic job-related situations and use appropriate criteria to assess their performance. Stated simply, an authentic assessment matches job tasks and the performances, conditions, and criteria that appear in the corresponding performance requirements. In this way, the performance assessment instrument is an essential element of "backwards design."

Authenticity is probably the aspect of developing a PAI that new IDs typically have the most difficulty with. This commonly shows up when they note mismatches that usually require changes in either the performance requirements or the PAI itself. A PAI is authentic when it matches:

- *The performances in the* performance requirements. The assessment items should literally match the performance in the performance requirements, which should match tasks in the task analysis. In other words, the assessment instrument should ask the learners to demonstrate the same performances as described in the performance requirements and the task analysis.

- *The conditions in the* performance requirements. Sometimes practical constraints (related to things such as time, cost, hazard, or distance) interfere with creating an assessment instrument that is a literal match with the real-world conditions described in the performance requirements. The solution is to require the same performance under simulated conditions. For example, you may decide that dumping hazardous chemicals as a way of assessing whether employees can clean up the spill is a little too risky. In a case like this, you may choose to ask the learners to clean up a spill of a less hazardous substance. The key is to get as close to the real conditions as possible. And notice that the performance should still be a literal match of the performance requirements.
- *The criteria in the* performance requirements. An assessment that doesn't match the criteria in the performance requirements is useless. Instead, an authentic performance assessment typically employs an assessment checklist based on the job-focused criteria in the performance requirements. Further, the mastery level specified in the assessment is the result of discussions that IDs, clients, SMEs, and other project stakeholders have had about a performance threshold that will best predict successful performance of job tasks in the workplace.

Taken together, performances, conditions, and criteria help you maximize the transfer of learned skills and knowledge to the job. This is based on Thorndike's law of identical elements (Thorndike & Woodworth, 1901). The military communicates this law in simpler terms with the adage "Train the way you fight. Fight the way you train."

For assessments of job tasks that learners must perform by recall in the workplace (without any job aids), authenticity also means administering any assessments several days after learners have completed their last practice exercises and received their last feedback. Allowing time for forgetting ensures that the assessment measures what learners can actually recall, rather than what's on the top of their minds after the last practice and its feedback are over.

Practical

The last consideration is to make sure the PAI is practical. There are five considerations here.

1. First, the organization of the PAI should align with workplace performance. The steps required to complete the job and the assessment should largely follow the same sequential order. Group like information together and maintain the sequence of steps.
2. Second, learners should be able to complete the PAI within the time allotted for the training program. For example, a PAI that requires 90 minutes to complete may not be realistic for a training program that is limited to 3 hours.
3. Third, the assessment needs to be feasible for the client and the sponsoring organization. An assessment approach that may be feasible for one organization may not be feasible for another.

4. Fourth, learners, their supervisors, your client, and other organizational stakeholders should approve the PAI and accept the results it will produce. Include them in reviews and tryouts of the PAI.
5. Last, the PAI needs to be easy to administer. It should be well organized and provide adequate and clear directions so that instructors administer the test in the same way from one learner and training session to the next. Assessments that are difficult to administer yield uneven outcomes, meaning that the test can be a poor predictor of job performance.

Create a PAI

Step 1. Determine Whether to Use a Process or Product Assessment

There are two basic types of performances to assess: product and process. You will need to determine which type to use.

- *Product assessment.* Choose this type of assessment when the learner's performance results in something tangible that can be evaluated. Examples include situations in which the learners have produced a widget, architectural blueprint, or marketing plan. Other examples of product assessments could include producing a table, installing solar panels, or developing a policy manual. Notice that in each of these examples, the primary focus is on a tangible product.

  In a product assessment, instructors or observers don't have to watch the learners completing the task itself. Instead, they review the finished product. Hence, product assessments can be less time consuming and costly to administer than process assessments.

- *Process assessment.* Choose this type of assessment when the learner's performance does not result in something tangible. Examples include situations in which the learners give a presentation, coach an employee, or perform a dance routine. Other examples could include teaching a class, evacuating an airplane, or facilitating a group meeting. Notice that in each of these examples, there is no finished product. In order to evaluate the learner's performance, an instructor, observer, or the eLearning must monitor it while it is occurring.

In some projects, IDs might use both types of assessments to determine mastery. If a job task requires complex decision-making, it could be helpful to base mastery decisions on both an articulation of the decisions as well as a review of the work products. Savvy IDs generally try to use the least expensive assessment type that will provide adequate evidence that learners should be able to perform their job tasks in the workplace.

Step 2. Determine the Number of Trials the Assessment Will Use

The PAI will also need to include an adequate number of trials that learners will complete during the test to indicate that they can perform their jobs in the workplace.

Depending on the nature of the job and its complexity, an adequate number of trials will vary. To make this decision, IDs need to consider:

- *The number of conditions under which learners typically perform the task in the workplace.* Some job tasks are fairly straightforward, and learners will encounter the same conditions and perform the tasks largely the same way each time on the job. For instance, line cooks in restaurants need to prepare menu items the same way each time.

  Conversely, some jobs occur under a greater number of conditions. For example, truck drivers are expected to drive in good and bad weather, on open highways and city streets, during the day and at night. To say that the individual has "mastered" truck driving, you would probably want to see the driver perform successfully in a variety of conditions.
  As a rule of thumb, the more conditions under which learners perform an objective, the more trials their assessment may need to include to provide a trustworthy promise that learners who pass the test can perform their jobs.

- *The length of time required to perform the task on the job.* Assessments for tasks that learners perform quickly may require more trials. For example, assembly line operators using microscopes to inspect stripped wire cables must identify when the cable is stripped correctly. They'll also need to identify several possible defects a cable may have. In this situation, conducting the inspection and identifying these defects doesn't take long. Given the short task time and the number of decisions operators make, there should be multiple trials for this assessment. Conversely, other assessments involve tasks that take a long time to complete. They will typically involve fewer trials.

- *Task complexity and novelty.* Assessments for tasks involving a lot of novelty, decision-making, and problem-solving can require more trials to ensure that the assessment measures the typical amount of novelty, varied decision-making, and different context for problem-solving that appear in the workplace. For example, a single role-play assessment is likely not going to be enough to determine mastery given the different people, mental states, and situations a learner will encounter on the job.

Savvy IDs often use formative evaluation to verify and adjust these initial guesstimates. Tryouts of assessment instruments during the design component and pilot tests of these instruments with supervisors and managers who provide workplace feedback after training completion can also provide additional data about the guesstimates.

- *Number of times learners need to demonstrate competence.* This would involve making sure the learners successfully perform the task enough times so that their success cannot reasonably be attributed to luck or chance. For example, hitting a golf ball straight once could be a chance occurrence. To say that the golfer has "mastered" this skill, you may want to see them hit the ball straight maybe eight out of ten times over several days.

In a similar vein, inspectors who verify that a manufactured product meets quality standards would need to inspect multiple products pulled from the assembly line and verify each one meets the appropriate quality standards. Looking at a single product alone wouldn't provide enough trials to reasonably determine that inspectors can perform this task in the workplace.

Clients, SMEs, other organizational stakeholders, and ID teams typically work together to determine an adequate set of trials for a performance assessment. The set should be large enough to show that people who pass the assessment are able to perform the tasks. Too small a sample, and learners could pass the assessment based on chance alone. Too large a sample, and the assessment takes more time to take, meaning that the organization incurs additional costs as learners remain off their jobs to complete their training.

Step 3. Construct Assessment Checklists

Performance-based interventions often involve performance requirements with multiple objective criteria. To determine if learners meet each criterion, performance assessment instruments often use yes/no checklists or rating scales. The question for *yes/no criteria* is "Did they perform well enough?" While a *rubric or rating scale* asks "How well did they perform?"

Either way, it's important to be sure to fully describe the "good enough" performance indicators for any criteria or level(s) used. The complexity of these checklists will vary with the number of criteria, number of levels used, and the number of trials to indicate mastery of job tasks. Good rubrics are much harder to write because they use more performance indicators for multiple levels of criteria, so they should be tried out to ensure their reliability. They also require observer training to produce consistent results.

An assessment checklist for a simple job task that learners perform twice in the assessment might look like the one in Table 7.2. The criteria that appear in the checklist:

TABLE 7.2 Assessment checklist template for a task performed twice (two trials)

Performance	[The performance from the corresponding performance requirement would go here.]		
Conditions	[The conditions from the corresponding performance requirement would go here.]		
Assessment Checklist			
Did the learner:	**Meet the criteria?**		**Comments**
	Trial 1	Trial 2	
Objective criteria 1	Yes ☐ No ☐	Yes ☐ No ☐	
Objective criteria 2	Yes ☐ No ☐	Yes ☐ No ☐	
Objective criteria 3	Yes ☐ No ☐	Yes ☐ No ☐	
Number of "Yes"			Mastery = 2 or more "yes" checkmarks for each trial

- Come from the criteria that appear in the performance requirements for the training.
- Represent each point on your task analysis.
- Follow the sequential steps of the task analysis and represent decision tables.
- May also include hot tips and cautions that appear in the task analysis.
- Read left to right, with important items on the left.
- Include space for comments on each performance criterion.
- Document observed performance. This documentation is especially important when failing the assessment results in job loss.

Step 4: Specify a Mastery Level

There is an important distinction between a criterion that appears in the assessment checklist and the mastery level (also called a "mastery threshold") for the performance assessment instrument. A checklist criterion in a performance requirement refers to the standard for *each time* the task is performed. Seen this way, checklist criteria reflect what the learner should do on the job.

Mastery level refers to *how many times or at what level* the learner must perform criteria to be judged successful in the intervention. What is "good enough" (not "perfect") to provide evidence that learners can perform their job tasks in ways that meet expectations? A mastery level sets a threshold that learners need to meet to show they should be able to perform the task in the work setting. In different situations, the mastery threshold may appear as a:

- Set level of correct responses over a set number of trials.
- Percentage of correct responses—specified as the total number of required correct responses required to master the assessment.
- Set of correct responses for each trial in the assessment.
- Set of correct responses for the entire assessment.

Mastery levels often appear at the bottom of performance assessment checklists, where a qualified observer:

1. Tallies the number of times the learner met objective criteria.
2. Reads the directions on the checklist for determining mastery.
3. Determines whether the learner's score meets or exceeds the stated mastery threshold.

Scores that are equal to or greater than the threshold indicate learners who have mastered the assessment. Scores that are less than the threshold indicate learners who have not demonstrated mastery and require remediation.

There are no hard-and-fast rules for determining a level of mastery. However, there are two factors to consider:

1. *The criticality of the performance.* The more critical the performance, the higher the mastery level should be. For example, people who operate nuclear reactors are

performing very critical tasks—the consequences of a misstep are potentially very dangerous and costly. Such tasks typically require high levels of human reliability. To determine that someone has mastered tasks related to operating a nuclear reactor, an appropriate level of mastery would require perfect or near-perfect performance.

Furthermore, some task criteria may be far more important than others. These criteria typically relate to safety, where unsafe behaviors during an assessment or in the workplace could produce significant injury or costly property damage. For example, an ID team created an intervention teaching US Coast Guard personnel how to dock ("tie up" or "moor") their sea-going ships. The occurrence of certain unsafe behaviors resulted in learners immediately failing the test and receiving remediation.

2. *The cost of attaining mastery.* Ultimately, there is no generic level of mastery. Savvy IDs need to collaborate with clients, SMEs, and other organizational stakeholders to make this decision for each assessment and in every ID project. You're looking to strike a balance between obtaining mastery and the time, cost, and organizational tolerance of doing so. The question is, "What level of performance is a 'good enough' indicator that learners who pass the test can perform their jobs in the workplace?" This is why savvy IDs work with clients and SMEs to specify realistic levels of mastery for each assessment. Set too low, and learners will pass the assessment who can't perform their jobs in the workplace. Set too high, and learners will need to spend additional, unnecessary time in training. And learners who can otherwise perform their jobs in the workplace will fail the test. Providing remediation so these learners can pass the test they failed is time consuming and costly.

Step 5. Write Instructions

Instructors will need directions to:

*   *Set up the assessment.* Specify any:
    *   Items or materials the instructor will use to collect to administer the assessment.
    *   Necessary room arrangements the instructor will need to make.
    *   Personnel arrangements the instructor will need to make. For example, assessments using role-play activities may require an instructor to find actors to play different roles and SMEs and other qualified job incumbents who can administer the assessment, assess performance, and provide feedback.

*   *Provide instructions for learners to complete the assessment.* The instructions should specify the time the test will take and provide step-by-step directions for completing the test. A mirror version of these instructions also needs to appear in the materials that learners use to complete the assessment.
*   *Administer the assessment.* The assessment should provide any step-by-step directions that instructors will use to administer each part of the assessment, including the assessment checklist and any rubrics.
*   *Determine if the learner's performance meets criteria.* It's common for assessment checklists to provide some sort of directions telling instructors how to complete the checklist.

- *Determine if the learner's performance meets a specified mastery level.* It's common for assessment checklists to provide directions for determining mastery. Typically, these directions require instructors to tally performances that meet objective criteria and compare them with a mastery level (threshold).
- *Provide remediation to any learners who fail the assessment.* The assessment needs to provide directions that instructors can use to provide necessary remediation to any students who fail. This remediation could consist of:

    - Immediate coaching on the things that a learner missed, followed by a retake of the assessment.
    - Immediate coaching followed by additional practice and a retake of the assessment.
    - Completing parts of the intervention again, followed by the assessment.
    - Completing the entire intervention over again, including the assessment.

Savvy IDs will generally provide any necessary remediation in the most time- and cost-efficient way possible.

Learners will also need directions for completing the assessment. They will need to know what is expected of them to complete the assessment.

To Ensure PAIs Are Culturally Relevant, Inclusive, and Equitable, Be Sure to Consider

- How and when to modify or provide accommodations for learners.
- Guidance on available remediation when learners don't achieve mastery.
- Feedback provided should be framed from a growth mindset, focusing on the future desired performance characteristics that would signal mastery, *not* centered on what was done wrong.
- Consider the cultures and identities of the learners to ensure that the language, examples, guidance, recommendations, etc. included in any feedback will be clearly understood by *all* learners.

KNOWLEDGE ASSESSMENTS

Why Use Knowledge Assessments?

There are times when it's appropriate to use knowledge assessments. Instead of checking learners' performance of workplace tasks, knowledge assessments check the knowledge learners have constructed during their learning experience. These assessments typically use interactions that you may have seen in printed or eLearning tests. They can include these types of questions:

- *Open-ended.* Similar to writing an essay, learners enter text in response to a question or instruction. Open-ended questions are the easiest to write but the most difficult to analyze, assess, aggregate, and report on because they require human reviewers. Open-ended questions require checklists or rubrics with behavioral descriptions for reliable and efficient grading.

- *Multiple-choice.* Learners select one or more best answers from a set of items that include incorrect answers ("distractors"). It's good ID practice for each distractor to correspond to a common learner misconception and to provide feedback correcting it.
- *True/false questions.* Learners indicate whether a statement is either true or false.
- *Fill-in-the-blank.* Learners input a short amount of text in response to a question or direction.
- *Ranking.* Learners indicate a ranked order in response to a question or direction.
- *Matching.* Learners match two things that go together. In eLearning, matching questions can appear as "drag and drop" items where learners use a mouse or finger to drag an item on the screen and tap when the item lays atop another.

Collections of these questions can take the form of two broad types of knowledge assessments:

- *Quizzes* ("knowledge checks" or "knowledge tests"), which are usually graded or scored in a way that indicates the extent to which a learner has met mastery requirements.
- *Self-assessments*, which are questions interspersed throughout instructional interventions. In addition to appearing as "ungraded" quizzes or tests that don't count towards determining whether learners have mastered a performance requirement, self-assessments may appear in the form of closed- or open-ended questions, polls, discussion prompts, surveys, rating scales, etc. Integrating these kinds of interactions can increase engagement of the learners, support reflection, and provide learners with risk-free feedback about their comprehension, progress, and performance.

There are other reasons to use knowledge assessments. Some regulatory situations require organizations to track knowledge test scores in Learning Management Systems (LMSs) as a record indicating that learners met a regulatory requirement. In some organizations, management sometimes requires L&D groups to report test scores in place of scores on performance assessments because they believe knowledge assessments are less expensive.

Savvy IDs generally avoid using final knowledge assessment scores when organizations or regulators don't require them. These scores can create anxiety that actually interferes with learning and performance. For online interventions, IDs can use learning analytics (computer recorded data) to track learners' progress without using knowledge assessment scores.

Like other assessment instruments, developing quizzes and self-assessments require tryouts and revisions. Whenever possible, we recommend using closed-ended question items for these types of assessment instruments because they are more efficient to analyze, assess, aggregate, and report on. One way to create these questions is to start with a set of open-ended questions. From there, you can come up with correct response item options and incorrect response item distractors as needed. Oftentimes, IDs seek help from SMEs to identify common misconceptions (i.e., plausible, but not possible, answers) to create distractors.

Guidelines for Creating Prompts and Questions

- Focus questions and expected answers on the key points and main ideas.
- Create questions that focus on one component of an objective or performance requirement (PR) at a time.
- Create questions that assess the desired knowledge or skills instead of common test-taking skills
  - Use care to ensure there are no grammatical cues for close-ended response options.
  - Create response options that are relatively equal in length and detail.
  - Avoid "all of the above" or "none of the above."
- Check out *Writing Quiz Questions* (Norman, 2016) for more tips.

Quiz Design

Quizzes can support comprehension, retention, and recall, in university or professional education environments. Some situations lend themselves to quizzes. These can include:

- An eLearning course that doesn't hold the learner's attention without breaks in the form of responses to content-sensitive questions.
- An intervention in which learners are required to read a lot of text.
- A performance setting where learners are expected to be able to spell and identify terms correctly from recall and the amount of information requires more practice or time on task than learners would normally spend on their own.
- A certification program in which a credentialing agency (e.g., SHRM, PMP) requires quizzes.
- Some regulatory environments that require a quiz.

In addition, quiz questions and knowledge checks are also helpful for learners who would benefit from feedback on their comprehension and progress towards learning new knowledge. IDs can mitigate learner anxiety by awarding completion credit and providing specific feedback on why a response is correct or incorrect, along with a score. In some situations, learner anxiety can be reduced and motivation to learn increased by turning the assessment into a game.

Self-Assessment Design

Like quizzes, self-assessments can be used to determine learners' ability to apply conceptual knowledge, procedural knowledge, and problem-solving knowledge. Question items can include reflection prompts, rating scales, and checklists or rubrics with behavioral descriptions.

In addition to providing risk-free assessments for learners' own information, self-assessments can also support learners' reflections related to their own skills and knowledge and their transfer to workplace settings. Self-assessment items for reflection can include:

- What have you found most valuable in this learning experience?
- How might you apply what you've learned in this experience to your work?
- What aspects of your performance on this job task went well?
- What aspects of your performance on this job task could be improved? How might you do that?
- What aspects of this learning experience are still confusing? How might you get help to understand them better?

Feedback Strategies

Authentic performance assessments integrate scoring instruments such as checklists with behavioral descriptions, rating scales, or rubrics that capture increasingly nuanced understanding to provide feedback (Smith & Ragan, 2004). Open-ended questions may also incorporate these approaches. Closed-ended questions will ideally incorporate one correct answer. Feedback almost always includes identifying incorrect answers. When possible, feedback should also explain why correct answers are correct, and why incorrect answers are wrong. When learners are not allowed to self-correct answers with a corresponding rationale, then feedback should include correct answers, provide a rationale, and explain where to find additional information.

A challenge with using self-assessments is that people (including learners) are not always good judges of their own performance—some tend to be over-critical and others tend to be under-critical. However, self-assessments can be used to guide learners' performance or develop their metacognitive skills by providing an interim check before assessment by an instructor. The value of this interim and metacognitive check can be increased by asking learners to evaluate one another's performance.

INSTRUCTIONAL STRATEGIES AND ACTIVITIES

L&D IDs can draw upon a variety of strategies to support learning and performance. IDs often spend a large portion of their time designing formal learning environments that will provide opportunities to access information, interact with others, practice, and receive feedback. These can include how instructors or LMSs relay information; the type of guidance instructors would provide for learners as they move through the module, course, or program; and feedback features.

Instructional activities operationalize select instructional strategies creatively; they incorporate content and represent the methods used to deliver or facilitate instructional interventions, engage the learners, and foster learning by *all* learners. They represent the art of ID. Instructional activities are often delivered by an instructor, or a supervisor, or found online in a learning management system (LMS). There is a continuum of instructional activities, ranging from less interaction to more interaction. They can be less structured or more structured. IDs create instructional activities with the contexts, performance outcome goals, performance requirements, diverse learner identities, needs, and preferences of the learners, in mind. In any one learning environment, IDs often combine several learning activities.

The best instructional strategies and activities would be grounded in inclusive design, adult learning theory, motivation theory, design justice principles, and evidence-based practice. This represents the science component of instructional design. Working from these foundations allows IDs to support deliberate, systematic, and systemic interventions.

To Ensure Learning Environments Are Culturally Relevant, Inclusive, and Equitable, Be Sure to Consider

- How to embrace contributions and a sense of belonging for all individuals, including those who representing diverse identities and backgrounds, bring to the table.
- How to incorporate the unique assets that all individuals, including those representing diverse identities and backgrounds, bring to the table.
- How to include perspectives from individuals representing diverse identities and backgrounds.
- How to help learners relate their past experiences to the new concepts, procedures, and problem-solving approaches they might encounter.
- How to help learners relate their past experiences to the new performance expectations and authentic project deliverables.
- How to help learners create valued, authentic, respectful, and meaningful relationships with instructors and other learners.
- How to attend to issues of power in instructional activities, guidance, and feedback design.
- How to provide guidance to help learners both identify and negotiate expectations for their performance.

Instructional Strategies

IDs can draw upon five instructional strategies. As shown in Figure 7.2, they range from those that are less interactive and learner-specific (such as information dissemination and static guidance) to those that are more interactive and learner-specific (practice with delayed feedback and practice with real-time feedback).

Whether as individuals or in groups, learners won't always need the same amount of formal instruction, coaching, or other support to achieve any given learning and performance goal (Pearson et al., 2022). Table 7.3 depicts the progression of instructional strategies from less interaction to more interaction and feedback. Each strategy

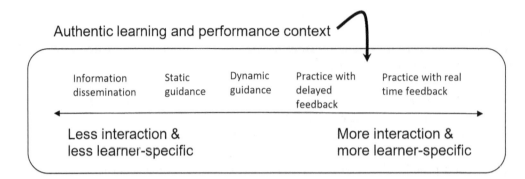

FIGURE 7.2 Instructional strategies continuum.

TABLE 7.3 Instructional strategies and example activities

Purpose	Instructional Strategy	Group or Individual?	Performance Assessed?	Examples
Awareness	Information dissemination	Can be learner-specific or not	Performance may or may not need to be assessed	Explainer video, story, lecture
Instructions regarding how to do something	Static guidance to elicit learner performance	Not learner-specific	Performance may or may not need to be assessed	Job aids, performance support systems, workbooks, deliverable instructions
Provide situated interaction between learners and potentially instructors, coaches, or mentors	Dynamic guidance to elicit learner performance	Can be learner-specific or not	Performance may or may not need to be assessed	Case study, simulation, authentic performance
Validate and reinforce desired behavior and offer correction. Provide situated interaction between learner and peers, or instructors, or managers, or coaches, or mentors	Delayed feedback to elicit learner reflection and correction	Can be learner-specific or not	Yes	Performance reviews, portfolio reviews, after action reviews, before action reviews, team charters
Validate and reinforce desired behavior and offer correction. Provides for situated interaction between learner and peers, or instructors, or managers, or coaches, or mentors	Real-time feedback to elicit learner reflection and often correction too	Learner-specific	Yes	Live classroom, coaching, mentoring, on the job training, cognitive apprenticeship

provides an à la carte menu of possible options for IDs to choose as part of "design" that would then be built during "development." Further, there's no empirical evidence to show that one instructional strategy sequence is any better than another (MacDonald, Shukla, & Giacumo, 2022).

In other words, you can create learning pathways such that individuals first receive content and instruction, next make content-sensitive decisions, and finally receive feedback. Or you can ask learners to first make decisions, next provide them with feedback on their decisions, and then finally provide only the instruction the learners actually need. Either way, learners will often, but not always, need opportunities to practice and receive feedback. If learners aren't performing well, it's often because they need more practice and feedback (Villachica et al., 2020).

Instructional Activity Examples

Instructional activities are based on one or more of the instructional strategies and can range from simple to very complex. Instructional activities are the learning experiences that IDs design to standardize instruction across multiple instructional events (e.g., delivered by instructors or eLearning software). Organizations utilize standardized instruction to ensure quality and to be more consistent, which helps manage expectations and,

How to Create Instructional Activities

1. Clearly indicate the activity alignment to critical tasks and performance requirements.
2. Use a task analysis approach with a seasoned instructor or facilitator to come up with the input required for an initial set of instructions.
3. Use select formative evaluation strategies (e.g., expert review, client feedback, learner input) and try them out with potential learners using prototype testing or a pilot implementation.

ultimately, improve performance throughout the organization. IDs can create a variety of example products for different instructional activities, as described below.

Information Dissemination Activity Examples

These might include: handouts, infographics, concept maps, readings, videos, lectures, or panel discussions. More simple microlearning examples might include a brief update or a few simple reminders. More complex examples might include an instructor, or group of experts, or a self-paced eLearning object. They might convey stories to learners that could include simple to complex scenarios and think-alouds. They might require learners to access email, a Learning Management System (LMS), another type of electronic delivery platform, or a physical location.

Static Guidance Activity Examples

These might include: job aids, tutorials, demonstrations, pre-planned discussion prompts or reflection questions, worksheets or templates, pre-planned collaboration prompts, scavenger hunts, observations, reflections, knowledge check questions, writing prompts, or short activities that require content-sensitive performance, and facilitation instructions. ELearning objects or games might also make use of a learning agent, faded support, and simple to complex scenarios through constrained navigation options or linear learning path options, as forms of static guidance that are identical for all learners. They might require learners to access email, an LMS, other electronic delivery platforms, or physical locations.

Wait, Are You Saying a Course on Diversity, Equity, and Inclusion (DEI) Is the Way to Go? That's Not Supported in My Context . . .

No. Well, it's complicated. Let's take a look at some types of applied decisions that avoid politically charged vocabulary in the United States but would lead to desired DEI performance outcomes.

First, we can teach organizational justice theory as concept knowledge to individuals. Interactional justice is the part that touches on respect and dignity in interactions and communications. Distributive justice is about the allocation of resources, being able to make judgments relating to fairness is distributive justice. It's the same for procedural justice—that's about fair processes. However, that's not the end of it. One might be aware that these things are useful but still not know how to do them. We also need to teach procedural knowledge and problem-solving knowledge that's aligned with DEI, so folks know how to make the desired decisions over time.

That's why you could build a second course for specific management functions. Let's consider ID leaders. They might need to learn how to build DEI into their processes without you ever using the words social justice, equity, inclusion, or diversity. In this situation, you would focus on building a course that would enable procedural knowledge and problem-solving knowledge. The topics might include: how to attend to all learner needs (e.g., including those who identify with marginalized and intersectional groups), how to select design team members (e.g., you demonstrate the value of representation and how this improves results in your context), prototyping, testing selection strategy, participant sampling strategy, and analysis with disaggregated data (Equitable Data Working Group, 2022) and reporting strategies.

Dynamic Guidance Activity Examples

These might include structured on-the-job training (OJT), case study discussions, coaching, mentoring, surveys, interviews, brainstorming, inquiry, problem-solving, creating authentic deliverables, live discussions, role play, projects, task-centered or problem-based learning, debates, projects, practices, and labs. They can also be project-based, or problem-based, or discovery-driven, where learners work in groups or on their own to plan their work and execute their plan to achieve a goal. The guidance might be in real time (e.g., synchronous) or delayed (e.g., asynchronous). They might use a cognitive apprenticeship model, where experts and learners interact socially while completing work, to facilitate learning how to make situational decisions. ELearning objects or games might also make use of coaches or advisors, faded support, simple to complex scenarios, multiple navigation options, or branching learning path options, as forms of dynamic guidance that are different for different learner actions.

Delayed and Real-time Feedback Activity Examples

Feedback can be focused on structured OJT, specific performances, general group performances, solutions, processes, growth, reflection, checklists, or rubrics. Ideally, formative feedback is kind, relevant, timely, actionable, and balanced. This means it should articulate what was done well, what was valued, and why. Ideally, for authentic performances, formative feedback would also articulate what could be done in the future, why it's important to do, and one example of how it can be done. For close-ended knowledge check questions, formative feedback would confirm a correct answer or incorrect answer, references to corresponding instructional materials, and suggest another attempt if an incorrect answer was selected. It should describe why each answer is correct or incorrect—in ways that address common misconceptions if you aren't going to allow learners opportunities to self-correct.

Planning for Feedback in Instructional Activities

It's helpful to manage learners' expectations and let them know up front when to expect feedback. Feedback should be timely but doesn't necessarily need to be immediate. In fact, some empirical research evidence (Corral, Carpenter, & Clingan-Siverly, 2021) shows that delayed feedback can lead to better learning outcomes. Feedback can be given in real time to validate and reinforce desired behavior, prompt reflection, and guide improved performance as needed. Feedback can also be given after a performance is over to let learners know the extent to which they met objective standards, to validate and reinforce desired behavior, and to guide improved performance.

One easy way to give prompt feedback is to share the expected answers or behaviors when learners submit their answers. Another way is to point out which answers or behaviors were expected and where learners can find correct answers, models, or examples. You can also aggregate results for a large group or small teams. This assigns the focus less on individuals' performance and more on how the group is doing. Individuals can then compare their performance with that of the rest of the group and use this feedback to decide when to approach a manager or leader with their concerns.

CASE STUDY

The online MBA program at Elite University (pseudonym) is proud to offer a competitively priced, high-quality degree program. The learning designers integrate a short survey at the end of each module to track learners' time-on-task and reactions. After running a new course design for two semesters, they notice learners who identify as female or Black are tracking twice as much time in responding to discussion prompts as those who identify as white males. The course design is primarily based on instructor lecture videos, select teachings from textbook chapters and journal articles, reading comprehension quiz questions, problem sets from publisher resources, and required asynchronous discussions each week. The retention rates of learners who are female or Black are three times lower than the white male population retention rate. The retention rates of female Black learners are four times lower than the white male population retention rate. The online MBA program manager at Elite University has decided to assign you as the lead instructional designer to remedy this situation.

Think back to Chapter 1 and the description of organizational justice in combination with design justice. Organizational justice emphasizes the idea that processes, procedures, policies, and interactions are respectful, dignified, fair, and equitable. Design justice emphasizes *everyone is an expert based on their own lived experience* and that *we all have unique and brilliant contributions to bring to a design process.*

- How might you apply that information to guide you in improving retention rates in this situation?

REFLECTION QUESTIONS

- Thinking back to Chapters 1–3, and building on what we covered in this chapter, when have you seen the minority of learners being more burdened as a consequence of the intervention design? What were the consequences? What could have been done differently to lessen the impact?
- What would you need to do to create instructional activities that are less biased against groups of historically marginalized learners?
- You just got hired as a learning and performance design consultant in an organization. If you had to select strategies for use in a new instructional intervention, where would you start? Why?
- How would you ensure a culturally relevant and equitable performance assessment instrument?
- How would you attend to issues of power, organizational justice, inclusive design, and design justice, in learning activity design?

REFERENCES

Corral, D., Carpenter, S. K., & Clingan-Siverly, S. (2021). The effects of immediate versus delayed feedback on complex concept learning. *Quarterly Journal of Experimental Psychology*, 74(4), 786–799.

Equitable Data Working Group. (2022). *A vision for equitable data: Recommendations from the Equitable Data Working Group*. https://www.whitehouse.gov/wp-content/uploads/2022/04/eo13985-vision-for-equitable-data.pdf

MacDonald, M., Shukla, S., & Giacumo, L. A. (2022). *How to get started with chunking & sequencing eLearning design*. https://www.learningguild.com/articles/how-to-get-started-with-chunking-sequencing-elearning-design/

Norman, M. (2016, July 15). *Writing quiz questions*. https://ctl.wiley.com/writing-quiz-questions/

Pearson, J., Giacumo, L. A., Farid, A., & Sadegh, M. (2022). A systematic multiple studies review of low-income, first-generation, and underrepresented, STEM-degree support programs: Emerging evidence-based models and recommendations. *Education Sciences*, 12(5), 333.

Peters, D. J. T., & Giacumo, L. A. (2020). Ethical and responsible cross-cultural interviewing: Theory to practice guidance for human performance and workplace learning professionals. *Performance Improvement*, 59(1), 26–34.

Smith, P. L., & Ragan, T. J. (2004). *Instructional design* (3rd ed.). John Wiley & Sons.

Thorndike, E. L., & Woodworth, R. S. (1901). The influence of improvement in one mental function upon the efficiency of other functions. *Psychological Review*, 8, 247–261; 384–395; 553–564.

Villachica, S. W., Stieha, V., Giacumo, L., Becker, L., & Fenner, J. A. (2020). A formative evaluation of a master's-level career-coaching course for performance improvement students. *Performance Improvement Quarterly*, 32(4), 427–459. doi:10.1002/piq.21302

CHAPTER 8

How to Select Appropriate Formal, Informal, Instructional, and Non-instructional Learning Solutions

INTRODUCTION

To this point, this text has described culturally relevant and equitable approaches for creating effective instructional solutions that include both learning and performance support materials. We've focused on creating learning experiences including classroom training, eLearning, structured on-the-job training, and job aids, among others. These learning experiences all involve instruction. They consist of sets of events or activities presented in a structured or planned way, using one or more media (Dick, Carey, & Carey, 2009). This instruction enables learners to achieve prespecified behaviors, such as performing their job tasks.

These are all formal types of learning and performance support materials because:

- *The organization formally supports the creation of these materials.* Clients in the organization sponsor the instructional design (ID) projects that create learning and performance support materials. The organization pays ID teams to create these materials. The organization provides release time for clients, subject matter experts (SMEs), learners, supervisors, managers, and other stakeholders to review and try out these materials. The organization implements these materials so that learners can complete their learning experiences.
- *The created learning and performance support materials meet the needs of clients and other organizational stakeholders.* To meet these needs, organizations sponsor the creation, implementation, and maintenance of learning and performance support materials. These needs should align with the mission of the organization, its strategic business objectives, and its current strategic initiatives.
- *The created materials produce standard outcomes.* Instructional designers (IDs) ideally use systematic and systemic approaches, such as the LeaPS ID model, to create learning and performance support materials. By working collaboratively

DOI: 10.4324/9781003360612-8

to complete the Empathize & Analyze, Design & Develop, and Implement & Evaluate components, they specify performance requirements and objectives that specify standard performances that the learning experiences should produce.

In contrast, IDs can also create non-instructional learning solutions. Organizations don't always employ formal instructional approaches to create learning and performance solutions. Formal instruction may not always meet the learning needs that learners have. At times, learners may turn to informal or even non-instructional learning solutions. Because they don't use instruction to build learner skills, non-instructional learning solutions typically don't use assessments. After reading this chapter, you should be able to:

- Compare formal and informal learning approaches.
- Argue that IDs can use and repurpose informal learning in their formal efforts.
- Explore the use of formal non-instructional learning solutions in ID practice.

FORMAL VERSUS INFORMAL LEARNING

It's common for IDs to spend a lot of time creating formal learning experiences and job aids. When these materials are inadequate or don't exist, learners often turn to informal learning. Merriam and Bierema (2013) note that informal learning consists of the impromptu ways that people learn to perform their jobs. In contrast to formal learning approaches, informal learning:

- *Arises organically.* These learning experiences arise as learners turn to accessible people and resources to answer their questions and meet their needs.
- *Meets the needs of participants.* Because learners are creating their own learning solutions, these solutions meet the needs of the learners themselves, and usually augment organizational performance, too.
- *Produces non-standard outcomes.* The quality of learning experiences can vary dramatically in informal learning, depending on the qualifications and willingness of the person a learner turns to with questions or learning needs. The person a learner asks for help may be as clueless as the learner in any given situation. Conversely, the person may be competent, but may not have the time or willingness to provide responses that are accurate and complete. Consequently, the outcomes of informal learning can vary from outstanding to dismal.

Scholars (Cross, 2007; Boileau, 2018) agree that there is a continuum between formal and informal workplace learning. Figure 8.1 depicts this continuum. As a rule of thumb, organizations use both informal and formal learning approaches. However, clients, executives, and managers may not be aware of the informal learning approaches that learners in their organizations are using. Savvy IDs are aware of these approaches and use them to meet learning needs.

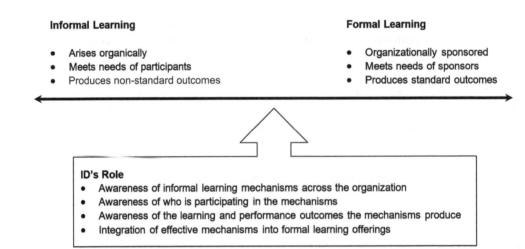

FIGURE 8.1 A continuum of formal and informal learning and the role of IDs.

People may complete formal learning experiences such as structured on-the-job training (OJT). As they transition from this training into independent performance, they may encounter more nuances, or uncommon situations that weren't handled in the OJT, out on their own. Or they may seek additional support through social interactions with their peers, colleagues, or an informal community of practice. Seen this way, learners could need both formal and informal learning. Furthermore, Kittel, Kunz, & Seufert (2021) linked informal learning with organizational learning culture. A supportive organizational learning culture is associated with increased motivation to transfer learning to performance, lower employee turnover, and increase job satisfaction (Egan, Yang, & Bartlett, 2004).

Given awareness of different informal learning mechanisms in the organization, IDs can identify who is participating in them. IDs can also identify the outcomes these informal mechanisms produce. Quite often, informal learning approaches can produce non-standard learning and performance outcomes. The quality of what an informal learning participant learns is largely based on the expertise and the willingness of the person they've asked for help. If that person is competent, willing to respond, and has the available time to do so, then learners will find the responses they receive are useful. Otherwise, the responses may not be useful—or could even lead to instances of poor workplace performance. Informal learning can also come with hidden expenses that organizational managers and accountants don't see. People requesting assistance in an informal learning situation often try, on their own, to find a competent person to answer their questions. And novice performers who are relying on informal learning can ask the same questions repeatedly. The cost of answering each question involves the combined time and rates of the novice and the competent performer. Each instance of question and response doesn't involve much time or cost. But multiply the time and cost of asking and responding to each question by the total number of times this exchange happens across the organization for a year, and the true cost of informal learning can be staggering!

Nonetheless, informal learning can provide valuable learning opportunities. That's why savvy IDs try to integrate appropriate informal learning opportunities into their formal learning offerings.

REPURPOSING INFORMAL LEARNING

With an awareness of the informal learning solutions that have already arisen organically within the organization, IDs can potentially repurpose them to serve as formal non-instructional learning solutions. For example, an ID who discovers that learners in an organization are using informal job shadowing may opt to formalize this existing practice so that the organization gains the standard learning outcomes that a formal job shadowing program could produce. Table 8.1 compares informal and formal learning solutions. Note that there are no clear distinctions; these represent more of a continuum of possibilities.

IDs may choose to use informal approaches when there are no other alternatives. And they may identify existing informal learning resources and repurpose them to formal learning solutions when:

TABLE 8.1 Informal and formal learning solutions

Informal Learning Solutions	Formal Learning Solutions
• *Informal job shadowing*: Learners follow a more experienced performer as they perform their job tasks. The experienced performer may or may not articulate thought processes and decisions that guide performance. There may or may not be opportunities for learners to reflect on and articulate what they've learned.	• *Formal job shadowing*: Learners follow a selected successful performer as they perform their tasks. The successful performer articulates their thought process and decisions as they perform their tasks—or shortly afterwards. Learners have frequent opportunities to articulate their reflections about what they've seen and learned.
• *Unstructured on-the-job training (OJT)*: An instructional solution where learners receive impromptu explanations or demonstrations from more experienced employees. Learners then try to imitate their behaviors through trial and error (Van Pamel, 2013). Unstructured OJT can arise organically as learners seek out help from others doing similar work. This approach is sometimes called, "Work with Joe."	• *Structured on-the-job training (OJT)*: An instructional solution where learners receive crafted explanations or demonstrations from instructors who are successful performers. The instructors also provide opportunities for practice and coaching. The instructors use checklists to verify learners can perform tasks in ways that meet specified criteria (Van Pamel, 2013).
• *Cheat sheets*: Quickly created guidance that a more experienced performer creates for someone else. Could include instructions for completing tasks or information that a learner needs on hand—for example, post-it notes that contain logins and passwords that people post on computer screens.	• *Job aids*: Guidance that has been systematically created. An ID or other qualified individual has converted the contents of a task analysis into a set of instructions for completing a job task. Job aids are an instructional solution.

(Continued)

TABLE 8.1 (Continued)

Informal Learning Solutions	Formal Learning Solutions
• *Accumulated content*: A collection of shared electronic folders and files that a group of people may use. People in the group add files and folders they feel may be helpful. It is hard for the group to locate the content they need.	• *Curated content repositories*: A collection of electronic folders and files that a curator has collected and organized so that a group of people may use it. Feedback from the group helps the curator ensure the content is relevant, complete, accurate, and timely.
• *Communities of Practice (CoPs)*: Groups of people who are informally bound together by shared expertise and passion for a joint enterprise. Members share their experiences and knowledge in ways that help them build new approaches to solving shared problems (Wenger & Snyder, 2000).	• *Organizational Communities of Practice (CoPs)*: An organizationally sponsored group deliberately designed to cultivate a learning structure where members can share their functional practices so they better perform their job tasks (Nithithanatchinnapat et al., 2016). • *Affinity groups*: A sponsored group deliberately designed to cultivate a learning structure where groups of people sharing common identity group characteristics, interests, or goals come together in a flat or hierarchical organization. Affinity groups are also called "employee resource groups" (Foldy, 2019).
• *Informal mentoring*: Informal mentoring occurs in a relationship between two people where a protégé gains insight, knowledge, wisdom, friendship, and support from a mentor. Either the mentor or the protégé may initiate the mentoring relationship (Inzer & Crawford, 2005).	• *Formal mentoring*: Formal mentoring occurs when organizations set up mentoring programs to identify and train mentors and then pair them with selected protégés as investments in its employees' maximum development (Giacumo, Chen, & Seguinot-Cruz, 2020).

- The non-instructional solution would help to address a skill or knowledge gap worth closing.
- They have adequate client and stakeholder sponsorship to make these conversions.
- They can provide adequate organizational support to maintain the converted solutions. This means:
  - Obtaining release time for job shadowing and structured OJT mentors, caretakers who support organizational CoPs and affinity groups, and curators for content repositories.
  - Ensuring that these solutions operate in organizationally just and culturally relevant ways, including expanding the range of learners to include relevant groups who may have been left out before.

Seen this way, IDs may select among a variety of approaches, including both formal and informal learning as well as instructional and non-instructional learning. Figure 8.2 depicts these options.

SELECTING FORMAL NON-INSTRUCTIONAL LEARNING SOLUTIONS

IDs select among non-instructional learning solutions to meet the needs of their learners and clients. Pragmatically, IDs might select an intervention given the constraints

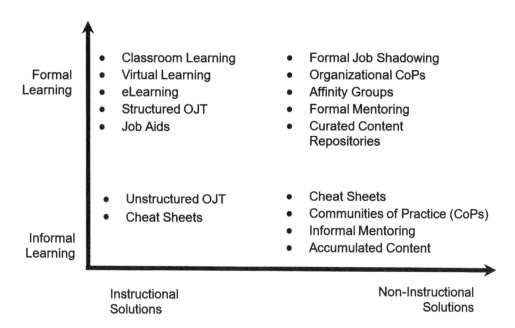

FIGURE 8.2 Formal/informal and instructional/non-instructional learning solutions.

of the potential level of leadership support, budget, and available talent. In general, there are two situations in which informal solutions might be a good choice. The first is when formal options aren't available for purchase or can't be integrated into existing systems.

The second is when the level of organizational support is insufficient to support formal solutions. With sufficient support, IDs can repurpose existing informal learning solutions to meet learners' needs and produce standard learning outcomes across the organization. However, the effectiveness of the learning solutions will suffer without sufficient support in the form of budget, available SMEs, and backing from organizational leaders, clients, and sponsors for design, development, and ongoing maintenance.

Table 8.2 illustrates the relationship among learner needs, learning outcomes, and levels of interaction and support for each type of formal non-instructional learning solution. If the formal options aren't available, then use their informal counterparts when appropriate.

PLANNING NON-INSTRUCTIONAL LEARNING SOLUTIONS

Once selected, IDs must plan the creation, implementation, and maintenance of non-instructional learning solutions. And this planning needs to support just, culturally relevant, equitable, and inclusive learning opportunities.

TABLE 8.2 Non-instructional learning solutions and assessments

When Learners Need to	And Learning Outcomes Are to	And Access to Interaction and Support Is Available	Then Formal Non-Instructional Learning Solution
• Interact with other people like them in the organization who share a similar interest to ask questions, discuss best practices, or seek expertise.	• Build skills to perform more complex tasks involving complex procedures and processes.	• Intensive support and interaction. Learners will interact as they need.	• Organizational CoPs • Affinity Groups
• Interact with a more experienced colleague who can provide coaching and suggest what to do in specific situations.		• Intensive support and interaction during mentoring sessions. Protégés may not be able to interact with mentors on demand.	• Formal Mentoring
• Accompany a successful performer as they perform their daily tasks.		• Medium support and interaction. The successful performer needs to split attention between performing their job tasks and interacting with the learner.	• Formal Job Shadowing
• Access useful, well-organized information appearing in the form they need at the time they need.	• Access timely, accurate, complete, and relevant information upon demand. • Integrate declarative, conceptual, simple procedural knowledge.	• Minimal support and interaction.	• Curated Content Repositories • Performance Support Systems

Planning

When possible, IDs should work with other stakeholders in the organization to plan non-instructional learning solutions. For example, setting up formal:

- Organizational CoPs and affinity groups may require working with members of existing informal CoPs and the people in those CoPs who are members of other related CoPs who might be part of the new solution.
- Mentoring programs may require identifying mentor candidates, training them to be mentors, and obtaining release time from other duties for them to be mentors. Without this release time, mentors may find themselves being punished as they assume additional mentoring duties without additional time to complete them. Every mentoring session they facilitate may come at the price of completing a growing amount of other work.

- Job shadowing programs may require working with supervisors and managers to identify those successful performers whom learners will shadow. Ideally these successful performers are not only experts at completing their job tasks, but also people who are good at explaining what they do and answering questions. These successful performers will also need release time to support their job shadowing efforts. IDs may also want to investigate whether the successful performers who facilitate job shadowing later become mentors to their learners.
- Curated content repositories may require IDs to work with supervisors and managers of the human curators to obtain adequate release time as well as the curators themselves. These efforts may also involve determining the information assets the repository should contain, how users will access them, and how curators will keep the content timely, relevant, useful, complete, and accurate. Because these solutions require some sort of digital infrastructure, IDs may need to work with the organization's Information Technology group to ensure that any technology they select will work with the organization's technology infrastructure.

Planning Tips: Inclusive and Equitable Intervention Design

1. Informal, non-instructional interventions can leave some valued learners without adequate support. Research findings show that learners who are historically marginalized tend to have more challenges finding informal mentors and coaches in organizations.
2. Don't assume you know what others value, or check your assumptions frequently. Instead ask for individual learners' preferences when considering any intervention. For example, learners with diverse identities may or may not want to be matched with other performers who have similar identities.
3. Post-intervention, celebrate each individual learner's self-selected accomplishments widely and equitably.
4. Collect and share personal narratives of diverse learners widely in intervention content and recruitment content.
5. Plan to educate allies of diverse learners, to prevent or intervene in pushback from colleagues who are unfamiliar with safeguarding space and expectations for those with underrepresented identities.
(Sisco, 2020)

Regardless of the cast of characters IDs work with to implement a formal non-instructional intervention, the planning process may include these major steps.

1. Specify the potential features the selected non-instructional solutions should possess.
2. Identify any limitations associated with the selected solutions.
3. Ensure the selected solutions that align with organizational culture.

4. Specify observable and measurable learning and performance outcomes. Ensure the outcomes align with the organization's strategic business goals.
5. Design the implementation of the selected non-instructional systems. More on implementation appears in Chapter 12 of this text.

Ensuring Formal Non-Instructional Solutions Are Culturally Relevant and Inclusive

Informal non-instructional learning solutions live outside an ID's responsibilities. These solutions serve the needs of their existing members and participants. However, the creation, implementation, and maintenance of formal non-instructional solutions also requires IDs to intentionally plan for just, culturally relevant, equitable, and inclusive learning opportunities.

Guidelines for Culturally Relevant and Inclusive Non-Instructional Solution Design

1. Ensure you consider input, participatory design, or co-design input from learners with diverse identities when selecting, designing, prototyping, testing, and piloting the selected solutions.
2. Ensure the creation, implementation, and maintenance of the selected solutions won't overburden any one group. If this is impossible, then be transparent regarding the logic behind any decisions that will overburden any group.
3. Include relevant groups in creating any necessary policies, procedures, or "playground rules" describing how these solutions will operate in ways that are inclusive and equitable.
4. Be transparent about how to access resources or programs. Ensure that a diverse and inclusive group of potential participants receives relevant information to help them:

   - Become aware that these solutions exist.
   - Communicate how these solutions can benefit them.
   - Access these solutions.

5. Ensure learners are adequately supported, equitably included, respected, and treated with dignity, when engaging with these tools.

CASE STUDY

The University of Innovation and Excellence (pseudonym) proudly offered a new employee mentoring program last year. The primary mentoring program outcomes are related to increasing retention, facilitating new employees' access to senior employees, and ensuring new employees are able to access other available organizational resources. Program participants should also develop positive attitudes towards the organization, their department leaders, and leaders' ability to create an inclusive community in support of all employees. Executive leaders decided to fund a minimum viable product approach. The ID would create an early, basic version of the mentoring program that met the minimum necessary requirements for a mentoring program Given protégé, mentor, and feedback from other stakeholders, the organization could then adapt and improve the mentoring program in the future.

The program coordinator was given one month to design and implement a mentor selection and matching process for the organization. They were also authorized to provide 20 minutes of training to on-board mentors and protégés. At the end of the year, aggregated participant surveys revealed mixed results. Aggregated ratings suggested mediocre attitudes towards the mentoring program, the organizational culture of inclusion, and department leaders. Approximately 40 percent of the new employees left the organization by the end of the year.

The program coordinator has sought you out to consult on the design of the next iteration of this program.

- What mentoring program design decisions could cause some of these results? Would you be able to influence any of these factors? Which ones should you try to influence? How?
- What else could cause these results? As an ID, would you be able to influence any of these factors? Which ones should you try to influence? How?
- Who would you suggest should be on the design team? Why?
- What process could you use to redesign the program that would result in increased participants' satisfaction with this program? What are the strengths of this process? What are the potential limitations of this process? How could you mitigate these limitations?
- What new or different features of the mentoring program would you advocate for? Why?

REFLECTION QUESTIONS

- Why should IDs create, implement, and maintain non-instructional learning solutions?
- Who else should be involved in the design of informal learning interventions?
- How would you become informed about designing a new-to-you informal learning intervention, should you be asked to work on one?
- What are the risks of designing informal learning interventions without including input from representatives of historically marginalized populations and intersectional populations?

REFERENCES

Boileau, T. (2018). Informal learning. In West, R. E. *Foundations of learning and instructional design technology: The past, present, and future of learning and instructional design technology.* EdTech Books. https://edtechbooks.org/lidtfoundations/informal_learning

Cross, J. (2007). *Informal learning: Rediscovering the natural pathways that inspire innovation and performance*. Pfeiffer.

Dick, W., Carey, L., & Carey, J. O. (2009). *The systematic design of instruction* (7th ed.). Pearson.

Egan, T. M., Yang, B., & Bartlett, K. R. (2004). The effects of organizational learning culture and job satisfaction on motivation to transfer learning and turnover intention. *Human Resource Development Quarterly*, 15(3), 279–301. doi:10.1002/hrdq.1104

Foldy, E. G. (2019, July). Employee resource groups: What we know about their impact on individuals and organizations. In *Academy of Management Proceedings* (Vol. 1, p. 10633). Briarcliff Manor, NY 10510: Academy of Management. https://www.researchgate.net/profile/Erica-Foldy/publication/352799741_Foldy--ERGs_and_Their_Impact--Narrative_table/links/60da34d792851ca94493efaf/Foldy--ERGs-and-Their-Impact--Narrative-table

Giacumo, L. A., Chen, J., & Seguinot-Cruz, A. (2020). Evidence on the use of mentoring programs and practices to support workplace learning: a systematic multiple-studies review. *Performance Improvement Quarterly*, 33(3), 259–303. doi:10.1002/piq.21324

Inzer, L. D., & Crawford, C. B. (2005). A review of formal and informal mentoring: Processes, problems, and design. *Journal of Leadership Education*, 4(1), 31–50. https://journalofleadershiped.org/wp-content/uploads/2019/02/4_1_Inzer_Crawford.pdf

Kittel, A. F., Kunz, R. A., & Seufert, T. (2021). Self-regulation in informal workplace learning: influence of organizational learning culture and job characteristics. *Frontiers in Psychology*, 12, 643748. doi:10.3389/fpsyg.2021.643748

Merriam, S. B., & Bierema, L. L. (2013). *Adult learning: Linking theory and practice*. San Francisco, CA: Jossey-Bass.

Nithithanatchinnapat, B., Taylor, J., Joshi, K. D., & Weiss, M. L. (2016). Organizational communities of practice: Review, analysis, and role of information and communications technologies. *Journal of Organizational Computing and Electronic Commerce*, 26(4), 307–322. doi:10.1080/10919392.2016.1228357

Sisco, S. (2020). Race-conscious career development: Exploring self-preservation and coping strategies of Black professionals in corporate America. *Advances in Developing Human Resources*, 22(4), 419–436.

Van Pamel, M. (2013, April 16). On-the-job training: Best practices: Structured v unstructured on-the-job training. http://onthejobtrainingbestpractices.blogspot.com/2013/04/structured-v-unstructured-on-job.html

Wenger, E. C., & Snyder, W. M. (2000). Communities of practice: The organizational frontier. *Harvard Business Review*, 78(1), 139–145. https://hbr.org/2000/01/communities-of-practice-the-organizational-frontier

CHAPTER 9

Strategies to Design & Develop Single Events and Multifaceted Programs

INTRODUCTION

As we noted in Chapter 7, savvy instructional designers (IDs) often use a backwards design approach. After you create the performance requirements and performance assessment instruments, you can use them to inform prototypes of interventions. This backwards design process keeps your focus on the desired authentic performance and mastery expectations you have for learners. In this chapter you'll read about the collaborative process strategies and technical output strategies that you can use to support learners' critical task development.

To get started, we'll offer decision support on selecting appropriate collaborative process strategies. Then, we'll turn to strategies you can use to turn the performance requirements into job aid prototypes and sequencing intervention solution components. At some point, you'll need to prototype and refine the larger learning system. Thus, the next project pushes will likely include the following design and development work:

- Prototype, test, and iterate learner intervention materials.
- Chunking and sequence plans for the whole intervention.
- Flipping the intervention prototypes into developed materials, technology, and/or embedded systems, in the organization.

Looking ahead, you may need to finalize a high-level design document that describes an intervention or multifaceted program. We will cover high-level design documentation in Chapter 10. You might also need to prototype, test, iterate, and develop facilitation and implementation guides so that other professionals can seamlessly use the intervention(s) you've built. In Chapter 11 we will go over facilitation guides. In Chapter 12 we will cover implementation guides, data-informed maintenance, and evaluation.

After reading this chapter, you should be able to:

- Given an organizational context, select collaborative process strategies to design and develop culturally relevant and inclusive interventions.
- Given learning and performance support needs, select relevant job aid types for intervention development.

DOI: 10.4324/9781003360612-9

- Use templates as a strategy to produce a variety of standardized deliverables that effectively support learners.
- Determine sequencing for different tasks that are included in an instructional event or multifaceted programs.

COLLABORATIVE PROCESS STRATEGIES TO BUILD LEARNING AND DEVELOPMENT (L&D) INTERVENTIONS

As you strive to create processes and outputs that are more contextualized and emphasize more equitable inclusion of groups and perspectives that haven't been included in the past, you might realize that it's not always possible to prioritize efficiency when you are working to produce more culturally relevant and inclusive interventions. The traditional goal to produce the most efficient, effective, and engaging interventions is too constraining.

Taking a humanistic approach means that we treat people with more dignity, respect, kindness, and compassion. We can't achieve this goal by following only how we think others want to be treated. We must engage with whom we seek to serve. IDs somehow must make space for diverse perspectives and participatory input.

In certain cases, we find ways to work with the diverse learners we want to serve. This takes time. The question then becomes, what strategies should we expect to use in different contexts? You might use Table 9.1 to help guide your work.

Hopefully, you have used some participatory design approaches, if not also some co-design approaches, in your work so far. It's best to spend a lot of time gathering this kind of input as early as possible in a project. These approaches often result in more inclusive, engaging, and effective design, sometimes with less iteration or revision work. However, they are not always possible.

TECHNICAL OUTPUT STRATEGIES TO BUILD EFFECTIVE L&D INTERVENTIONS

The technical output strategies savvy IDs use often begin with identifying relevant job aid types for desired learner decision-making, creating or borrowing templates, and planning formative evaluation for prototyping.

TABLE 9.1 Implementation context and selecting co-design, participator, and consulting strategies

If the implementation context is	Then consider using
A community organization	Co-design strategies
A not-for-profit business, healthcare, or educational organization	Co-design or participatory design strategies
A for-profit business or B Corporation	Participatory design and expert consultant design strategies
A military or government organization	Participatory design and expert consultant design strategies

JOB AIDS: WHY USE THEM AND HOW TO BUILD THEM

We introduced job aids to support learning and performance earlier in this book. However, job aids can also help instructional design (ID) teams get their work done, too. In workplace settings, job aids help learners and performers make decisions using conceptual knowledge, procedural knowledge, and problem-solving knowledge. In this sense, it may help to think of a job aid as a task analysis in a visual format that is easier to decode than the written task analysis.

Savvy IDs generally use job aids wherever and whenever possible to eliminate training time (using job aids alone), reduce training time, and provide post-training performance support in the workplace. Specifically, IDs can use job aids in the following ways:

- Standalone job aids.
- Job aids with introductory training.
- Job aids with extensive training.

To determine how to use job aids, IDs collect additional data about the job tasks that learners perform, the characteristics of the learners themselves, and the environmental factors that affect learning and performance. These data will help in making decisions about the specific job aid formats to be used and how to use them in ways that will support workplace performance.

Combine Multiple Job Aid Formats to Create Systems of Instruction and Performance Support

Willmore (2018) identifies ten different job aid formats. Table 9.2 shows a wide variety of design possibilities.

In some situations, a single job aid format will provide all the support performers need to complete a given job task. However, some job tasks are complex enough to require a combination of job aid formats. For example, warehouse personnel operating manual pallet jacks to move items may require a combination of job aid formats:

- Steps listing the sequence for raising the skids, moving the jack, lowering the skids.
- Photos and callouts of each action.
- Checklist for safe operations.
- Reminders (signage) for safe operations, especially at turns, corners, and uneven floors.

In any case, it's important for IDs to create a system of job aids that provides the guidance performers need, when they need it, and in the format(s) they need. More specifically, the job aids should:

- Align with aspects of exemplary performance.
- Be concise.
- Provide adequate focus and specificity for performers to perform the task.
- Provide any necessary directions about who should use them and how to use them.
- Be easy to use during the training and in the workplace.

TABLE 9.2 Job aid formats, descriptions, and examples

Format	Description	Examples
Reminder	Provides a simple set of instructions to prompt performer behavior.	• A calendar reminder on your smartphone or computer. • A car alarm that sounds when your eyes aren't on the road or your head falls. • A sticky note on a computer screen containing login and password information.
Match	Provides an example or non-example for comparison.	• A sign for bartenders depicting a legitimate driver's license and its components. • Photos depicting how a restaurant arranges food on different menu items. • Photos and callouts illustrating steps in a process. • Sample form letters.
Step	Provides step-by-step instructions to complete a procedure or process.	• A recipe. • Acronyms that depict a sequence (e.g., ADDIE). • Product assembly guides. • An online wizard that guides users through completing a process.
Checklist	Provides a reminder of multiple items to complete or check.	• To do list. • Grocery list. • Airplane preflight checklist. • Packing list. • Surgical checklist.
Worksheet	Provides a format for calculating, recording information, or making decisions.	• Form for determining a tax refund. • Form for determining the value of a customer return. • Online app for recording and calculating trip expenses.
Process table or flowchart	Graphically depicts a series of actions to complete a process or task.	• A simple flowchart. • A swimlane flowchart.
Decision table	Displays information for performers to help them discriminate among data and sort through various options to reach a decision or make an evaluation.	• Decision table to determine types of gunshot wounds. • Online app to determine whether a person is a frequent flier. • If/Then decision tables.
Troubleshooting diagram	Provides a flowchart depicting how to solve a problem. Combines a series of decisions.	• Mager and Pipe's (1997) performance analysis flowchart. • Machine repair guide troubleshooting aids.
Data array	Provides an organized set of data relevant to a given job task so performers can pick out relevant information without having to memorize it.	• A list of customer phone numbers. • An online information system that provides standardized information about securities products. • A list of nearby restaurants, their menus, hours, and distance from you.
Script	Provides text that a performer is supposed to follow.	• Script describing Miranda rights. • Cold-calling script for a sales representative.

- Employ useful and authentic acronyms and mnemonics.
- Be part of a larger, accessible repository that performers can access as needed.
- Employ a common look and feel.

As Willmore (2018) notes, job aids can employ a variety of modalities, from hand-written sticky notes to printed forms and signage to online apps that enable users to perform a task.

When to Use a Job Aid

- If feasible modalities are cost-appropriate, and
- It's safe and easy to use in the workplace, and
- It's appropriate for the organizational culture, and
- It's technologically sound, and
- It's easy to maintain, and
- It supports a complex performance that people do regularly but easily forget how to do, or
- It supports a simple task that people won't remember because they don't do it often enough.

Flipping a Task Analysis into a Job Aid

One way to develop a job aid (JA) for use by learners in an instructional setting, or by performers in a job setting, is to flip a task analysis (TA) into a JA. As described in Chapter 5, a TA is a text outline of the steps and concepts relevant to the desired learner performance. In a text format, the steps are easier to review and revise. However, using visual design can transform a TA into something that's easier for learners to decode and still provides the right amount of information to perform the task.

Figure 9.1 shows a job aid that began as a TA and was developed through collaboration with a graphic designer. This example regrouped information, eliminated information that is useful to instructional designers but not necessary for learners, incorporated color and photos, added organizational branding, and applied a required organizational style guide. It represents Wilmore's (2018) step type of job aid.

Job Aid Templates for Prototyping and Developing Interventions

In addition to supporting learners, job aids can help IDs organize a wide variety of inputs for making valued decisions in ID projects. In other words, savvy IDs often create and use job aids as templates to organize their own work throughout an inclusive ID process. Select common job aid examples you might consider using are introduced below, organized by the Willmore (2018) categories.

Worksheet Job Aid Template

Figure 9.2 shows a worksheet template example to plan an ID team kickoff meeting. As Willard (2018) notes, worksheet job aids provide a format for calculating, recording

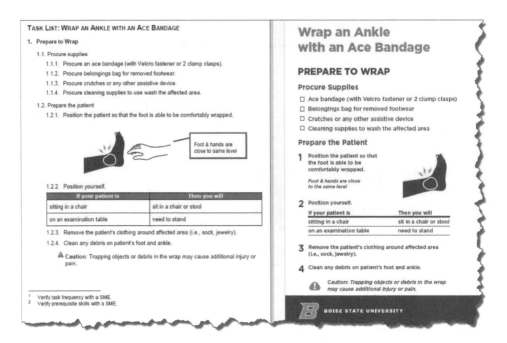

FIGURE 9.1 Example of a task analysis flipped into a step job aid through collaboration with a graphic designer. Branded job aid used with permission from Mrs. Brandalyn Athons and Dr. Seung (Yonnie) Chyung.

information, or making decisions. Different teams can reuse and modify this template for different specialized project needs.

You'll likely encounter situations where you will be called upon to help upskill junior IDs or guide subject matter expert (SME) contributions. Another common example of a worksheet template that IDs can create and/or use is a knowledge check questions template. They can include areas for the item number, an objective number, question, correct responses, distractors, and feedback.

Checklist Job Aid Example

Figure 9.3 illustrates an example performance assessment checklist for wrapping an injured ankle. The authors created this example to support authentic performance in an on-the-job training program. This specific version is for a paper format. However, previous ID teams have created a similar tool in an electronic version using Google Forms and Google Sheets for a pilot study (Frazier-Aich et al., 2023). To turn this into a template you would:

1. Delete the text in the light gray rows and far-left white cells.
2. Add prompt text for new project teams to add information specific to their projects.
3. "Save as" a checklist template.
4. Distribute the checklist to new ID teams.

Decision Table Template

Figure 9.1 includes a two-column decision table embedded in a step job aid. In a similar vein, Table 9.3 depicts a template for a three-column decision table. The leftmost two

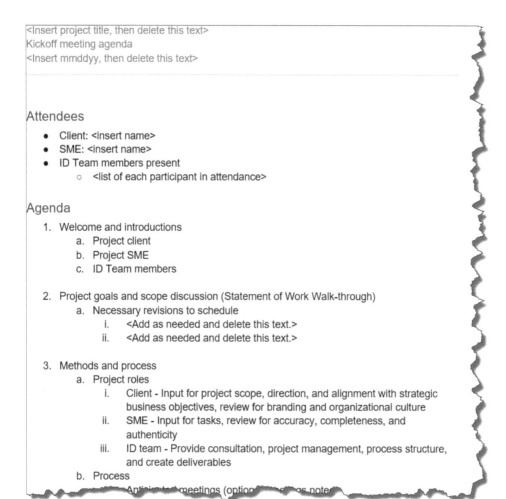

FIGURE 9.2 Example worksheet template for a kickoff meeting agenda.

columns specify conditions. The third column specifies an appropriate decision based on the conditions. Similar decision tables can help organize information for learners and performers when they need to make simple decisions. They are often components of larger step job aids that guide performance of a larger task.

Data Array Job Aid Template for Electronic or Mobile Displays

Figure 9.4 shows a dashboard template. These screens can help organize information for learners and performers when they need to make complex decisions. You can choose from a wide variety of data array visualization displays from different data sets relevant to inform individuals' decision-making.

A set of mobile app templates would be another example of a data array template. The screen wireframes can show designers different ways they might help organize information for learners and performers when they need to either learn or access information to support decisions.

ASSESSMENT CHECKLIST

OBJECTIVE: WRAP AN INJURED ANKLE IN AN ACE BANDAGE, USING A JOB AID

Learner Name:			Instructor Name:
Criteria	**Meet the criteria?**		**Comments**
	Trial 1 Date:	**Trial 2** Date:	
Patient Positioning			
• The foot can be comfortably wrapped.	☐ Yes ☐ No	☐ Yes ☐ No	
• Patient's foot and wrapper's hands are close to the same level.	☐ Yes ☐ No	☐ Yes ☐ No	
• Clothing is removed from affected area.	☐ Yes ☐ No	☐ Yes ☐ No	
• The patient's foot and ankle are clean.	☐ Yes ☐ No	☐ Yes ☐ No	
• The patient's foot and ankle are free of debris.	☐ Yes ☐ No	☐ Yes ☐ No	
The Base Wrap			
• Ensures the wrap doesn't unravel.	☐ Yes ☐ No	☐ Yes ☐ No	
• The wrapper uses both hands to secure the base wrap.	☐ Yes ☐ No	☐ Yes ☐ No	
• There is no slack between the skin and the bandage.	☐ Yes ☐ No	☐ Yes ☐ No	
Foot Wrapping			
• Foot is wrapped from the toes to the ankle.	☐ Yes ☐ No	☐ Yes ☐ No	
• Foot is wrapped twice in a spiral.	☐ Yes ☐ No	☐ Yes ☐ No	
Near the Heel			
• Bandage is wrapped in a figure 8 format.	☐ Yes ☐ No	☐ Yes ☐ No	

FIGURE 9.3 Example performance assessment checklist.

TABLE 9.3 Three-column decision table template

If <insert condition, delete this text>	And <insert condition, delete this text>	Then <insert decision, delete this text>
<Describe condition, delete this text>	<Describe condition, delete this text>	<Describe decision, delete this text>
<Describe condition, delete this text>	<Describe condition, delete this text>	<Describe decision, delete this text>
<Describe condition, delete this text>	<Describe condition, delete this text>	<Describe decision, delete this text>
<Add more rows or delete, as need>		

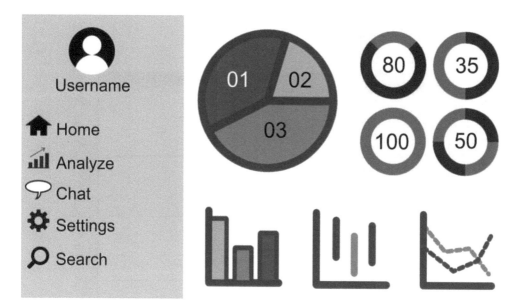

FIGURE 9.4 Dashboard template.

Script Job Aid Template

Figure 9.5 shows a two-column video storyboard template. In the left column, IDs can add the audio script and specify any other sounds that should be included in the video. In the right column, IDs can add simple text descriptions of the visuals that should appear on the screen. This is a great approach to use, especially when you can collaborate with a videographer who might be able to help evolve and iterate design ideas.

A set of eLearning or mobile app storyboard templates can also serve as a script and worksheet type job aid. They can save a lot of time in situations where you are unsure of the amount of support you have for your design ideas. Of course, in projects where you are confident of the knowledge components and that your design decisions will be accepted and you will be responsible for developing the eLearning or mobile learning object, you might choose to skip this step.

While these are more complex than the video template, the idea is the same. You can use simple text descriptions to communicate high-level ideas and solicit input from other design team members and client reviewers. This saves time by guiding feedback and discussion centered on the content and big ideas first. More refined prototypes can address look and feel later, once the specific knowledge components are approved. Common input areas often include the following: project title, module title, screen title, screen number, visual display, onscreen text, animation, interactions, navigation instructions, and development notes.

Checklist-Worksheet Combination Job Aid

Figure 9.6 (see p.147) depicts a performance assessment instrument template. This template specifies information that could appear in an authentic assessment for an instructor-led

Video Storyboard

Project title:

Script	Visuals

FIGURE 9.5 Two-column video storyboard template.

course. An instructor could then use the resulting document to consistently deliver the assessment to students. Whenever you need to work on projects with authentic performance assessments, it can be helpful to work from a template similar to this one. It helps organize bits of information that might come from a variety of different sources and reminds you of any outstanding questions you might need to ask before you try to build a more polished prototype for testing.

You will likely encounter situations where you will be called upon to help formalize specific processes and procedures that relate to learning and performance but aren't related to training programs. Employee self-assessment templates are another common form of a checklist-worksheet job aid that IDs can create. There are many examples available online. As long as you start with a basic task analysis, these too will be relatively straightforward projects, even if you have never worked on one before.

Job Aid Prototypes and Formative Evaluation

In larger ID projects involving more unknowns and greater complexity, IDs often create a series of increasingly refined prototypes to guide their development efforts. In most instances, IDs and their clients agree on the number of prototyping, tryout, and revision cycles before the formal start of work on the project. You may have completed this when the statement of work was finalized, you wrote a project plan, or set up a project charter, or somewhere in between.

Performance Assessment Instrument Template

[Use this template to create a performance assessment instrument.][1]

Type of performance Assessment and Rationale

Type of assessment	Rationale
¨ Product assessment ¨ Process assessment	

Instructor Directions

Assessment Set Up

[Provide step-by-step directions and checklists that the instructor can use to set up the assessment.]

Instructions to Learners

[Inform learners how long the test will take. Provide step-by-step directions that the instructor can use to provide direction to the learners who will complete the test.]

Determining Mastery

[Specify a level of performance for determining mastery.]

Providing Remediation

[Describe how the training will provide remediation for learners who fail the assessment.]

Assessment Checklist

[Provide a yes/no checklist that instructors can use to verify that learners met objective performances and their criteria. The checklist should enable the instructor to comment on items that learners missed, tally correct items, and determine whether learner performance met a mastery threshold.]

Operating Assumptions

[List any assumptions that the ID team has made to date to meet project quality or schedule. Be sure to share any assumptions with your client, SMEs, and stakeholders. Collect any data you need to either verify or reject your assumptions.]

---

[1] Delete all instructions that appear in brackets before submitting templates to your instructor or client.

FIGURE 9.6 Performance assessment instrument template.

Once you have a general idea about your learner personas, the performance context, and available resources, and you have made some decisions about the intervention type(s) you'll build, it's time to prototype. As you build the prototype(s), savvy IDs usually follow an iterative process, which includes some formative evaluation activities. This includes stakeholder reviews, intended learner/performer try outs, design iterations, revisions, and refinements, before eventually building out the final products.

Prototypes initially start as low-fidelity, potential products that IDs create to try out and refine ideas, identify problems, and clarify project scopes. They can range from early sketches on paper or whiteboards through preliminary interactive digital experiences, which are subject to iteration or substantial change and evolution. Examples of prototypes in eLearning or online learning include but are not limited to: storyboards; screen layouts; wireframes that might show structure, buttons, or other interactive elements; digital mock-ups with color, typography, and graphics; and videos. Prototypes in instructor-led interventions can include types of job aids, portions of assessments, instructor guides, and participant guides.

It can be helpful to prototype and try them out in sets. First prototypes often center on key components of technology or events and testing them. The next set of prototypes tend to show how the components work together, especially if a tool or program will become quite complex. What's sometimes hard about prototyping is that you must be prepared to change it significantly as you learn more about the learners' experiences and outcomes after interacting with a prototype (Svihla, 2021). However, once you have settled on components of technology or materials that are working well, it becomes easier to prototype, test, and finalize a larger system. So you may go through several rounds of building and testing when you begin prototyping before you are ready to finalize a product design.

There is often an alpha and beta test for learning and performance support products after the design is finalized. Alpha testing refers to a tryout with a small group of learners done during the early stages of development. The feedback gathered during an alpha test can be used to improve the user experience, design, content, and functionality of the program.

Beta testing refers to a larger-scale tryout of a learning program when it's in its final stages of development. This allows IDs to gather feedback from a larger pool of diverse participants with more varied backgrounds and experiences. This results in additional insights into how a product will work when it's fully rolled out to all potential users and learners. Both alpha and beta testing are intended to improve the quality, effectiveness, and usability of the products.

There are several ways to create these feedback loops. One of the best ways is to observe a small group (e.g., three to five) of each intended user type (e.g., learners, instructors, facilitators) using the prototypes. As part of the observations, IDs might note what is easy, what is difficult, and where participants tend to get stuck, and to what extent using the prototype results in expected behaviors. Another way to obtain feedback is for IDs to ask three to five users to think out loud when they are interacting with an intervention. Another way to test the prototypes at this stage is to request key stakeholders (e.g., client, SME, instructors, facilitators) to review the prototypes and provide written feedback. You might come up with other ways to create these feedback loops as well.

Is it possible to skip this kind of iterative tryouts and testing? It's not a good idea, particularly in larger projects. Even in small projects, the benefits of testing and revising performance support products outweigh the costs. Smaller projects might require fewer iterations but the testing and revision is still less costly than moving directly from the first prototype to full implementation only to find out that revisions are necessary when end users aren't able to effectively perform their required tasks.

SEQUENCING MULTIPLE PERFORMANCE OUTCOMES AND TASKS INTO AN INSTRUCTIONAL INTERVENTION

In Chapter 5, you learned how to identify critical tasks and arrange other associated learning and performance requirements under those critical tasks. Each of the critical

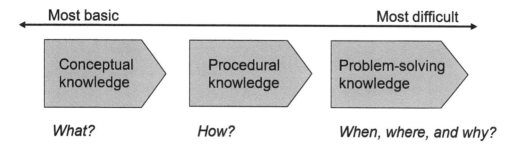

FIGURE 9.7 Knowledge types continuum from most basic to advanced. Adapted from MacDonald, Shukla, & Giacumo (2022), used with permission from The Guild.

tasks served as inputs for your task analysis. Then in Chapter 7, you learned how to identify three different types of knowledge (e.g., conceptual, procedural, and problem-solving) that organizational members use to make decisions. Figure 9.7 shows a knowledge types continuum, from most basic to advanced, and organizes each type as it becomes more difficult or complicated to attain.

Some scholars (Merrill, 2018; Schalk et al., 2018) recommend a basic sequence of learning or instruction, starting with conceptual knowledge, followed by procedural knowledge, culminating in problem-solving knowledge. However, there's no evidence to suggest that this is the only sequence that learners can follow. Further, many times learning and performance interventions must be designed to include multiple outcomes that require mastery of all three different knowledge types (MacDonald et al., 2022). Then the question is how to chunk and sequence them.

When you chunk lesson-level interventions down into smaller modules or components with one to three desired performance outcomes, you can help build learners' capacity to achieve larger or even overarching performance outcomes (Shipley, Stephen, & Tawfik, 2018). Giacumo et al. (2021) recommend creating a visual map of how subordinate learning and performance outcomes can contribute to larger and overarching learning and performance outcomes. Figure 9.8 shows one way to chunk and sequence a set of performance outcomes associated with a task analysis. Specifically, it depicts a sequence of eight lessons with performance outcomes and knowledge types that range from most basic to most advanced (Giacumo et al., 2021).

In that sequence example, each lesson chunk is complementary, and there are no explicit dependencies between them. This means that we can offer learners access to the conceptual knowledge before the procedural or problem-solving knowledge. Further, when we design sequences that allow learners to build on prior knowledge or experience with new knowledge in a tell-and-practice sequence (Merrill, 2018; Schalk et al., 2018) that's well designed and aligned with a larger learning and performance outcome, learners tend to be successful (Kraiger & Ford, 2021; Longo & Rajendran, 2021). Thus, IDs can start with conceptual knowledge before jumping to procedural knowledge, such as is indicated by lesson 1 and lesson 2. This approach allows IDs to build reinforcement of lesson 1 into lessons 2, 4, and 7, to better support learning, given a required sequence structure embedded into the intervention.

However, it is important to note that a tell-and-practice sequence is not the only way to organize chunks of a learning intervention. While a tell-and-practice sequence may

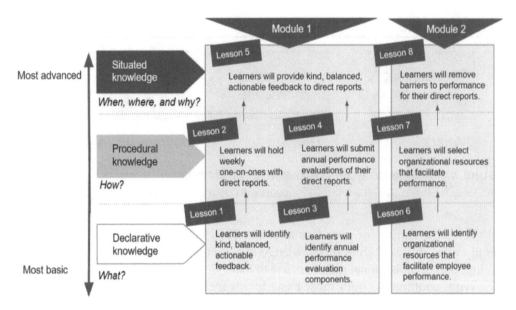

FIGURE 9.8 Sequence of eight lessons with performance outcomes and knowledge types that range from most basic to most advanced. Used with permission from The Guild.

be more efficient, a problem-solving-then-instruction (PS-I) sequence, although more time-consuming, can be superior if in-depth understanding, persistence, and grit are more important (Schalk et al., 2018). Either sequence type can be initiated with a story and problem to get learners interested and focused on the task at hand to be learned (Doolani et al., 2020; Rea, 2021).

When working on module-level or even program-level sequencing, you could consider a few different approaches. These might include the following:

- *Familiarity.* Starting with familiar tasks and progressing to tasks that are less familiar.
- *Difficulty.* Starting with easier tasks and progressing to more difficult ones.
- *Frequency.* Starting with tasks that are performed more frequently and progressing to those that are performed less frequently.
- *Criticality.* Starting with tasks that have particularly important consequences and progressing to those that are less critical.
- *Chronology.* Starting with the first task or step to be performed, *or* with the last task or step to be performed.
- *Prerequisite.* Starting with tasks that must be learned before other tasks can be learned. For example, learning to operate a computer is typically a prerequisite skill for programming one.

In short, it's been our experience that, if we have identified more than one or two key groups of performance requirements, we have also created more than one learning intervention. Additionally, other heuristics can guide ID decisions regarding multifaceted programs. For example, you can ask SMEs how long it usually takes them to explain and orientate someone or a group to the specific task such that a new learner becomes independently competent to a reasonable standard and what that has entailed. When you couple that information with information about the intended learning environment (e.g., classroom, online, mentoring, coaching, number of learners) it becomes easier to gauge whether your intervention might be best suited for a series of quick email microlearnings, a 6-minute eLearning, a 15-minute Zoom conference, a 1-hour classroom event, a 6-month mentoring program, or something more involved. As with all ID decisions, experience over time will also help you refine your ability to more accurately predict and determine what set of interventions will resolve a given performance gap.

Program-Level Structure Organization Decisions

Common structural decisions you might make can be to take a modular structure, integrated structure, or some combination of the two.

- Modular structure, standalone components with no prerequisite knowledge or skills.
  - Positives—anyone can enter into a module as needed and they are easier to update and change because other components don't rest on top of them.
  - Negatives—careful planning is needed to refresh, reinforce, and extend the knowledge and skills covered in a module over time. May also require some sort of tool to help learners select the content associated with their needs.
  - Typical uses—for learning and performance objectives that are relatively finite and require a smaller chunk of content and little practice or feedback for competency or mastery.
- Integrated structure, progressive units that build on previous units.
  - Positives—reinforcement and extension of previous new knowledge and skills can help learners integrate new knowledge and advance skills with spaced learning over time (Thalheimer, 2006).
  - Negatives—learners will have to follow a planned sequence to gain access to some knowledge and skills, which can have implications for motivation, enrollment, and performance.
  - Typical uses—to support larger knowledge and skills gains which require more time, practice, coaching, and feedback for competency or mastery.

MULTIFACETED PROGRAM DESIGN AND DEVELOPMENT

Multifaceted intervention programs are a collection of multiple interventions required to adequately support learners' knowledge and skill development. They may include both instructional and non-instructional learning components. These systems of interventions often address highly contextualized or individualized feedback loops to support complex and highly nuanced decision-making. In Chapters 7 and 8, you learned what to consider in selecting each type of intervention.

To get started with planning a multifaceted program, savvy IDs often begin with a general idea of the learning activities, or instructional interventions, to include in a multifaceted program. Or, sometimes the need for multifaceted programs only becomes apparent after IDs prototype and test materials for a single intervention, or an object such as a game. Regardless of where an ID team starts, when a collection of intervention types occurring across a period of time is required to improve the L&D system, savvy IDs often take a step back to make decisions relevant to a larger program structure and logistics.

Map the Multifaceted Program Out at a High Level

One way to show how multiple interventions can work together to support a desired L&D systems change is to build a logic model. A logic model shows the process and relationships between program components and short-, mid-, and long-term outcomes. The process of creating one can help you identify the inputs, activities, outputs, short-term outcomes, mid-term outcomes, and long-term outcomes, as shown in Figure 9.9. It shows the purpose of the program interventions, why the program is important, and serves as a reference point. A complete model can also inform planning, budgeting, and evaluating.

Figure 9.10 shows a realistic, although generic, example of a completed logic model for a professional education program.

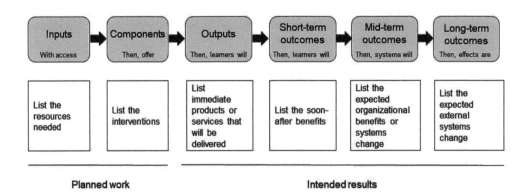

FIGURE 9.9 Logic model components.

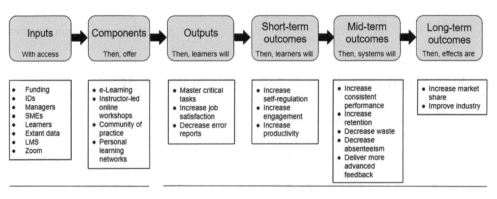

FIGURE 9.10 Logic model of a professional education program.

Once you have a logic model, you can begin to design the multifaceted program intervention components, assessments, and activities. You can use the same basic process that we've covered so far in this book to achieve this at the program level (e.g., solicit stakeholder input, complete task analyses to support required decision-making, select instructional and/or non-instructional strategies, begin prototyping, testing, iterating, and piloting).

To Build a Culturally Relevant and Equitable Logic Model

- Start by articulating a meaningful performance problem or a new performance opportunity that your stakeholders agree on or want to seize.
- Create an observable, measurable, overarching goal statement related to a desired comprehensive program outcome.
- Identify the root causes, facilitators, and barriers associated with the critical tasks. Be sure to include diverse intended learners' input, center their needs, and work to build on this information.
- Map the causes to a set of intervention solutions. This should be done through evidence-based practices, informed both by relevant theory and empirical research gathered from scholarly literature and the organizational context. If there's no evidence of previous practices in your organization, a literature review will at least provide some insight. As always, be sure to include diverse intended learners' input when selecting potential solutions.
- Submit the logic map for stakeholder review and feedback.

As previously mentioned, we generally recommend starting with a smaller tryout or pilot approach and then revise and scale it up as needed. Including potential learners as members on your design team, who can help you ideate and provide diverse, representational input, can help inform these decisions. As always, it's important to be intentional and clear about who is best and least served, so you can think critically to ensure your decisions result in culturally relevant and equitable programs.

FORMATIVE EVALUATION OF INSTRUCTIONAL AND NON-INSTRUCTIONAL INTERVENTIONS AND PROGRAMS

As we mentioned before, there is no one standard approach to setting up an ID project process. Over time, you will find what works for you and modify as needed for different contexts and needs. You may have to advocate for what you need to prototype, try out, and iterate the rest of the materials, technology, and/or embedded systems. No matter what process you use, after you gather or build the templates, and perhaps test some prototypes, it's time to revisit your design work. At this point, your project likely has the following resources:

- Documentation and/or organizational intelligence created during the Empathize & Analyze component, which includes information that describes the organizational culture, the learners, the performance context, desired performance outcomes and associated knowledge types (e.g., conceptual, procedural, problem-solving), learning requirements, task analyses, and performance requirements.
- Documentation and/or organizational intelligence created during the Design & Develop component, which includes some prototypes and some testing results.

CASE STUDY

Rain (pseudonym; they/them) is the Chief People Officer for a regional healthcare organization that's growing. They just hired Juan (pseudonym; he/him) as the organization's first learning and development manager. Rain has asked Juan to begin with the job aids that are used by ancillary diagnostic staff throughout the organization (e.g., lab technicians, medical imaging technicians). Juan has used job aids such as worksheets and templates in the past to complete assignments for school and share information with others.

- Thinking back to the principles of "inclusive design" from Chapter 1, how might Juan assemble a design team to review and revise existing job aids and develop new job aids where necessary?

REFLECTION QUESTIONS

- What worksheets or templates have you used to guide your work on job aids in the past? What did you notice while you used the job aids? What worked and what didn't? How might you use this experience to revise the process you use to develop job aids in the future?
- With any past projects, have you tried to include a diverse and representative group of learners on your ID team, including learners who have different identities and perspectives from you or others on the team? How did that go?
- What arguments could you now use with a reluctant client to include a diverse and representative group of learners on your ID team?

REFERENCES

Doolani, S., Owens, L., Wessels, C., & Makedon, F. (2020). vIS: An immersive virtual storytelling system for vocational training. *Applied Sciences, 10*(22), 8143. doi:10.3390/app10228143

Frazier-Aich, L., Beaudry, J., MacDonald, M., & Giacumo, L. A. (2023). Instructional design for socially distanced compliance audit. *TechTrends, 67*, 68–83. doi:10.1007/s11528-022-00772-3

Giacumo, L. A., MacDonald, M., Shukla, S. (2021). How to Get Started with Chunking & Sequencing eLearning Design. https://www.learningguild.com/articles/how-to-get-started-with-chunking-sequencing-elearning-design/

Kraiger, K., & Ford, J. K. (2021). The science of workplace instruction: Learning and development applied to work. *Annual Review of Organizational Psychology and Organizational Behavior, 8*, 45–72. doi:10.1146/annurev-orgpsych-012420–060109

Longo, L., & Rajendran, M. (2021, November). A novel parabolic model of instructional efficiency grounded on ideal mental workload and performance. *International Symposium on Human Mental Workload: Models and Applications* (pp. 11–36). Springer. doi:10.1007/978–3-030–91408–0_2

MacDonald, M., Shukla, M., S., & Giacumo, L. A. (2022, May 12). How to get started with chunking & sequencing eLearning design. *Learning Solutions*. https://www.learningguild.com/articles/how-to-get-started-with-chunking-sequencing-elearning-design/

Mager, R. F., & Pipe, P. (1997). *Analyzing performance problems: You really oughta wanna* (3rd ed.). CEP Press.

Merrill, M. D. (2018). Using the first principles of instruction to make instruction effective, efficient, and engaging. *Foundations of learning and instructional design technology*. BYU Open Textbook Network. https://open.byu.edu/lidtfoundations/using_the_first_principles_of_instruction

Rea, E. A. (2021). Changing the face of technology: Storytelling as intersectional feminist practice in coding organizations. *Technical Communication, 68*(4), 26–39.

Schalk, L., Schumacher, R., Barth, A., & Stern, E. (2018). When problem-solving followed by instruction is superior to the traditional tell-and-practice sequence. *Journal of Educational Psychology, 110*(4), 596. https://psycnet.apa.org/doi/10.1037/edu0000234

Shipley, S. L., Stephen, J. S., & Tawfik, A. A. (2018). Revisiting the historical roots of task analysis in instructional design. *TechTrends, 62*(4), 319–320. doi:10.1007/s11528-018-0303-8

Svihla, V. (2021). Design thinking. In McDonald, J. K., & West, R. E. (Eds), *Design for learning: Principles, processes, and praxis*. EdTech Books. https://edtechbooks.org/id/design_thinking

Thalheimer, W. (2006). Spacing learning events over time: What the research says. https://www.worklearning.com/wp-content/uploads/2017/10/Spacing_Learning_Over_Time__March2009v1_.pdf

Willmore, J. (2018). Job aids basics. American Society for Training and Development.

CHAPTER **10**

Strategies to Design Learning and Performance Ecosystems

INTRODUCTION

This chapter will deal with a menagerie of similar interventions, all related to supporting performance at the moment of need. These interventions include performance support, electronic performance support systems, performance support systems, mobile performance support systems, and learning and performance ecosystems. These interventions have evolved over time, and different practitioners and authors have used different terms to describe similar approaches to supporting performance. Seen this way, "job aids" have become "performance support." Online job aids and tools have become "electronic performance support systems" (EPSSs). And EPSSs combined with instructor-led learning interventions have become "performance support systems" (PSSs). PSSs delivered over wearable and mobile devices have become "mobile performance support systems" (MPSSs). And, more recently, PSSs and MPSSs delivered over the Internet have become "Learning and Performance Ecosystems." In our view, these similarities are far more important than their minor differences.

To this point, this text has mentioned the role of job aids in supporting performance. Job aids come in many forms. When combined with introductory training or extended training, job aids can reduce the amount of time learning experiences would otherwise take for learners to complete. This chapter will build on what job aids can do to improve workplace learning and performance. After reading this chapter, you should be able to:

- Describe performance support.
- Specify different approaches to providing performance support, including EPSSs, PSSs, MPSSs, and learning and performance ecosystems.
- Describe the benefits of these performance support approaches.
- Discuss the design and maintenance of culturally relevant and equitable learning and performance ecosystems.

As previously mentioned, instructional design (ID) is scalable. Individual instructional designers (IDs) and ID teams may find themselves working with a large cast of other characters from the organization to create large-scale learning and performance ecosystems. Conversely, an ID or small ID team might be responsible for smaller solutions involving the creation of a few performance support solutions.

DOI: 10.4324/9781003360612-10

PERFORMANCE SUPPORT

One of the long-standing challenges in ID is that the field is full of different terms that mean approximately the same thing. And there are times when the same term can mean very different things. One place where terminology gets messy lies in the area of performance support and related interventions. Depending on who is using them, terms related to performance support can mean the same or different things. Some people use these terms interchangeably. When using terms related to any form of performance support, it's good ID practice to mention both the term and its key features as well.

Considered the "mother of performance support," Gery (1991) compared job aids to performance support (p. 50). Table 10.1 summarizes their differences. These comparisons gave rise to the notion that performance support was akin to "extreme job aids."

Quinn (2014) notes that performance support delivers information at the moment of need, rather than breaking away from the workflow to find them. Adequate performance support would provide these resources before, during, and after "moments of need" to improve the performance and turn them into learning experiences.

Narum (2018) lists ten different types of performance support tools:

1. *Quick reference guides*. Reference content that quickly provides learners with the information they need to keep working in the moment. These can provide step-by-step instructions or information needed to complete a specific task.
2. *Infographics*. Visual representations using charts, graphs, instructions, and diagrams to provide visual representations of useful content that assists learning.

TABLE 10.1 A comparison of job aids and performance support

Job Aids	Performance Support
Typically support simple, linear sequential procedural tasks.	Can support performance of simple or complex tasks; with multi-path branched, integrated processes via expert systems.
Do not accept user input or data. Structuring occurs in advance of need and addresses limited situations.	Can accept user input or data as a basis for situationally specific branching, advice, information presentation, etc.
Provide task structuring but not related information.	Provide task structuring, advice, and related information.
Structured in advance and do not accommodate individual user requirements.	Can present customized views of the system to individual users.
Typically paper-based with possibility of passive multiple modes (i.e., text and still images). When electronic, it could incorporate multiple modes, but is mostly text and still images.	Can incorporate multiple modes of information presentation (e.g., text, audio, images, animated sequences).
Typically provide predetermined and structured access. Because the information base is not integrated, the path is usually linear.	Can provide alternative access to the information (using menus or alphabetical listings), hierarchical access using outlines, or relational access using hyperlinked media.

3. *Process maps.* Provide a big picture view of processes that cut across organizational departments and silos. They specify the steps comprising the process, including upstream and downstream processes.
4. *eLearning.* Online learning experiences learners complete to learn new skills or as a refresher. eLearning can help new employees build the skills they need and existing employees with their professional development.
5. *Mobile apps.* Computer programs or software applications designed to run on mobile devices such as phones, tablets, or watches. Mobile apps can support employees who don't have immediate access to computer or printed resources. Users turn to these apps to complete their job tasks, entering information they need while receiving information and guidance they need.
6. *eBooks/Interactive PDFs.* Use of online files containing interactive features such as buttons, videos, and other attached files. Learners navigate these documents to find the information they need.
7. *How-to-videos.* Online video demonstrations describing how to perform a task.
8. *Frequently asked questions (FAQs).* Lists of questions that users may have and their answers.
9. *Checklists.* Help users complete complex tasks by ensuring users address all key points. They help ensure users have completed all steps comprising a given task, have all the resources they need to perform a task, and have met all of the criteria associated with a task. Checklists also help ensure users perform procedural tasks the same way each time.
10. *Learning portals.* A centralized repository of all learning content users need to access on the job. They can provide access to all of these performance support tools.

EPSSS, PSSS, AND MPSSS

Performance support can provide a single repository of information and guidance via learning portals and learning management systems (LMSs). However, accessing these portals requires users to stop working on a given task, access the learning portal, and find the support they need. How can users more easily access what they need, when they need it, in the form they need it? ID teams can work with others in the organization to integrate individual performance support components into a system. EPSSs, PSSs, and MPSSs provide such on-demand access within the flow of work itself.

EPSSs

Work itself has become increasingly computer-mediated. Knowledge workers often use computers and software to perform their job tasks. Gery (1991) coined the term "EPSS" to denote a new type of software designed to enable users to become productive on the job on the day the software is implemented—without classroom training. Raybauld (1990) described an EPSS as "a computer-based system that improves worker productivity by providing on-the-job access to integrated information, advice, and learning experiences" (p. 4).

TABLE 10.2 A continuum of performance support integrations

Configuration	Description
Offline external	Either an offline or online performance support that requires users to stop what they are doing on the computer to consult an offline, external resource, such as a colleague or a printed reference manual. Users are responsible for integrating what they access into the performance of the task.
Online external	Performance support that is "bolted on" to the application itself. Users must stop what they are doing and invoke a separate PSS, such as a learning portal. The performer is either using the application or the PSS, but never using both at the same time. Users are responsible for integrating what they access into the performance of the task.
Online extrinsic	Performance support within the application itself, where there are built-in mechanisms to access relevant, just-in-time, context-sensitive performance support components.
Online intrinsic	Performance support is fully integrated (or fused) with the application. The application's user interface helps users establish goals, structure work processes, access embedded knowledge, monitor their progress, and automate task performance. One example would be a "wizard" that enables novices to perform various tasks. Another example would be a context-sensitive link in the application that invokes relevant eLearning supporting a given job task.

As people use software to complete their job tasks, Gery (1995) notes they can access supports in the form of:

- Cue cards that provide sequential or logical guidance about completing a task.
- Explanations about the job task.
- Demonstrations showing how to complete the job task.
- Coaches or guides that provide interactive walk-throughs of system-related tasks.
- Searchable references consisting of content or knowledge databases that include concepts, products, processes, equipment, facts, principles. These online references would be organized for flexible searches, retrieval, and navigation.
- Checklists.
- Process maps.
- Examples of work processes and outcomes in a database of instances.
- Templates, consisting of pre-structured formats or shells.
- Tips, hints, and suggested alternatives.
- Interactive practice activities (eLearning).
- Assessments.

Villachica and Stone (1999) note a variety of EPSS configurations that provide a continuum of performance support, as shown in Table 10.2.

PSSs

Villachica and Stone (1999) define a PSS as

an optimized body of coordinated online and offline methods and resources that enable and maintain a person's or an organization's performance. The goal is to give performers what they need, when they need it, and in the form in which they need it so that they perform in a way that consistently meets organizational objectives.

(pp. 443–444)

In their view, a PSS is an integrated intervention, with online intrinsic components designed to work together to improve performance. A PSS consists of the people who use it, the processes it supports, and the devices it uses. A PSS facilitates performance across multiple levels in an organization. Rossett and Shafer (2007) broadly divide PSSs into

- "Sidekicks," which users employ as they complete their work.
- "Planners," which provide support when users are preparing to perform or reflecting on their completed actions.

This definition of a PSS is broader in scope than the computer-centric definitions of EPSSs and MPSSs. As illustrated in Table 10.3, the integrated online and offline components of a PSS can include:

TABLE 10.3 Potential PSS components (Villachica, Stone, & Endicott, 2006, p. 543)

• Online evaluation or feedback system	• Instructor-led training	• Automated reporting
• Employee videos	• Compliance training	• Compliance database
• Handheld wireless devices	• Jobs database	• Online checklists
• Video conferencing or teleconferencing	• Automated data collection	• Operational excellence
• Print-based job aids	• World Wide Web	• Electronic communities of practice (CoPs)
• Policy and procedure manuals	• Online database reports	• Self-paced workbooks
• FAQs	• Multimedia scenario-based training	• Supervisor workbooks
• Software tools	• Employee workbooks	• Learning management systems/learning content management systems
• Supervisor videos	• Distance learning	• Experts
• Glossary	• Mentors and coaches	
	• Help desk	

MPSSs

MPSSs emerged with EPSS. Essentially, an MPSS is a handheld or wearable version of an EPSS that resides on mobile devices. Huang and Klein (2023) note that a MPSS assists users who don't often sit at the same locations. MPSS users include drivers, facility workers, salespeople, nurses, police officers, and other mobile workers.

Handheld devices are digital computers that users can hold in their hands or carry in their pockets, such as personal digital assistants (PDAs), digital readers, smartphones, and tablets. For example, Amazon and UPS delivery drivers use handheld MPSSs that schedule their routes, guide them en route, and track their deliveries. Wearable performance support includes smart glasses, earpieces, digital watches, and head-mounted devices for users who need to use their hands as they perform their job tasks. For instance, a bartender in a restaurant system may use an earpiece connected to an MPSS that provides guidance about how to mix drinks, enters orders in the point-of-sale system, and requests help from an expert in the organization in novel situations.

MPSSs share characteristics of other performance support solutions. They can also provide guidance and assistance based on geolocation. Geolocation helps users navigate, receive location-based information, and collect geographic data for analysis. Users from field engineering, gaming, logistics, aviation, sales, tourism, agriculture, and architecture have used geo-specific guidance and information on MPSSs to complete their tasks. MPSSs can also employ augmented reality by providing digital and other types of information placed on top of the physical environment. Mechanics repairing a car can use an MPSS on smart glasses to guide them through the procedure while keeping their hands free to use their tools.

Learning and Performance Ecosystems

Over time, learning and development (L&D) thought leaders began to recommend a combination of various instructional and non-instructional interventions, with approaches such as EPSS, PSS, and MPSS. These dynamic systems of intervention combinations are known as learning and performance ecosystems, sometimes called "learning ecosystems." Bannan, Dabbaugh, and Walcutt (2019) note that an ecosystem is composed of dynamic interconnected components, with the behaviors of many individual agents affecting each other, as well as the environment's overall holistic pattern. According to Foreman (2022), these ecosystems are not technologies per se. Instead, they are ways of "integrating learning and working to achieve strategic results. They are enabled by the right mix of content, technology, processes, and metrics." They make learning and working seamless activities by connecting knowledge, guidance, learning, colleagues, and experts in ways that optimize individual performance and organizational productivity.

According to Rosenberg and Foreman (2014), learning and performance ecosystems enhance performance effectiveness at the individual and organizational levels by connecting people and supporting them with a broad range of content, processes, and technologies. A learning and performance ecosystem introduces new capabilities that integrate learning and performance solutions into the work environment. These ecosystems minimize the need for users to leave work in order to learn, reduce work disruption, and place more learning opportunities directly into the flow of the work. As described in Table 10.4, these ecosystems consist of six major integrated components that enable users and organizations to pursue multiple goals.

Dillon (2022) layers similar components in what he calls a "learning ecosystem."

- *Shared knowledge.* A "look it up" layer that includes all tools and tactics users need to access and apply information within the flow of their work. These tools can include organizational intranets, knowledge management systems, wikis, shared drives, cloud repositories, sales enablement tools, customer relationship management platforms, company websites, and learning content management systems.
- *Performance support.* A layer embedded in the natural workflow that provides just enough context-specific information to complete a task when and where the performer needs it.
- *Reinforcement.* A layer consisting of the minimal need-to-know information related to a given task and use of strategies to help learners learn, practice, apply, and remember how to perform the task over time.

TABLE 10.4 Learning and performance ecosystem components, individual goals, and organizational goals (Rosenberg & Foreman, 2014)

Component	Individual Goals	Organizational Goals
Talent management	Help individuals seeking to advance their careers and find the best place for themselves in the organization.	Manage and develop the workforce.
Performance support	Provide performance support assistance at the moment of need within the context of job tasks.	Improve productivity and reduce errors.
Knowledge management	Provide access to content that supports the work. Research a topic and quickly get answers.	Provide easy and reliable access to information.
Access to experts	Find and consult with experts to resolve problems or issues, or grow user capabilities over time.	Effectively leverage expertise.
Social networking and collaboration	Share information and insights so the collective knowledge and experience of a group helps users solve problems and improve performance.	Encourage the exchange of knowledge and ideas.
Structured learning	Access formally designed learning experiences (classroom and online) that help build skills and knowledge.	Train, certify, and meet compliance requirements.

- *Coaching.* A layer where supervisors and managers act as guides or mentors for people on their teams. This layer selects coaches and provides them with access to relevant and timely data and reporting so they can provide insightful feedback. This layer also trains coaches to build trust, ask good questions, listen actively, recognize strengths, monitor emotions, demonstrate care, and communicate recommendations. This layer provides coaches with adequate release time to focus on their team members.
- *Pull training.* Optional online courses, instructor-led sessions, and hands-on training programs that users can complete as they desire for their own self-directed learning and career development, without deadlines.
- *Push training.* Mandatory online courses, instructor-led sessions, and hands-on training programs that users are required to complete by specified deadlines.

Learning Programs versus Learning Ecosystems

Like learning programs, learning and performance ecosystems can contain interactive learning experiences. They can also contain job aids, online tools and apps, and other forms of performance support. Unlike learning programs, the focus of these ecosystems isn't always on learning new knowledge and skills. Instead, the focus is on providing on-the-job performance support—often without any formally designed learning experiences. Learning and performance ecosystems enable users to perform parts of their job tasks without necessarily remembering learned concepts and steps.

Deciding which of these alternatives to use involves determining how much instruction is really needed. Can a learning program provide the information, practice, and guidance that learners need to meet specified criteria when they perform their jobs?

Will providing access to learning activities and guidance alone enable them to perform? Or will learners need the additional support that learning and performance ecosystems provide? If successful performance requires access to experts, social networking, and access to rapidly changing information, then a learning ecosystem may be appropriate.

In addition, IDs should consider the goals of these efforts. Learning programs can support substantial goals that are finite and immediate. One example could be how to assess warehouse management operations for a number of locations for a multi-national organization such as Amazon or for the US Air Force. In contrast, learning and performance ecosystems can support larger, longer-term goals that may be infinite in nature. For instance, a goal of creating a pipeline of software developers who can lead innovation teams to deliver novel solutions some years from now might lend itself to a learning and performance ecosystem. Likewise, a streamlined onboarding process that provides timely access to information, learning resources, and access to others in the organization may lend itself to an ecosystem approach.

BENEFITS

The primary benefit of learning and performance ecosystems lies in decreased time to obtain and maintain skilled performance over time. In other words, learners can become proficient faster and keep performing at skilled levels longer with these ecosystems than with learning programs alone. Villachica and Stone (1999) contend that in some situations PSSs can produce near expert-like performance from day one with little or no training. Traditional training often occurs away from the job site, focuses on disseminating information, and employs massed practice. Courses typically cover a large amount of content within a short space of time (hours or days in single lengthy sessions or multiple sessions separated by short intervals (American Psychological Association, 2018). Massed practice often occurs at the expense of providing adequate practice, coaching, and feedback. Consequently, transfer of learning to the workplace setting is low. Subsequent on-the-job training (either formal or informal) ultimately produces near-expert performance with additional time. This can be interrupted by new releases of software or changes to policies and procedures, resulting in short-term drops in performance that require additional interventions.

In contrast, the highly modular and contextualized advice that a PSS provides quickly produces near-expert performance. Because any necessary training occurs on the job, employs distributed practice, and provides various forms of feedback, transfer of learning is high. Novices can complete initial training quickly. Like a well-designed job aid, a fully integrated PSS can also often enable near-expert performance from the first day, with no training at all. As new software releases or policies and procedures changes are built into the PSS, few if any associated drops in performance appear. Use of a PSS often makes it possible to obtain near-expert performance almost immediately and to sustain it indefinitely.

As an example, Stone and Villachica (1997) describe the creation of a large-scale PSS named "CornerStone," which helped examiners perform audits of securities firms to ensure they:

- Possessed enough funds to trade on the securities market.
- Complied with appropriate sales practices.

An EPSS lay at the heart of CornerStone. It consisted of integrated computer-based training (eLearning), a product information system, custom software for conducting examinations and reporting their results, an online reference system, and a help system for using the EPSS. The EPSS was supported by an integrated set of offline components, including an electronic brochure that introduced the PSS to its users, self-paced foundations training using self-paced printed workbooks and instructor-led training that introduced new examiners to their job tasks, printed job aids describing job tasks, a mentoring program, on-the-job training, and a formal training program for the mentors. CornerStone also featured a low-fidelity, authentic simulation of a larger-scale examination, where examiners worked in teams. The simulation included case files, financial information, and actors playing the roles of different people in the securities firm. The examiners used the CornerStone EPSS to complete their examination and then presented their report to a panel of expert stakeholders from the organization.

The CornerStone PSS (Villachica & Stone, 1998) cited the following financial and business benefits (pp. 448–449).

- Produced ROI of 42.3% with payoff in 2.2 years.
- Reduced training delivery costs 43% by providing on-demand training.
- Decreased the potential that regulatory violations might harm the investing public during the time a novice examiner comes up to speed.
- Provided experienced examiners with new opportunities for career advancement. After five years on the job, these individuals can be selected as mentors, a role in which they also receive formal training.
- Increased employee satisfaction.
- Eliminated the possibility that novice examiners might rely on members of the securities firms they investigate to teach them about new products they encounter during exams because they can now access this information on demand.
- Increased consistency in exam performance and decreased unnecessary District variation in the exam processes by providing explicit learning [based on] experts' decision processes.
- Supervisors, managers, and legal personnel return fewer exam reports for rework.
- Improved the appearance of professionalism.

These specific benefits align with general benefits that appear in the professional literature. Nguyen (2010) notes these benefits of PSS include:

- Increased performance.
- Improved user attitudes.
- Reduction in monetary costs.
- Providing users with memory support for infrequently performed tasks.
- Rapidly distributing updated information to broad groups of users.
- Exposing users to broader ranges of support content that isn't possible or practical to provide in training.

Rosenberg and Foreman (2014) note that learning and performance ecosystems produce these benefits:

- Expanded capabilities and choices with a full array of components that users can combine in different ways to support learning and performance.
- Increased organizational innovation and agility using an appropriate combination of approaches, some embedded in workflow itself.
- Complementary support for learning, mastery, transfer, reinforcement, enrichment, and sharing.
- Improved productivity and lower cost to add value to the organization and its customers.
- Improved framework to organize the learning and performance improvement framework function within organizations.

DESIGN AND MAINTENANCE CONSIDERATIONS

As you've come to realize over the last few chapters, designing one performance-based learning experience that is culturally relevant and equitable requires more input from people with diverse perspectives. Designing a learning program composed of multiple, connected learning experiences will involve more consideration. And designing a learning and performance ecosystem can be even more complex. One reason is that these interventions (PSS and learning and performance ecosystems) may consist of more interacting parts than learning programs. The other reason is that much of the ecosystem will contain information and guidance that will require continual updating. Because of the size and complexity of these interventions, IDs should work with clients, learners, subject matter experts (SMEs), managers, supervisors, IT professionals, and other stakeholders to maintain what they have created and implemented.

Phase 1: Identify the Embedded Components

One way to begin identifying the components of a learning and performance support system is to review the contents of a previously conducted needs assessment. A useful needs assessment will typically include:

- A description of one or more gaps between existing and desired performance that the organization wants to close.
- A compelling argument that the gaps are worth closing.
- A description of the sources of the gaps and how they interact.
- Selected feasible solutions that address the sources.

Using information about the sources of the gap and the solutions that might address them, IDs can collaborate with others to identify the major components of a learning

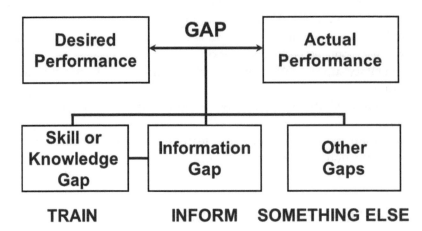

FIGURE 10.1 Pass 1 selecting components for a learning and performance ecosystem (Villachica & Moore, 1997). Given a gap between existing and desired performance, identify sources of the gap arising from a lack of adequate skills or knowledge, information, or other causes. Used with permission from Deborah L. Stone and Andrea K. Moore.

and performance ecosystem. Villachica and Moore (1997) suggested an approach for PSSs that can be updated for the components that could comprise an ecosystem. Using the results of a needs assessment, they suggest that the ID team complete several passes, with each pass making a set of decisions about the components. As illustrated in Figure 10.1, Pass 1 focuses on determining whether the sources of the gap and their solutions are about closing a skill and knowledge gap, an information gap, or some other type of gap.

As shown in Figure 10.2, Pass 2 focuses on revisiting decisions about skill, knowledge, and information gaps to determine whether users will need to practice performing a task to master it. If users will need to practice the task while receiving coaching (real-time error detection and correction) and feedback, then they will need to complete formal learning experiences. Tasks that don't require practice to mastery should be supported with different types of information embedded in the ecosystem. Other tasks that computers can better perform—or help users perform, should be supported with online tools embedded in the ecosystem. These tools could include both apps and larger-scale software solutions that IT groups create.

Pass 3 focuses on investigating potential tools that can work with corresponding information and guided practice. Potential tools could include business process re-engineering and custom software applications that operate over desktop, mobile, and handheld devices. This exploration of potential tools often requires L&D professionals to work with the organization's IT group.

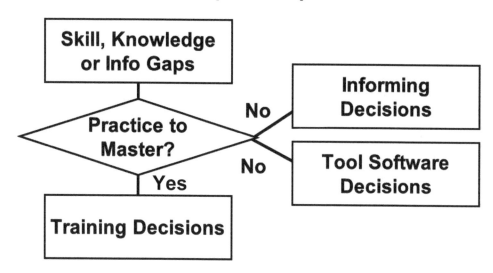

FIGURE 10.2 Pass 2 selecting components for a learning and performance ecosystem (Villachica & Moore, 1997). Given skill, knowledge, or information sources of a performance gap, determine whether users need to practice tasks to master them. If so, the ecosystem should provide learning experiences for those tasks. If not, the ecosystem should provide information or automated tools. Used with permission from Deborah L. Stone and Andrea K. Moore.

Pass 4 focuses on determining the types of information and guidance that will be embedded in the ecosystem. A partial list of information solutions appears below:

- Chatbots.
- Checklists.
- Cloud repositories.
- Company websites.
- Cue cards.
- Demonstrations/How-to videos.
- Digital coaches.
- eBooks.
- Examples.
- Explanations.
- Frequently asked questions (FAQs).
- Infographics.
- Interactive online coaches, guides, or PDFs.
- Job aids (printed or online).
- Knowledge management systems.
- Nudges/Reminders.
- Organizational intranets.
- Process maps.
- Quick reference guides (QRGs).
- Shared drives.
- Software/Apps.
- Templates.
- Tips, hints, and suggested alternatives.
- Wikis.

Pass 5 focuses on selecting appropriate instructional and non-instructional, formal and informal learning solutions that will be embedded within the ecosystem. These solutions could include instructor-led training (classroom or virtual), self-paced manuals, eLearning, simulations, case studies, problem-based learning, on-the-job training, coaching, and mentoring. Additional learning solutions could also include personal learning networks, workflow learning, cognitive apprenticeships, stretch assignments, internships/fellowships, certifications, and badges.

Pass 6 focuses on determining the social supports the ecosystem should provide.

- Experts.
- Knowledge brokers (members of multiple different CoPs).
- Social networking.
- Collaboration.

Phase 2: Map Out Success Measures

Donovan (2022) recommends creating a measurement map to determine whether the organization's investment in creating the learning and performance support ecosystem is contributing positively to the organization's strategic objectives. These maps specify relationships between the investment, a list of leading indicators (i.e., metrics that would predict performance), specific expected business results, aligned with select strategic goals. Figure 10.3 depicts a measurement map for a job site safety training program.

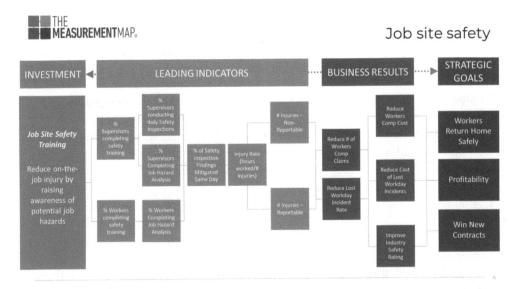

FIGURE 10.3 A measurement map for a job site safety training program. Used with permission from Matt Donovan and Bonnie Beresford. The Measurement Map® and the Measurement Map logo are registered trademarks of Bonnie Beresford and licensed by GP Strategies.

Phase 3: Organize the Components

This phase starts with the decision to use the interface of an existing software system or create a custom user interface. Ecosystems built into existing software typically help users understand the software's features and how to use them. They can also include hyperlinks to related learning, information, and social networking features.

Another approach for organizing the components of an ecosystem is to create a custom user interface that supports task performance itself. With a custom interface, ecosystem components appear as they are needed on the job. While these interfaces can take more time to create than using an existing one, they typically require less support for users to use than existing interfaces.

Phase 4: Create Prototypes and Journey Maps

Having determined the approach for organizing the learning and performance ecosystem, the ID team can start working with stakeholders to iteratively:

- *Create personas depicting key types of users with diverse identities.* Donovan (2022) recommends identifying the key types of people who will interact with the ecosystem and how they will use it. According to Donovan, personas are useful to different user groups: model performers who will provide data for specifying learning and performance goals, SMEs who will contribute content, the performance support network of people that enable the work experience, and business stakeholders.
- *Create, review, and try out prototypes of key ecosystem components.* These prototypes will depict the user interface and how different personas use them to complete learning and performance activities. Prototypes could illustrate learning components, informational components, and social components of the ecosystem as personas would use them in the flow of their workday. Reviews and tryouts of the prototypes should lead to their increasing refinement. The final iteration of prototypes should operate on the online platforms the ecosystem will use.
- *Create and review journey maps.* According to Donovan (2022), these maps depict how different types of users will interact with the ecosystem to perform their tasks. These maps should also depict how users will complete their learning and performance experiences. These maps can help the ID team plan for the touchpoints, resources, and logistics the ecosystem will need. They should describe how one or more of the personas use the elements of the prototype to complete a learning or job task. These experiences should establish relevance to job tasks and strategic organizational objectives, create connections, respect user/learner time, generate interest so that users/learners will want to use the ecosystem again, and enable insights for the ID team to create the next iteration of the ecosystem.

Phase 5: Build High-Level and Detailed Design Documents

Complex solutions like learning and performance ecosystems often require two sets of design documents to adequately describe these solutions for the clients, ID teams, learners/users, SMEs, and other stakeholders who will create, implement, and maintain them. In these situations, a high-level design document describes the major components of the ecosystem, as a whole, and how users will interact with them. This document may also describe the development and integration of these components into a system that satisfies the performance and technical requirements for the ecosystem project. The high-level design document should also contain plans for implementation, maintenance, and evaluation of the ecosystem itself.

Corresponding detailed design documents would describe the workings of each major component comprising the learning and performance ecosystem. One detailed design document might describe the learning components, using a format similar to what appears in Chapter 9. Other detailed design documents might describe the online performance software and how users interact with its features and benefits to perform their tasks, along with how the features meet specified technical and performance requirements.

Users employ the different learning and performance features of this ecosystem over time and at multiple moments of need. Gotfredson and Mosher (2011) specify five moments of learning need:

1. Learning for the first time.
2. Learning more.
3. Applying and refining what's been learned.
4. Adjusting to change.
5. Reacting to failure.

The high-level design document should describe these experiences and the strategies the ecosystem will use to keep them engaging.

Donovan (2022) notes that a learning and performance ecosystem that supports talent development might also need to support roles involving innovation and career growth for the next role. Owing to the dynamic content of a learning and performance ecosystem, other roles might include consumers of ecosystem content, moderators of chat and discussion groups, content curators, content contributors, content creators, and collaborators. He also mentions roles that support connected learning across the organization: learning connectors, learning bridgers, coaching and mentoring specialists, and information brokers.

TOWARDS INCLUSIVE DESIGN FOR LEARNING AND PERFORMANCE ECOSYSTEMS

In one sense, creating, implementing, and maintaining learning and performance ecosystems is similar to creating the other instructional and non-instructional solutions already addressed in this text. To meet goals to improve organizational performance, these ecosystems should provide culturally relevant and equitable learning and performance experiences. The ID team should work with stakeholder representatives.

These stakeholders should include the client, learners, and users of the ecosystem, supervisors, managers, and other organizational stakeholders. They should come from all levels of the organization and include individuals representing diverse identities and abilities.

Representatives from these groups could work as part of steering committees and technical review teams (see Chapter 4) who specify requirements and review project deliverables. Other representatives could participate in tryouts of the project deliverables. As always, it's important to be intentional with "expanded collaboration" so the project team can think critically to ensure interventions that are culturally relevant and equitable.

An inclusive and diverse cast of characters collaborating in creating, implementing, and maintaining larger-scale learning and performance ecosystems can be enormous. The larger the cast of characters, the more additional time the ID team will need to spend managing the project and negotiating potentially conflicting needs. And the more people involved in the project, the more time and effort clients will need to spend arranging for release time and coordinating reviews and tryouts.

CASE STUDY

"As the 10,000-person marketing and sales organization of this international communications company moved to 'solutions selling,' there was a great need to increase the size and revenue of each sale. A learning and performance ecosystem composed of five components was deployed. It included: (1) a knowledge base to provide sales collateral, product information, competitive analysis and positioning information, and market research data anytime and anywhere; (2) sales performance support to provide guidance to the sales force around the solutions-selling process; (3) a unique online 'ask an expert' feature that allowed sales representatives to consult with peers who were star performers in selling high-revenue solutions; (4) communities of practice for networking; and (5) a revamped learning and mentoring program that provided opportunities for sales people to practice solutions-selling encounters with retired CEOs. The results? The organization reached or exceeded its overall revenue target two of the first four quarters of its solution-selling initiative and continued to increase the percentage of revenue achieved through solution sales over the following years. After years of selling discrete products to middle managers, the sales culture gradually evolved into selling high-revenue solutions that included entire product suites to C-level executives" (Rosenberg & Foreman, 2014, p. 36).

- As part of the ongoing evaluation, how might you use personas and journey maps to assess the effectiveness of this learning and performance ecosystem?
- How would you use the principles of "inclusive design" to create these personas and journey maps?
- How would you use principles of "inclusive design" to identify and counter any organizational barriers, perhaps related to the way sales commissions are paid, to the emphasis on "solutions selling?"

REFLECTION QUESTIONS

- Have you ever helped to design a learning and performance support ecosystem for an organization?

  - What kinds of deliverables did you or the team create?
  - To what extent did the ID team employ an "inclusive design" approach to create, implement, and maintain the ecosystem? How did it identify learners and users from underrepresented groups?

- Have you ever helped to implement a learning and performance support ecosystem for an organization? What kinds of resources did the organization provide to you? To what extent were those resources sufficient to provide a learning and performance support ecosystem that was culturally relevant and equitable?

REFERENCES

American Psychological Association (APA) (2018, April 19). Massed practice. https://dictionary.apa.org/massed-practice

Bannan, B, Dabbaugh, N., & Walcutt, J. J. (2019). Instructional strategies for the future. In Walcutt, J. J., & Schatz, S. (Eds), *Modernizing learning: Building the future learning ecosystem* (pp. 223–242). *Advanced Distributed Learning Initiative*. Retrieved from https://adlnet.gov/assets/uploads/Modernizing%20Learning.pdf

Dillon, J. (2022). *The modern learning ecosystem: A new L&D mindset for the ever-changing workplace.* ATD.

Donovan, M. (2022). *6 essential elements to develop a learner experience playbook.* GP Strategies. https://transform.gpstrategies.com/hubfs/eBook-LearnerExperiencePlaybook%20v1.0%2009.07.22(OL)opt.pdf

Foreman, S. (2022, April 17). *The learning and performance ecosystem.* eLearning Trends. https://elearningindustry.com/the-learning-and-performance-ecosystem

Gery, G. (1991). *Electronic performance support systems: How and why to remake the workplace through the strategic application of technology.* Gery Performance Press.

Gery, G. (1995). Attributes and behaviors of performance-centered systems. *Performance Improvement Quarterly, 8*(1), 47–93. doi:10.1111/j.1937–8327.1995.tb00661.x

Gottfredson, C., & Mosher, B. (2011). *Innovative performance support: Strategies and practices for learning in the workflow.* McGraw Hill.

Huang, Y., & Klein, J. D. (2023). Mobile performance support systems: Characteristics, benefits, and conditions. *TechTrends, 67,* 150–159.

Narum, C. (2018, April 20). 10 Types of performance support tools from quick reference guides to mobile apps. [Blog] eLearning Industry Corporate eLearning. https://elearningindustry.com/performance-support-tools-quick-reference-guides-mobile-apps-10-types

Nguyen, F. (2010). Electronic performance support systems. In Watkins, R., & Leigh, D. (Eds), *Handbook of improving performance in the workplace* (Vol. 2), pp. 325–343. Pfeiffer.

Quinn, C. N. (2014). *Revolutionize learning & development: Performance and innovation strategy for the information age.* Wiley.

Raybould, B. (1990). Solving human performance problems with computers—A case study: Building an electronic performance support system. *Performance & Instruction, 29*(10), 4–14.

Rosenberg, M. J., & Foreman, S. (2014). *Learning and performance ecosystems: Strategy, technology, impact, and challenges.* eLearning Guild. https://www.learningguild.com/publications/53/learning-and-performance-ecosystems-strategy-technology-impact-and-challenges/

Rossett, A., & Schafer, L. (2007). *Job aids and performance support: Moving from knowledge in the classroom to knowledge everywhere*. Wiley.

Stone, D. L., & Villachica, S. W. (1997). Performance support for knowledge workers: Practical strategies based on research and practice. *Performance Improvement, 36*(3), 6–12. doi:10.1002/pfi.4140360304

Villachica, S. W., & Moore, A. K. (1997, April). Using technology to leverage performance: How to ensure you select the right interventions for the right reasons. Paper presented at the conference of the International Society for Performance Improvement, Anaheim, CA.

Villachica, S. W., & Stone, D. L. (1998). CORNERSTONE: A case study of a large-scale performance support system. In Dean, P. J., & Ripley, D. E. (Eds), *Performance improvement interventions: Performance technologies in the workplace* (pp. 437–460). International Society for Performance Improvement.

Villachica, S. W., & Stone, D. L. (1999). Performance support systems. In Stolovitch, H. D., & Keeps, E. J. (Eds), *Handbook of human performance technology: Improving individual and organizational performance worldwide* (2nd ed., pp. 442–463). Jossey-Bass/Pfeiffer.

Villachica, S. W., Stone, D. L., & Endicott, J. E. (2006). Performance support systems. In Pershing, J. A. (Ed.), *Handbook of human performance technology: Improving individual and organizational performance worldwide* (3rd ed., pp. 539–566). Jossey-Bass/Pfeiffer.

CHAPTER 11

How to Develop Instructional Materials, Learning Resources, and Guides

INTRODUCTION

In Chapter 9, you read about sequencing and chunking at the program level. Sometimes, you don't need to organize a multifaceted program. In this chapter, you will read about creating materials for a *course or single intervention*. This includes:

- Sequencing the performance requirements you've created for a smaller unit of learning.
- Converting detailed performance requirements into abbreviated learning objectives.
- Sequencing the instruction for each unit composed of one or more objectives. In each unit, your instruction will build on what the learners already know, demonstrate the new tasks they will perform, provide the learners with opportunities to practice, and help the learners integrate their new skills into their on-the-job performance.
- Creating instructor and participant guides to support any instructor-led courses.

To this end, the conditions, performances, and criteria embedded within the instructor guide and other instructional materials you may create (job aids, participant guides, slides, etc.) need to align with the performance requirements, performance assessment instrument, task analysis, learner and environmental analysis, and learner requirements analysis you've already created. Any items in the instructional materials that don't align with these other instructional design (ID) deliverables can produce interventions that are neither efficient nor effective—thereby wasting the time and resources of the client and sponsoring organization.

After reading this chapter, you will be able to:

- Sequence performance requirements.
- Sequence units of instruction.
- Write instructor guides.
- Write participant guides.

DOI: 10.4324/9781003360612-11

TOWARDS INCLUSIVE DESIGN IN DEVELOPING INSTRUCTION

Creating instructional environments and materials that are culturally relevant and equitable requires design practices that center learners' dignity and respect. This means ensuring that all learners have access to the systems, information, and resources they need. While much of this work can occur during the Empathize & Analyze (E&A) stage, not all instructional designers (IDs) will work on those components of a given project. Therefore, IDs who are jumping into Design & Develop (D&D) may bring fresh perspectives and suggest adjustments to the assessments, design documents, and other existing project deliverables.

For example, there are times when IDs don't do initial E&A work. Instead, a more senior manager, a dedicated "front-end analysis group," or someone above them, completes this work. These individuals can make decisions that present problems later in the project, often related to being culturally relevant and equitable. IDs can address these issues later in the project. When this happens, it can be an opportunity to "shape the culture" of the organization, as described in Chapter 1. IDs can use *expanded collaboration* to include stakeholders with diverse perspectives and take advantage of their varied perspectives and insights, which can help create an intervention that is culturally relevant and equitable. While it can take time, organizational change can occur. This is more likely if IDs continue to advocate for learning and development interventions that center inclusion and belonging.

SEQUENCE THE PERFORMANCE REQUIREMENTS

Performance requirements act as a "north star" for IDs and clients because they provide all relevant information about a given performance. As such, they specify a performance by describing relevant:

- Conditions (cues and resources) under which the performance will occur.
- Criteria (standards) that the performance should meet.

A relatively straightforward job task may correspond to a single performance requirement. In this case, there is no need to consider sequencing. On the other hand, a more complex task may correspond to several different performance requirements. And, larger blocks of learning addressing multiple job tasks often correspond to multiple performance requirements. In this case, the question is: in what order should the instruction present the performance requirements to the learners?

If your intervention consists of more than one performance requirement, you may have already begun thinking about how to sequence them, as part of creating the "design document," described in Chapter 9. There are several sequencing strategies to consider:

- *Familiarity*. Starting with familiar tasks and progressing to tasks that are less familiar.
- *Difficulty*. Starting with easier tasks and progressing to more difficult ones.

- *Frequency*. Starting with tasks that are performed more frequently and progressing to those that are performed less frequently.
- *Criticality*. Starting with tasks that have particularly important consequences and progressing to those that are less critical.
- *Chronology*. Starting with the first task or step to be performed *or* with the last task or step to be performed.
- *Prerequisite*. Starting with tasks that must be learned before other tasks can be learned (for example, learning to operate a computer is typically a prerequisite skill for programming one).
- *Part-to-whole*. Starting with one component, then the next, until the whole component is constructed. Kirschner and van Merriënboer (2013) recommend using this type of sequencing sparingly—only when whole tasks are too complex and abstract to understand.
- *Whole-to-part*. Presenting an overarching logic or a whole task in its simplest, most representative form first. Then present an increasingly complex version of the task. This type of sequencing helps learners quickly acquire a complete view of the whole skill, which is then embellished during learning (Kirschner & van Merriënboer, 2013). Interventions for knowledge workers often employ this type of sequencing.

CONVERT PERFORMANCE REQUIREMENTS INTO LEARNING OBJECTIVES

The detailed representations of performance requirements primarily benefit the IDs who are creating the interventions and the clients who need to know their workplace performance requirements are being met. However, these detailed performance requirements are simply too cumbersome for use in the materials comprising the intervention itself. Thus, when a short summary statement is needed, you would transform detailed performance requirements into lean learning objectives by pruning much of the details. These abbreviated learning objectives often appear in instructor guides and other related materials.

After having sequenced the performance requirements, you're now ready to write learning objectives. Learning objectives consist of key conditions, performances, and criteria abbreviated from the performance requirements. Use a short, one-sentence format that mentions only the most important aspects of successful performance. For example, a detailed performance requirement about recommending appropriate Medicare plans to AARP clients would contain numerous conditions and criteria. This detailed performance requirement could appear as the following learning objective:

> *Using software and job aids, recommend several Medicare plans that will match client needs.*

This objective could appear in the instructor guide for this intervention and other related materials. IDs will generally convert other parts of the performance requirements as well. For example:

- The conditions under which people perform the objectives can turn into module and lesson headings with names such as, "When You Do This," and "Resources You Will Use."
- The criteria that the objective should meet can appear in module and lesson headings such as "On-the-Job Criteria" or "Standards to Meet." Criteria also work their way into the checklists that performance assessment instruments use to determine mastery.

Chunking Objectives into Manageable Components

Writing objectives that correspond to smaller task parts can make sequencing decisions easier. A common heuristic is to write objectives where approximately one objective can be covered in an event that ranges from a few minutes up to 30 minutes. Most audiences and systems will benefit from smaller chunks.

For example, smaller chunks can facilitate more frequent breaks. A shorter block of time can allow busy adults to focus on the intervention in the moment. Short breaks then often allow attention to other responsibilities. Of course, this isn't true for all contexts and all audiences. The more experience you gain with an audience and system context, the better you'll be able to chunk manageable components.

SEQUENCE UNITS OF INSTRUCTION

It can be helpful to think about the instructional building blocks that IDs use to create interventions. Seen this way, IDs aggregate smaller blocks into larger structures.

- A collection of one or more learning activities forms an instructional event.
- A collection of instructional events forms a component (learner preparation, demonstration, application, transfer support).
- A collection of components forms a unit.
- A collection of units forms a module.
- A collection of modules forms a course.
- A collection of courses forms a curriculum.

Note that different learning and development (L&D) organizations may use different names for these building blocks. The point is that learning interventions are built by combining small parts into larger parts.

Chapter 9 introduced how to sequence critical tasks into one or more learning interventions. But how can you sequence the learning experience within a lesson or a smaller chunk of a larger intervention? IDs often use instructional models to create units of instruction that contain one objective or several related objectives that address a specific job task.

Useful instructional models typically work across all delivery methods, including:

- Instructor-led classroom learning.
- Instructor-led virtual classroom learning.
- Self-paced printed workbooks.
- Self-paced eLearning.
- Structured on-the-job learning.

As depicted in Table 11.1, the LeaPS Instructional model itself consists of five components and specifically combines:

- Brethower and Smalley's (1998) sequence of guided observation, guided practice, and demonstration of mastery.
- Gagné's nine events (Gagné & Briggs, 1979).
- Merrill's (2002, 2007) first principles.
- Keller's (2016) ARCS-V.

Possible learning activities for each component are suggested, which are intended to illustrate the types of activities that can be included. The specific activities will depend on the particular learning and development intervention.

Write an Instructional Unit

- Bundle features and discrete activities into five major components: (1) I Belong Here, (2) Set Me Up, (3) Show Me, (4) Let Me (a combination of guided practice and performance assessment), and (5) Watch Me.
- Describe specific learning activities for each component. For instructor-led learning, focus on describing what the instructor will do. For self-paced learning, address how learners will move through the environment.
- Specify the resources the learners and instructor will use to complete each learning activity.
- Specify estimated time for each component and every learning activity.

Scalability of Instructional Units

Not *all* performance-based interventions require all five components of the LeaPS Instructional model. Think about the last time you watched YouTube to learn how to do something. It's a safe guess that the video didn't state an objective using ID language, provide feedback on your performance, or ask you to reflect on what you've learned.

So, how do IDs know which components and activities to include and what activities to use? Several important resources are available, including:

- Your past experience.
- Input from E&A activities/deliverables.
- Input from others in the organization who have experience supporting similar changes in performance.

TABLE 11.1 The LeaPS Instructional model: components and sample learning activities

LeaPS Instructional Components	Sample Learning Activities
1. Culturally Relevant and Equitable Framework A.k.a. "I Belong Here" Initiate motivation to learn by sharing: • organizational resource allocation and processes that enable equitable access and trust building • learning experience design key features of specific interest to diverse learner identities • opportunities for voice, choice, relationships, collaboration, and empowerment.	• Communicate diverse learner recruitment and access processes that are equitable and inclusive. • Offer accessible, intuitive, and aesthetically pleasing user interface and materials. • Create a welcoming, inclusive, respectful, and comfortable environment. • Offer flexible options and equitable scaffolds. • Offer appropriate resources, amenities, schedules, and accommodations.
2. Learner Preparation A.k.a. "Set Me Up" Maintain motivation to learn by describing: • the goal of the intervention • the relevancy and value (i.e., "What's in it for them?") • how what they already know and do relates to what they will be learning and doing on the job.	• Surprise the learners with a compelling story that builds an emotional connection to what they are learning. • Post thought-provoking questions or an intriguing problem. • Present a new or interesting situation that provokes curiosity. • Present an engaging challenge. • Describe what learners will be able to do back on the job after completing the learning experience. • Explain how the learning experience will benefit learners personally. • Explain how the learning experience will benefit the organization. • Provide a metaphor or analogy to compare what learners will learn with something they already know or do. • Ask learners to discuss their previous experiences with the job task, or something similar to the task.
3. Demonstration A.k.a. "Show Me" Provide at least one demonstration that prepares learners and shows them how to complete the task(s) described in the task analysis. In addition to showing overt behaviors, show what is critical, difficult, and complex—including otherwise invisible situation recognition, decision-making, and problem-solving. For more complex job tasks, use multiple demonstrations and ask participants to compare them.	• Introduce workplace cues and resources. • Specify general principles that guide exemplary performance. • Provide advance organizers using pictures, diagrams, stories, charts, or oral descriptions depicting the job task. • Provide a mnemonic to remember and perform the job task. • Provide a job aid for the task. • Provide a demonstration of the entire job task (Demonstration 1 in a "whole-part" sequence). • Divide the entire task into segments (chunks) and demonstrate each segment, highlighting what is critical, difficult, and complex (Demonstration 2 in a "whole-part" sequence). • Demonstrate the task in different situations, beginning with the simplest yet representative version of the task (a "difficulty" sequence). • Relate stimulus information to specific actions in the demonstrations. • Discuss the demos to compare and contrast versions of the tasks and what was critical, difficult, and complex about them.

(Continued)

TABLE 11.1 (Continued)

LeaPS Instructional Components	Sample Learning Activities
4. Application (guided practice and mastery assessment) A.k.a. "Let Me" Provide at least one authentic practice exercise where learners perform the job task in a safe learning environment while the instructor provides coaching (real-time error detection and correction). Provide at least one authentic performance assessment where learners perform the job task in a safe environment—with no coaching at all. Provide feedback after each practice exercise and assessment about the extent to which the performance met the criteria from the objective(s), and how to improve overall performance. For more complex job tasks, provide a series of increasingly difficult authentic practice exercises and decrease the amount of coaching from one practice to the next.	• Have learners practice performing the job tasks. • Provide real-time coaching that provides error detection and correction for early practice exercises. • Fade, or gradually reduce and remove, the coaching in subsequent practice exercises. • Start with simple, but representative versions of the job task (a "difficulty" sequence). • Increase the difficulty of each practice exercise. • Facilitate discussions after each practice exercise to summarize and explore what learners learned. • After each practice, inform learners of the extent to which they met performance standards. • Inform learners how they can improve their performance. • Be positive and objective. • Provide one or more authentic performance assessments that replicates on-the-job performance requirements. • Do not provide coaching during the assessment. • Provide feedback after the assessment is over.

5. Transfer Support A.k.a. "Watch Me"
 	
Provide activities at the end of the learning experience that enhance retention and planned transfer.
 	
Ask supervisors and managers to facilitate activities in the workplace setting after the intervention is over to ensure skill transfer to the workplace.
	• Towards the end of the intervention, ask learners to (a) summarize content, (b) reflect on what they've learned, (c) create plans to transfer what they've learned to the workplace.
	• After the intervention is over and learners have returned to the workplace:
	  ○ Ask managers or supervisors to provide feedback and coaching.
	  ○ Ask learners to demonstrate and share their new skills to others.
	• Telling learners that managers expect learners to transfer their learned skills to the job.
	• Providing additional time to practice applying learned skills in the workplace.
	• Using mirror versions of the performance assessment checklist to provide feedback about workplace performance.
	• Meeting with learners after they return to the workplace setting to identify any potential barriers in the workplace that interfere with skill transfer or job performance.

At the very minimum:

1. Provide a brief overview of the performance outcomes the intervention will address.
2. Demonstrate how to complete workplace tasks and describe any knowledge-based decisions (e.g., conceptual, procedural, problem-solving) that you want to observe learners make after the intervention is over.

It's worth noting:

- If learners need more support to demonstrate performance criteria, it's likely to be opportunities for authentic practice, feedback, and reflection.
- If learners still need more support, it's likely that there's a progression in decision-making complexity required with more demonstration, practice, feedback, and/or reflection.
- If a task has extreme consequences, then there's a good reason to integrate a substantial amount of authentic practice in varied situations, with embedded feedback loops. Provide additional opportunities for on-the-job practice and feedback after learners return to the workplace to ensure the skills remain mastered—especially if these skills are critically important and rarely needed.

Some ways to accomplish more authentic practice, feedback, and reflection are to:

- Provide frequent reflection opportunities for individuals and small groups. Depending on the factors in the learning environment and learner preferences appearing in personas, ask learners to reflect on past experiences, recent learning experiences, and implications for future performance.
- Have managers facilitate additional practice, coaching, and feedback once learners return to the workplace.
- Ask learners to share their experiences and demonstrate new skills to others.

IDs may choose to omit instructional components and learning activities that aren't considered necessary or that the sponsoring organizational culture won't support. For example, an ID who is creating an "introductory" intervention that uses job aids may choose to omit certain instructional components and activities altogether.

Effective interventions for *complex tasks* require learning by doing, and that typically requires some sort of organizational support for providing learner preparation, guided observation, application, and transfer support. However, for *simple tasks*, this could be "instructional overkill." In addition, organizations using structured on-the-job learning may not always have personnel available to support each instructional event or all of their learning activities.

Table 11.2 compares the decisions that IDs may make about scaling instructional components in introductory and extensive learning.

TABLE 11.2 Approaches to scale LeaPS Instructional model components in introductory and extensive learning units

Scaling Approach and LeaPS Instructional Model Components	Introductory Learning	Extensive Learning
Scaling approach	Given straightforward tasks performed the same way each time and well-designed job aids, IDs pick any, or all, of the instructional events that the client organization can support and that will produce valued behavior.	Given more complex tasks that aren't performed the same way each time and any specified and well-designed job aids, IDs need to include all of the instructional events to provide adequate practice, coaching, feedback, and transfer support to change behavior in the workplace.
1. Culturally relevant and equitable	Required	Required
2. Learner preparation	Optional	Required
3. Demonstration	Optional	Required
4. Application	Optional	Required
5. Transfer support	Optional	Required

Common Errors Writing Instructional Units

Culturally Relevant and Equitable

- A framework and approaches that are built solely by individuals with identities, experiences, and abilities that are different from downstream stakeholders and intended learners without adequate input from said groups.

Learner Preparation Errors

- *A Learner Preparation component that is too long for the intervention.* The temptation to add "nice-to-know" content to the learning intervention "just in case you may need this someday" is great. An effective Learner Preparation component provides only enough information and learner activities to prepare learners for the demonstrations that will follow. This means that the Learner Preparation component should be as short as the ID can get away with, so more time can go to the Demonstration and Application components.

Demonstration Errors

- *Demonstrations that include "nice-to-know" content.* Good demonstrations provide just enough information for learners to move on to the subsequent Application component, where learners learn job tasks by practicing them in a safe environment while receiving coaching and feedback.
- *The demonstrations that mistakenly focus on telling learners about their job tasks.* Guided Observation is about showing learners how to perform the tasks while providing guidance about what's important. Demonstrations should model how an exemplary

performer performs the job task in the workplace and highlight what is critical, difficult, and complex—as the exemplary performer is completing the job.

- *The set of demonstrations doesn't depict a realistic range of situations in which learners will perform the task in the workplace.* For simpler job tasks that learners will perform the same way each time, one or two short demonstrations may suffice. More complex job tasks typically require multiple demonstrations. These tasks typically involve some level of novelty or variation from one time to the next. Demonstrations for these tasks should show an exemplary performance recognizing situations, making decisions, solving problems, and communicating with others. They should also show how to compare and contrast critical aspects of job performance.

Application Component Errors

Writing good Application components is hard because they contain multiple moving parts. IDs can easily find themselves making mistakes like these:

- *Practice exercises or performance assessments (mastery tests) don't align with performance requirements.* Just as it can be tempting to add "nice-to-know" information to demonstrations, it is also tempting to add "just for fun" or "because it's good for you" practice exercises or assessment items that don't align with performance requirements.
- *There are not enough practice exercises to ensure learners pass the performance assessments.* Learners build the necessary skills to perform their jobs by practicing them in authentic situations while receiving real-time coaching and feedback. Application components should provide enough practice opportunities for IDs, clients, and other stakeholders to reasonably expect that learners will pass the mastery assessments.
- *The set of practice exercises doesn't depict a realistic range of situations in which learners will perform the task in the workplace.* Because learning interventions typically address complex job tasks, an application component should provide sufficient practice exercises to represent the common situations that learners will encounter in the workplace.
- *The difficulty of the practice exercises doesn't increase from one practice to the next.* A well-crafted Application component begins with learners performing the simplest, yet realistic, version of the task. Each subsequent practice exercise is more difficult, representing the more complex situations learners typically encounter in the workplace.
- *Real-time coaching doesn't fade systematically over the set of practices.* Early practice exercises should employ real-time coaching strategies that encourage learners while helping them detect errors in their performance and correct them (real-time error detection and correction). This coaching should systematically decrease over the set of practice exercises. By the time learners complete the last practice exercise and during their performance assessments, they should be "flying solo"—without receiving any coaching at all.
- *Practice exercises and performance assessments don't provide delayed feedback.* At minimum, this feedback should inform learners about the extent to which their performance met mastery criteria and how to improve their performance itself. Delayed feedback should follow each practice exercise and assessment.
- *A mastery assessment doesn't entail a big enough sample of performances to ensure skill transfer to the workplace.* Clients and organizational stakeholders should be able to trust that

learners who pass mastery assessments return to the workplace largely ready to perform their job tasks, with minimal amounts of manager and supervisor coaching. This means that mastery assessments should include a realistic range of situations in which learners perform the task in the workplace as well as a reasonable number of repetitions to ensure that they don't pass the assessment simply because they were lucky.

Transfer Support Errors

- *There aren't opportunities for learners to engage in "Reflect," "Create," and "Watch Me" learning activities that support skill transfer to the workplace.* It costs money and time to create, implement, and maintain interventions. To offset this cost, these interventions should produce skill transfer to the workplace in ways that produce valued behavior change. Odds are such skill transfer won't occur unless IDs, clients, and organizational stakeholders plan and support it. Learning activities supporting transfer need to occur both towards the end of the learning intervention and after learners return to their jobs.
- *The Transfer Support component doesn't specify what supervisors and managers should do after learners return to the workplace.* Even the best designed intervention will fail if it doesn't produce valued behavior change in the workplace. Supervisors and managers have a role to play in facilitating "Reflect," "Create," and "Watch Me" activities in the workplace.

WRITE INSTRUCTOR GUIDES

The last items to build in the D&D component of the LeaPS ID model are often [but not always] either any required eLearning, instructor guides, and participant guides. Instructor guides are sometimes called "facilitator guides" or "leader guides." Regardless of what an L&D group calls them, instructor guides are typically single documents that include everything an instructor needs to deliver a course. The rest of this section on instructor guides will describe:

- Typical components of instructor guides.
- Scripts that provide instructor guidance.
- Other supplemental instructional resources.
- Common instructor guide conventions.
- Standard facilitation vocabulary.

Components

A minimally useful instructor guide for an instructional unit typically contains these components:

- *Course title.*
- *Table of contents.*
- *Course welcome to students.*
- *Course structure.*

- *Session titles.*
- *Session at a glance.* Describes the purpose of the intervention, its learning objectives, any document and physical resources learners will need to complete the intervention, and the classroom setup.
- *Advance preparation.* Provides directions for setting up the classroom before the intervention begins.
- *Content you should know.* Provides an overview of any concepts or techniques that are important for instructors to know before they begin facilitating any intervention.
- *Timeline.* Tracks the times that learning activities should start and end.
- *Overall course purpose.*
- *Objectives.*
- *Required document and physical resources.*
- *Room setup instructions.*
- *Script.* Things that the instructor says and does to facilitate each component of the unit and its corresponding learning activities.
- *Permissions to use copyrighted materials.*
- *Resource indicators.* If using slides, handouts, or other materials, note which should be used and at what point in between script components.
- *Time indicators.* For each chunk of the script or activity, note the approximate time a facilitator should spend.

Copyright permissions are important for legal and ethical reasons. It's important to make sure all of your instructional materials are copyright compliant. It's okay to use existing relevant materials within an intervention. In fact, it's often a good idea because it's usually quicker and cheaper than creating new materials. However, it's important to make sure that you comply with relevant copyright laws.

If you use any already-produced materials "as-is," explicit, written permission from the copyright owner is often critical. It's worthwhile to note that ideas, principles, and procedures cannot be copyrighted. And if you create new materials that are based on someone else's ideas or principles but are sufficiently different from the original materials and you reference the original author/creators, there should be no problem. However, any time you aren't sure, it's a good idea to check with someone more experienced before proceeding.

To obtain permission, first find out who owns the copyright for the materials you want to use. Make sure you have found the actual copyright owner. For example, for many books the copyright owner isn't the author of the book, but the publisher. Second, contact the copyright owner in writing (this can often be done by email). Explain what you would like to use and how you plan to use it, and ask for permission. Be specific. Your request doesn't have to be long, but it should tell the copyright owner exactly what you want to borrow and what you plan to do with it. Attach any copyright permissions to this assignment.

Scripts

Whether in abbreviated, bulleted format or a longer, more verbatim form, scripts should provide instructors with the guidance they need so that:

- The same instructor delivers the same course the same way each time.
- Different instructors deliver the same course the same way each time.

An adequate script typically includes:

- Directions for providing an introduction and a summary for the unit.
- Directions for facilitating the learning activities in each component, including directions for setting up the activity, directions for facilitating the activity, and directions for debriefing the activity and helping learners reflect on what they learned and will be doing in the workplace.
- Questions to begin and end learning activities and discussions.
- Expected answers to the questions.
- A summary for the intervention.

The key is to create instructor guides that provide instructors with what they really need—no more and no less. If the instructors are primarily:

- Subject matter experts (SMEs), then instructor guides may skimp on technical content instructors already know to provide more detailed information for facilitating the learning activities.
- Facilitators, then instructor guides may skimp on facilitation directions instructors already know to focus on providing more technical content.
- Familiar with the technical content of the course and how to facilitate the course, then the instructor guide may be abbreviated. In these cases, an instructor guide could be a few pages long—or even a set of bulleted notes in a presentation slide deck.

Organizations committed to ensuring that their instructor-led interventions produce even learning outcomes typically collect data from classroom observations, surveys from learners and managers, and on-the-job observations and surveys to monitor the performance of instructors and learners during and after the intervention delivery.

An Appropriate Level of Guidance in Scripts

One way to find this level of detail is to conduct tryouts of the draft instructor guides to ensure that instructors find them complete and easy to use. If necessary, provide formal interventions to teach the instructors how to use their instructor guides and instructional resources to facilitate the course. These interventions are often called "train-the-trainer" courses.

Other Supplemental Instructional Resources

Other materials can supplement instructor guides, including:

- Job aids.
- Photos, diagrams, forms.

- Presentation slide decks.
- Videos.
- Role-play materials.
- Games.
- Simulations.
- Posters.
- Learning journals.
- Skill transfer plans for learners and their supervisors and managers to be used on the job after learners return to the workplace setting.

Instructor guides should provide scripts with directions for using any supplemental materials.

Conventions

First and foremost, an instructor guide should be easy to read and to use as it facilitates the learning activities during the intervention. An instructor should never feel they have to struggle to use an instructor guide. To create friendly and useful instructor guides, IDs often follow conventions like these:

- Provide a *suggested* script. The suggested script acts as a guide for what to say and do. But it should not be a *required* script. Instructors should be able to adapt the script as they need.
- *Provide ample white space.* Use larger margins, tables, and bullets so instructors can scan the instructor guide. Leave space for instructors to add their own annotations.
- *Use short, bulleted sentences and short paragraphs.* Avoid long paragraphs that are hard to read. Avoid long sentences that require more than a breath to say.
- *Use the imperative mood.* Use second-person pronouns ("you, we") or the imperative mood, starting sentences with verbs. For example, the sentence "Park the car" uses imperative mood.
- *Use the active voice.* In an active voice, the subject of the sentence is the agent that produces the action. The direct object is the recipient of the action. Active voice is clearer and easier to understand than passive voice for two primary reasons. First, sentences in the active voice contain fewer words. Second, active voice is more logical, as most people tend to think about the agent before they think about the recipient.

Standard Facilitation Vocabulary

A useful instruction guide uses a limited and consistent vocabulary to describe what the instructor needs to say and do to facilitate the course. While specific vocabularies can vary greatly across organizations and courses, scripts in instructor guides often include terms like these (**in bold**):

- *WELCOME*: Greet participants as they arrive at the beginning of the course or return from breaks.

- *ASK*: Pose a question to pique interest, begin a learning activity, start a discussion, respond to a question.
- *GET ANSWERS*: Wait for and repeat answers to questions. Compare learner answers with expected answers.
- *SET UP*: Provide directions and other relevant information to set up a learning activity.
- *DISCUSS*: Facilitate a class or group discussion.
- *DEBRIEF*: Facilitate a specialized discussion at the end of a learning activity that helps learners reflect on what they've learned.
- *DEMONSTRATE*: Perform a job task while providing a "talk-aloud" that tells learners what the demonstrator is doing as they perform the task. Call out aspects of performance that are critical, difficult, or complex. Use any available job aids during the demonstration as learners would use them back on the job.
- *COACH*: Recognize errors as learners complete a practice exercise. Provide guidance about how to correct performance as learners are performing.
- *GIVE TIME WARNING*: Watch the allotted time for the learning activity. Start and stop learning activities and instructional components in a given unit on time. Give warnings about remaining time.

Instructor guides for interventions delivered virtually using online meeting software like Zoom typically contain additional terms describing how to use the software's features to facilitate the intervention. Feel free to adapt these terms or use others in your instructor guides when you feel they are more appropriate. Then use the terms consistently.

WRITE PARTICIPANT GUIDES

It's common for organizations to provide participant learner guides, sometimes called "learner guides," that learners use to complete the course. These are often a single document or binder that includes everything the learners will need during the intervention and to reference after the intervention is over. Thus, they typically include an overview of the intervention, agenda-type information, and any other relevant materials (e.g., content summaries, handouts, job aids, discussion questions, knowledge check questions, answer keys, workbook activities). Common template headings for participant guides include: course title, table of contents, welcome, structure, session titles if more than one session, purpose, objectives, advance organizers, content summaries, job aids, workbook activities. They typically include less information than instructor guides.

As a rule of thumb, savvy IDs strive to place only what learners need to complete their intervention in participant guides. Information that changes often shouldn't appear in participant guides. Instead, this information should appear in a format that is easily updated and distributed as it changes—a shared drive, an information system, workplace posters, a learning and performance ecosystem etc.

Different organizations and IDs often approach writing instructor and participant guides differently. Some IDs prefer to write instructor guides first. Then they create a copy of the instructor guide file and delete all the instructor-specific materials. Other IDs prefer to write participant guides first. Then they create a copy of the participant guide file and add the instructor details. It doesn't matter which guide is created first, as long as the process is efficient and the instructor and participant guides align well.

CASE STUDY

After the pandemic, headquarter employees at Family Sanitation Partners (pseudonym; a non-governmental organization (NGO)) continued to work from a distance. All of the face-to-face learning and development programs were hastily switched to online delivery. The only change to the face-to-face modality design was to add live video conference (e.g., Zoom) lectures, replacing the live classroom lectures. Recently, the Chief Learning Officer (CLO) has developed a new intervention strategy in which all interventions are delivered in a fully online delivery mode. The CLO has asked the learning and development department to provide consultation, recommendations, and appropriate instructional design support to department heads who request new training programs. If you were in charge of implementing this strategy:

- How would you apply principles of "inclusive design" (from Chapter 1) to ensure the resulting interventions were culturally relevant and equitable?
- What information would you gather to fulfill the CLO's request? Who would you gather this information from?
- How should your department work with SME instructors to facilitate adoption and implementation of the new delivery modalities?

REFLECTION QUESTIONS

- Would you create an instructor guide for a fully online course? If so, why? If not, why not? In a particular situation, what would your decision be based on? How would you ensure that instructors use the instructor guides you create?
- What would an instructor guide include for a fully online course? A blended course? A webinar?
- Think back to a learning and development program you helped create or completed as either a participant or instructor. Were the materials you were given adequate and helpful? If not, what would you do to improve them? What would you do to make them more culturally relevant and equitable?

REFERENCES

Brethower, D., & Smalley, K. (1998). *Performance-based instruction: Linking training to business results.* Jossey-Bass/Pfeiffer.

Gagné, R. M., & Briggs, L. J. (1979). *Principles of instructional design* (2nd ed.). Holt, Rinehart and Winston.

Keller, J. M. (2016). Motivation, learning, and technology: Applying the ARCS-V motivation model. *Participatory Educational Research, 3*(2), 1–15. doi:10.17275/per.16.06.3.2

Kirschner, P. A., & van Merriënboer, J. J. (2013). Do learners really know best? Urban legends in education. *Educational Psychologist, 48*(3), 169–183. doi:10.1080/00461520.2013.804395

Merrill, M. D. (2002). First principles of instruction. *Educational Technology Research & Development, 50*(3), 43–59. doi:10.1007/BF02505024

Merrill, M. D. (2007). A task-centered instructional strategy. *Journal of Research on Technology in Education, 40*(1), 5–22. doi:10.1080/15391523.2007.10782493

CHAPTER 12

How to Plan for Implementation, Evaluation, and Maintenance

INTRODUCTION

At this point in the instructional design (ID) process, developed learning and performance support materials are ready to roll out. After rollout, instructional designers (IDs) and other stakeholders will likely need to maintain these materials to keep them current over time. After rollout, organizational decision makers could be interested in evaluating them. This chapter will describe the Implement & Evaluate (I&E) component of the LeaPS ID model, as depicted in Figure 12.1. Most IDs, clients, and other stakeholders may believe these activities are important. However, Marker et al. (2014) have noted that implementation, evaluation, and maintenance are often treated as orphans or afterthoughts in most current performance-based learning and development models.

After reading this chapter you should be able to describe three important elements of the I&E components:

- Implementation.
- Summative evaluation and continuous improvement.
- Maintenance.

TOWARDS INCLUSIVE ID I&E PRACTICE

As with the other LeaPS ID model components, it's important to approach the I&E component in an inclusive and collaborative manner that will employ inclusive design in ways that will produce interventions that are culturally relevant and equitable. As in other LeaPS ID model components, IDs should collaborate with a diverse and representative set of the different learners, supervisors, managers, and other stakeholders who will have a voice in determining whether the ID project is successful.

- *Implementation.* Work with the client and stakeholders, including learners, across the organization to ensure that the implementation process is culturally relevant and equitable as the learning and performance support materials are rolled out. In addition, include all stakeholders in supporting and assisting learners, supervisors,

DOI: 10.4324/9781003360612-12

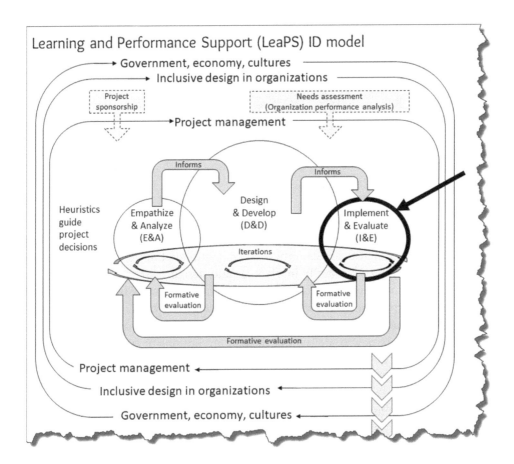

FIGURE 12.1 LeaPS ID model depicting Implement & Evaluate (I&E) components.

and managers as they work through new ways of performing their jobs. Learners will need release time to receive coaching and feedback after they return to the workplace. Supervisors, managers, and other peers may need training and release time to provide this coaching and feedback.

- *Summative evaluation.* Work with the client and stakeholders to determine the questions the evaluation will ask and the framework or model the evaluation will use. Obtain release time for learners to provide data in the form of observations, surveys, or interviews. Share draft evaluation findings with clients and stakeholders. Ask them for input in revising the findings. Use the same approach to share the draft recommendations. Communicate a rationale for accepting or rejecting each evaluation finding and recommendation.
- *Maintenance and continuous improvement.* Expect that materials created today will become obsolete. Make it easy to provide suggestions to fix or improve the learning and performance support materials. For example, QR codes could link to a portal to collect this information continuously. A software change control team with representatives from diverse learner groups could make recommended changes. Communicate a rationale for accepting or rejecting each change request.

IMPLEMENTATION PLANS

With ID projects, implementation is about successfully putting the designed and developed learning and performance support materials into use in their intended settings (Smith & Ragan, 2005, p. 304). Seen this way, implementation involves two major parts:

- Logistics.
- Adoption.

Logistics

The learning and performance support materials that IDs and others have created don't produce valued learning outcomes until learners complete their learning experiences. In some situations, IDs will actually implement and deliver learning and performance support interventions. But in other situations, implementation will be the responsibility of someone else. Experienced IDs who implement their own learning and performance support interventions probably don't need much of a guide to perform this job well. However, IDs who are new to delivering these interventions or hand off the materials they just designed or developed to someone else will need to coordinate a large number of moving parts:

- Preparing instructors, coaches, and mentors to deliver the training in classrooms, online (virtual classrooms), or on the job.
- Ensuring that instructors and learners have access to instructor guides, learner guides, and performance support resources as they need them.
- Ensuring that learners can access and complete eLearning using available online platforms.
- Preparing supervisors and managers to help learners apply what they've learned back on the job by observing them, providing coaching and feedback, and holding them accountable for meeting specified criteria.

To be successful, all this coordination requires planning. And without this planning, the hard work that went into creating the learner-ready materials can be in vain.

As a rule of thumb, people will remember the things that get in the way of successfully implementing learning and performance support interventions. For example, learners will remember if the eLearning crashes because the server has been overloaded; they will remember if their instructors seemed unprepared and uncomfortable facilitating their learning experiences. Both learners and facilitators will remember materials that are incomplete or late. In addition, supervisors and managers may tell their employees, "That training is fine. But that's not really the way we do things around here!" All of these will interfere with successful implementation.

If enough of these things get in the way, learners may not want to complete the learning experiences or use the performance support materials. They could even complete the training but be unwilling to apply it in the workplace. Supervisors and managers may be unwilling to help their learners apply what they've learned back on the job. Without successful implementation and planning for learning transfer to performance, the time and funds the organization has invested in the intervention are lost.

The larger the scale of the project, the more planning the implementation will require. Stone and Villachica (2003) argue that implementation efforts should be a consideration of ID teams and project stakeholders on day one of the project. Seen this way, part of the I&E component of the LeaPS ID model is about understanding the different people in the organization, the roles they play, and the changes the project will bring to their workplace tasks. Likewise, part of the Design and Development (D&D) component is about using iterative prototyping and tryouts to determine the extent to which the learning and performance materials serve the needs of their populations, ensuring they contain attributes that learners find desirable (see Chapter 3).

Part of the D&D component of the LeaPS ID model recommends creating an implementation plan for larger projects, especially when many people are involved. Implementation plans may not be needed for smaller projects or when the ID is also the only person involved in implementation. This plan can include the following information, as needed for any specific project:

- Staff roles (e.g., instructors, aids, facilities, helpdesk, administrative, transportation, safety), their responsibilities, and available support for each role.
- A description of any learning and performance support experiences offered or required for each staff role and their responsibilities.
- A description of any technical support provided for learners, instructors, and guest speakers.
- A description of any instructional support provided for learners and facilitators.
- A description of any instructional support that supervisors and managers will provide to learners after they return to the job.
- Descriptions of the items included in any participant and instructor materials package.
- Specifications for any required equipment, software, and hardware.
- Maintenance and continuous improvement plans for the materials, including scheduled updates and sundown (retirement) dates.
- Project management guidance (e.g., high-level workflow diagrams, sample Gantt charts showing overlaps, dependencies, concurrent tasks, critical paths, and deadlines).
- Deployment plans for materials and live events (e.g., sample timelines, calendars, schedules, planned session breaks, customization options, relevant policies).
- Communications plans and materials such as for marketing, testimonials collections, announcements, and adoption requirements.
- Modalities and locations for delivery (e.g., face to face, online, blended, video conferencing).
- Delivery interactions (e.g., synchronous, asynchronous, self-paced).
- Administrative systems associated with accessing class rosters, guest speakers, and learning management systems (LMSs).

Adoption

As noted in Chapter 3, interventions can cause changes in the ways people perform their tasks, the roles they play in the organization, and the organizational culture. Part of successful implementation is helping learners and other stakeholders adopt new ways of working. Dormant (2011) notes that people will tend to resist change they feel is forced upon them. They may accept changes they have a voice in. She advances four general principles:

1. Change is not just an event; it's a *process*. People will need to work through several phases as part of a process to adopt new ways of doing things.
2. Change takes *time*. Stone and Villachica (2003) note: "Stated simply, people require time to accept new products, adopt new innovations, address their concerns about them, and commit to the change" (p. 45).
3. Lacking good information, people can *horribilize*, fearing the worst (Dormant, 2011). When organizations force employees to change their job roles and how they perform their job tasks, employees can fear the potential adverse consequences the changes could bring, which can produce anxiety and inaction. A savvy change team often avoids this situation by observing, listening, asking questions, and offering reassuring and valid information.
4. Faced with change, people *resist* (p. 4). Changing people's roles and the way they perform their job tasks can be scary, especially when change is something that happens to people, rather than with their involvement.

Bottom-Up Support for Adoption

Successful adoption supports change from the bottom up of the organization and from the top down. Chapter 3 already mentioned how the collaborative design and formative evaluation of ID project deliverables can produce solutions that possess characteristics that lend themselves to adoption:

- Relative advantage.
- Simplicity.
- Compatibility.
- Observable.
- Trialable.

These characteristics can provide bottom-up support for the adoption of changes that the learning and performance support interventions will bring. Another source for bottom-up support for change can come from opinion leaders (Dormant, 2011; Rogers, 2003; Stone & Villachica, 2003). Collaborating with opinion-leading subject matter experts (SMEs) and other opinion leaders in the organization as part of reviewing and testing project deliverables can lead to their telling others in their social networks about the favorable changes that the learning and support materials can bring. Given enough of their "good word" communications, learners and other stakeholders can actually start looking forward to positive changes, rather than fearing them.

Top-Down Support for Adoption

There are numerous top-down approaches that provide support for adopting new ways of doing things on the job (e.g., Hall & Hord, 2011; Hiatt, 2006; Rogers, 2003). Dormant (2011) provides a model based on changes, adapters, change agents, and organizations (CACAO). She notes that chocolate is highly palatable to most people, and changes made more palatable are more likely to succeed—hence the Chocolate Model of Change. She maintains that potential adopters work through five stages to adopt new ways of doing things:

1. *Awareness.* The potential adopter is passive about the change, has little or no information about the change, and has little or no opinion about the change.
2. *Curiosity.* The potential adopter is more active regarding the change, has personal concerns and opinions, and asks questions about the impact on themselves.
3. *Mental tryout.* The potential adopter imagines how it will be with the change made, has job-focused concerns, asks questions about task and job impact.
4. *Hands-on tryout.* The potential adopter is ready to learn how to use the change, has opinions about the change and its use, asks questions about the organization and other impact.
5. *Adoption.* The adopter uses the change on the job, makes suggestions for improvements, asks detailed questions, and may need help (Dormant, 2011, p. 47).

This top-down approach for supporting change is often called "change management." With learning and performance support interventions, change management relies on change agents within the organization to choreograph adoption by helping learners and other stakeholders work through stages of adoption. Given time and appropriate support, learners and other stakeholders who transition through these stages will successfully adopt the changes caused by the intervention. Learners and stakeholders who don't transition through all of the stages are likely to resist new ways of working on the job.

The implementation plan contained in the design document for a larger-scale ID project should specify the strategies the change team will use to support each phase of the adoption process. These plans should also specify how change agents will collect data throughout the process to monitor and facilitate the change.

These top-down and bottom-up approaches to supporting change work together. Bottom-up approaches create buy-in for change based on the support of opinion leaders and building characteristics into learning and performance support interventions that will naturally lend themselves to adoption in the workplace. Top-down approaches essentially "grease the skids" for change by supporting learners and stakeholders over time as they work through the change process. On its own, bottom-up support for change can stall when it encounters organizational inertia. Alone, top-down support for change can encounter resistance or sabotage of the change effort.

SUMMATIVE EVALUATION AND CONTINUOUS IMPROVEMENT

The LeaPS ID model employs two different types of evaluation: formative and summative. Formative evaluation is used to help IDs, learners, and other project stakeholders ensure that the learning and performance support interventions they create will work as planned. Organizations use summative evaluations to determine the value, effectiveness, or efficiency of a learning and performance support intervention. Recall from Chapter 1 that the measures for the workplace performances that performance-based learning and development (PBL&D) should produce arise early in the project. They can appear in a needs assessment that precedes the PBL&D effort. They can be something that the client, stakeholders, and IDs specify early in the effort.

Six to twelve months after successful PBL&D is implemented, these individuals may become interested in determining its impact on the organization. The goal is to provide organizational decision makers with trustworthy information they can use to make decisions about the materials, instructors, instructional strategies, facilities, or the Learning and Development function itself. These questions typically answer decision makers' broad questions regarding "how good is it," or "did it meet our needs?"

Decision Makers

Traditionally, organizational decision makers consisted primarily of executives and senior managers who sponsor learning and development interventions. After all, they approved the budgets that sponsor these projects and provided the release time for learners, SMEs, and other stakeholders to collaborate in the design and development of the interventions. This once-limited definition of "decision makers" can now be expanded to include all those who have a voice in determining whether the learning and performance support effort is successful.

As organizations begin making decisions about evaluating learning and development interventions, they would be wise to consider more inclusive definitions such as "stakeholders" to include a diverse group of individuals, as well as the purpose of the evaluation. Both of these considerations will guide the selection of the questions the evaluation will address and the data collection methods it uses.

Answering Executives' Questions

The questions that executive leaders, or clients, likely want addressed will guide the direction and scope of any evaluation. Of course, some may be interested in the overall value of their training investment. Others could be interested in one or more specific types of value (Bukhari et al., 2017):

- *Direct value.* The extent to which the learning and performance support materials provide a direct benefit to learners, facilitators, or other specific stakeholder groups.
- *Social value.* The extent to which the materials benefit society (e.g., quality of a governmental service, impact on environment, impact on health or healthcare, etc.).
- *Operational value.* The extent to which the learning and performance support materials benefit the internal operations of the organization (e.g., decrease in waste, increase in productivity.

- *Strategic value.* The extent to which the materials help the organization to meet strategic business objectives, such as producing a just organizational culture, creating sustainable systems, seizing a new opportunity, etc.
- *Financial value.* The extent to which the materials increased revenue, reduced costs, etc.

Given different types of value, decision makers may have different interests in conducting an evaluation. These interests shape the types of questions an evaluation should answer. As depicted in Table 12.1, different types of evaluation questions can guide IDs to using different evaluation models.

TABLE 12.1 Common types of evaluation questions and useful evaluation models

Evaluation Questions	Evaluation Models
What is the return on the investment in the learning and performance support materials the organization has created?	• Kirkpatrick: Based on the work of Raymond Katzell (Thalheimer, 2018a) and introduced in 1956, the Kirkpatrick model is one of the most widely used models for evaluating training programs (Giacumo & Breman, 2020). Kirkpatrick (2004) uses four levels of evaluation: learners' reactions, learning, behaviors, and results. • Phillips (2012): The Phillips ROI model is a five-level model that assesses the effectiveness of training in terms of return on investment (ROI). It promotes five levels of evaluation: learners' reactions, learning, behaviors, results, and ROI. • Beresford (2019): The Measurement Map is an evaluation model that graphically depicts the return on the organization's investment in learning and performance. It links the organization's investment to the leading indicators of improved workplace performance to expected business results to the organization's strategic goals.
Do we have the right components in place to support learning and transfer? What is the impact of transferred learning?	• Thalheimer (2018b) Learning-Transfer Evaluation Model (LTEM): This model consists of eight levels: attendance, activity, learner perceptions, knowledge, decision-making competence, task competence, transfer, and positive and negative effects of transfer on the organization. In addition to determining the impact of learning, IDs can use this model to determine how to continuously improve the learning experience.
How can organizations leverage learning into improved workplace performance?	• Brinkerhoff's (2005) Success Case Method: This model involves identifying performers who are the most and least successful after participating in a program. IDs then analyze these individuals' stories and use the insights gained to improve the effectiveness of intervention.
To what extent can the program produce long-term, sustainable improvements?	• CIPP Model (Stufflebeam, 2007; 2015): The Context, Input, Process, and Product (CIPP) model is a comprehensive evaluation framework that can be applied to an intervention's goals, plans, actions, and outcomes.
To what extent do the materials contribute to the organization and society?	• Kaufman's Five Levels of Evaluation (Kaufman, Keller, & Watkins, 1996): This model includes five levels of evaluation which consider: inputs, processes, individual or small group payoffs, organizational payoffs, and societal contributions. It emphasizes the importance of measuring the impact of training on business results as well as contributions to clients and society.
What is the overall quality or value of a program targeted at improving individual, workplace, or societal performance?	• Chyung's 10-Step Evaluation model (Chyung, 2018): This model uses a ten-step process distributed over three different phases: Identification (analysis), Planning (design and development), and Implementation.

COMBINED EVALUATION AND NEEDS ASSESSMENT

This list of common evaluation questions and models isn't exhaustive. Still other decision makers could be interested in answering other questions. They could include:

- Are learners receiving support for transfer from their peers, managers, and supervisors when they return to the workplace?
- Are learners facing any emerging barriers as they try to perform the tasks they were trained on?

Answering questions like these requires IDs to blend approaches for evaluation with approaches for needs assessment. The evaluation part of answering these questions involves making decisions about overall value, worth, and merit. The needs assessment component involves using cause analysis models such as:

- Gilbert's (2007) Behavior Engineering Model (BEM).
- Chevalier's (2008) updated BEM.
- Rummler's (2006) Human Performance System.
- Mager and Pipe's (1997) performance analysis flowchart.

In general, using these cause analysis models will enable IDs to determine whether learners have the environmental and individual supports they need to apply their learning and performance support experiences in the workplace. This text won't comment much more on evaluation or needs assessment because there are many great references that exist to guide this component of ID work.

MAINTENANCE AND CONTINUOUS IMPROVEMENT

Interestingly, neither maintenance nor continuous improvement appear in the ADDIE family (Molenda, 2003) models of instructional design. However, both of these efforts are typically in the minds of executives and senior managers who oversee ID and other projects. For example, Ruparelia (2010) notes that most models of software development life cycle mention maintenance. It's certain that over time there will be changes in an organization, industry, society, and people's expectations. These changes could be gradual or rapid. They will necessitate updates to learning and development interventions, design, content, delivery mechanisms, and evaluation processes. Further, the information contained in an intervention can quickly become dated because of changes in the organization, the organization's learners and customers, or the larger society. These changes can result from market pressures or other societal events (e.g., a pandemic, natural disaster, or the death of well-known software such as Adobe Flash). Information in job aids is particularly subject to changes that can render any existing version of these materials obsolete, inaccurate, irrelevant, or incomplete. Stated simply, learning and development (L&D) organizations need to maintain the materials they create.

Maintenance Guidelines

The maintenance and continuous improvement plan that appears in the design document for a learning and performance support intervention specifies how the L&D group will work with stakeholders to:

- Keep the learning and performance support materials current and error free.
- Improve the materials and the performances they support over time.

Routine maintenance might include regularly scheduled tasks such as copying materials into new course shells, adjusting dates, checking links, populating learners in systems, registration updates, and just-in-time systems reminders. Routine maintenance also fixes known errors and software bugs. It can also include scheduled updates of information sources to keep them current.

Below are some general indicators of more urgent maintenance needs:

- Organizational members still are not meeting expectations due to a continuing knowledge or skill gap.
- The needs of the organization's customers have changed.
- The organization will be implementing a new process, tool, or performance standard.
- The organization will be dramatically changing existing performance standards, process, or tool.
- The organization will be changing the software it uses, owing to software updates or discontinuation.

These maintenance projects will need to fit into a budget to ensure appropriate resource allocation and cost-effective updates. The updates should align with strategic organizational goals and stakeholder needs (e.g., learners, facilitators, managers, clients). In addition, decisions associated with updates should be data-driven through a variety of performance criteria, indicators, feedback loops, and formative evaluation methods.

Continuous Improvement Guidelines

In learning and performance support, continuous improvement generally involves IDs working with stakeholders to monitor instructional and non-instructional solutions. Through a collaborative process of data collection, aggregation, analysis, and interpretation, IDs and stakeholders specify revisions to the intervention and determine the value of specific ongoing revision cycles with the purpose to improve future interventions.

For maintenance and continuous improvement, IDs can draw upon the software change control process that information technology (IT) professionals commonly use (Satyabrata, 2021). The authors have modified this process to focus on learning and performance support efforts.

1. *Create requests for change.* Changes could involve either requests to fix existing materials or to improve them. Learners and other stakeholders can submit these requests.
2. *Review and assess requests for change.* A change control team consisting of a group of representatives from the client, learners, the L&D group, and other stakeholders review each submitted change request. The team investigates details associated

with the change, the cost of making the change, and whether the requested change fits within the existing maintenance and continuous improvement budget(s). They prioritize the requested changes that the L&D group will make in the next release of the materials.

3. *Plan the change*. The change control team creates a plan to implement the approved changes.
4. *Test the change*. The change control team conducts tryouts of draft changed materials and tests any software changes.
5. *Create a change proposal*. The change control team creates a proposal documenting all the changes they will make in a given update/revision effort.
6. *Implement the changes*. The L&D group and other stakeholders implement the changes to the learning and performance support materials.
7. *Review changed performance*. The change control team collects data from clients, learners, and other stakeholders indicating if they are satisfied with the updates.
8. *Close the process*. The change control team closes out the last set of changes to the materials and begins collecting change requests for the next.

DATA COLLECTION

As in other components of the LeaPS ID model, I&E is an evidence-based process that requires IDs to collect and analyze data from a variety of sources. During formative evaluation during implementation, IDs typically collect preliminary data from clients, learners, supervisors, managers, and other organizational stakeholders indicating the extent to which learners are moving through the adoption stages and able to perform their roles. During summative evaluation, IDs typically collect data to answer the evaluation questions and determine any effects on organizational performance or societal impacts, often from the same people in addition to downstream stakeholders. Giacumo, MacDonald, & D'Jeane (2021) note that, when working across cultures, additional considerations must be made.

As a rule of thumb, direct performance observations and interviews can yield more useful data than surveys or questionnaires. Watching individuals perform tasks holistically and asking follow-up questions about decisions can yield rich data describing what is actually happening, along with how it happens and why. That said, interviews and observations can take time to complete and analyze. In contrast, questionnaires are much faster and lower in cost to implement. IDs need to do the best they can using the resources and project budgets available to them.

Steps to Ensure that Your Intervention Is Culturally Relevant and Equitable

- Consider a hybrid needs assessment-program evaluation integrated approach whenever significant, new organizational performance gaps appear. Program evaluations alone, while useful, do not always consider the larger organization-level performance context.

- Collect feedback from participants with diverse identities, who would potentially implement, deliver, or participate in any specific intervention and who are willing to provide feedback.
- Consider individual stories and other kinds of disaggregated data in testing, feedback loop design, and evaluation reporting, whenever possible, to characterize experiences and check to see if there are differing patterns between groups of participants, especially those of underrepresented groups. Make changes designed to better support performance across these groups (Equitable Data Working Group, 2022).

CASE STUDY

A new external ID consultant was hired by the learning and development department at Feed the World Headquarter (pseudonym), an international non-governmental organization (NGO). The ID project purpose was to update training for partner NGOs in specific locations, so they could upskill their staff and prepare a talent pipeline for promotions. The organization and their partner organizations in the network planned to adopt a new logistics software that the IT department had selected in partnership with the logistics department. Once the ID started the project, the ID realized that the software would require drastic changes to the current organizational logistics process. Thus, an organizational process re-engineering project would be necessary prior to updating the training program.

- Before the process re-engineering project starts, should the ID propose an evaluation of the existing process, new training program, or both? Why or why not?
- If yes, what would be the purpose for the evaluation? What evaluation model(s) should be considered for adoption? Why?

REFLECTION QUESTIONS

- How could you promote adoption of a learning and development intervention with "bottom-up" marketing materials?
- When is it appropriate to propose a summative evaluation? Why?
- How would you ensure your evaluation is culturally relevant and equitable?

REFERENCES

Beresford, B. (2019, September 23). So you want to measure impact. Now what? Chief Learning Officer. https://www.chieflearningofficer.com/2019/09/23/so-you-want-to-measure-impact-now-what/

Brinkerhoff, R. O. (2005). The success case method: A strategic evaluation approach to increasing the value and effect of training. *Advances in Developing Human Resources*, 7(1), 86–101. doi:10.1177/1523422304272172

Bukhari, H., Andreatta, P., Goldiez, B., & Rabelo, L. (2017). A framework for determining the return on investment of simulation-based training in health care. *Inquiry*, 54, 1–7. doi:10.1177/0046958016687176

Chevalier, R. (2008). The evolution of a performance analysis job aid. *Performance Improvement, 47*(10), 9–18. doi:10.1002/pfi.20034

Chyung, S. Y. Y. (2018). *10-step evaluation for training and performance improvement*. Sage.

Dormant, D. (2011). *The chocolate model of change*. Diane Dormant. http://www.chocochange.com/index.html

Equitable Data Working Group. (2022). *A vision for equitable data: Recommendations from the equitable data working group*. https://www.whitehouse.gov/wp-content/uploads/2022/04/eo13985-vision-for-equitable-data.pdf

Giacumo, L. A., & Breman, J. (2020). Trends and implications of models, frameworks, and approaches used by instructional designers in workplace learning and performance improvement. *Performance Improvement Quarterly, 34*(2), 131–170. doi:10.1002/piq.21349

Giacumo, L. A., MacDonald, M., & D'Jeane, T. P. (2021). Promoting organizational justice in cross-cultural data collection, analysis, and interpretation: Towards an emerging conceptual model. *Journal of Applied Instructional Design, 10*(4), 1–13. doi:10.59668/329.5268

Gilbert, T. F. (2007). Human *competence: Engineering worthy performance* (Tribute ed.). Pfeiffer.

Hall, G. E., & Hord, S. M. (2011). *Implementing change: Patterns, principles, and potholes* (3rd ed.). Pearson.

Hiatt, J. M. (2006). *ADKAR: A model for change in business, government and our community*. Prosci Learning Center.

Kaufman, R., Keller, J., & Watkins, R. (1996). What works and what doesn't: Evaluation beyond Kirkpatrick. *Performance and Instruction, 35*(2), 8–12. doi:10.1002/pfi.4170350203

Kirkpatrick, D. L. (2004). A T+D classic: How to start an objective evaluation of your training program. *T&D, 58*(5), 1–3.

Mager, R. F., & Pipe, P. (1997). *Analyzing performance problems: You really oughta wanna* (3rd ed.). CEP Press.

Marker, A., Villachica, S. W., Stepich, D., Allen, D., & Stanton, L. (2014). An updated framework for human performance improvement in the workplace: The spiral HPI framework. *Performance Improvement, 53*(1), 10–23. doi:10.1002/pfi.21389

Molenda, M. (2003). In search of the elusive ADDIE model. *Performance Improvement, 42*(5), 34–36. doi:10.1002/pfi.4930420508

Phillips, J. J. (2012). *Return on investment in training and performance improvement programs* (2nd ed.). Routledge.

Rogers, E. M. (2003). *Diffusion of innovations* (5th ed.). Free Press.

Rummler, G. A. (2006). The anatomy of performance. In Pershing, J. A. (Ed.), *Handbook of human performance technology: Principles, practices, and potential* (3rd ed., pp. 986–1007). Pfeiffer.

Ruparelia, N. B. (2010). Software development lifecycle models. *SIGSOFT Softw. Eng. Notes, 35*(3), 8–13. doi:10.1145/1764810.1764814

Satyabrata, J. (2021, August 18). *Change control: Change management in software engineering*. Geeks for Geeks. https://www.geeksforgeeks.org/change-management-in-software-engineering/

Smith, P. L., & Ragan, T. J. (2005). *Instructional design* (3rd ed.). John Wiley & Sons.

Stone, D. L., & Villachica, S. W. (2003). And then a miracle occurs! Ensuring the successful implementation of enterprisewide EPSS and e-learning from day one. *Performance Improvement, 42*(3), 42–51. doi:10.1002/pfi.4930420308

Stufflebeam, D. L. (2007). *CIPP evaluation model checklist* (2nd ed.). https://wmich.edu/sites/default/files/attachments/u350/2014/cippchecklist_mar07.pdf

Stufflebeam, D. L. (2015). *CIPP evaluation model checklist: A tool for applying the CIPP model to assess projects and programs*. http://rszarf.ips.uw.edu.pl/ewalps/dzienne/cipp-model-stufflebeam2015.pdf

Thalheimer, W. (2018a). *Donald Kirkpatrick was NOT the originator of the four-level model of learning evaluation*. https://www.worklearning.com/2018/01/30/donald-kirkpatrick-was-not-the-originator-of-the-four-level-model-of-learning-evaluation/

Thalheimer, W. (2018b). *The learning-transfer evaluation model: Sending messages to enable learning effectiveness*. https://www.worklearning.com/wp-content/uploads/2018/02/Thalheimer-The-Learning-Transfer-Evaluation-Model-Report-for-LTEM-v11.pdf

Navigating ID Practice in the Real World

INTRODUCTION

In the preceding chapters, you've encountered several themes to guide your inclusive and culturally relevant instructional design practice. These include:

- Focus on what really affects diverse learners' experiences.
- Communicate, communicate, communicate.
- Learn the business side of instructional design (ID).

In this chapter we focus on three common real-world ID challenges to these themes:

1. Unreasonable client expectations.
2. Contradictory organizational truths.
3. Moving away from traditional ID approaches, towards a diversity, equity, and inclusion (DEI)-focused process and collaborative consulting.

To support instructional designers (IDs) facing these challenges, we provide three solutions:

1. Increasing organizational intelligence.
2. Increasing credibility and trust.
3. Keeping clients happy.

Approaches to engage in "collaborative consulting" require gathering organizational intelligence over time and permission. Consulting is like great choreography. It's important to learn how to gracefully step forwards, side, or back and in ways that don't confuse your dance partners. You should also be able to find ways to dance together that are safe and mutually beneficial. Building your credibility can help you obtain the client permission and stakeholder buy-in that's required to do great work.

Further, savvy IDs are often visionaries. Ground truth keepers may not yet be ready to implement the official truth. And that's okay, too. One of the hardest things to learn might be that while savvy IDs generally serve as change agents, they really can't change clients or the organization overnight. Change is hard, even when it's wanted. Thus,

DOI: 10.4324/9781003360612-13

it can be harder when it's not your clients' or other stakeholders' idea. But, there are approaches you can use to find great opportunities and help build healthy working relationships.

After reading this chapter, you should be able to describes techniques to:

- Grow sources of useful organizational intelligence.
- Grow your own credibility so clients can trust you.
- Keep clients happy (and not annoyed).

BACKGROUND: THE ID'S DILEMMA

IDs often need to obtain permission from their clients and organizations to use the full range of techniques in the LeaPS ID model—or any model of performance-based learning or performance improvement. And obtaining this permission means that IDs have to gain clients' trust to use the resources the organization provides to create learning and performance support materials that will improve on-the-job performance. Ideally, clients and their organizations also believe that the creation, implementation, and maintenance of these materials will support goals of organizational justice, diversity, equity, and inclusion. If clients don't provide these permissions, IDs can find themselves in situations where they can't employ their best practices, models, and techniques.

Observational Apprenticeships

All clients have gone to school. They know what teachers do. They know what classrooms are like. They've completed in-person and online courses. They've used the Internet to "do their own research." While clients are familiar with the behaviors they've observed, they may be unaware of the otherwise invisible design decisions and content knowledge that produce these behaviors (Christopherson, 2019).

Lortie (1975) coined the phrase "observational apprenticeship," which is defined as "a method novices can use to gain confidence but also insufficient expertise by observing some aspects of others' performance without any other training, adequate guidance, or practice." The phenomenon of gaining an incomplete understanding from an apprenticeship that is "observational" alone can afflict IDs as well. Figure 13.1 depicts this iceberg.

Owing to these observations, some clients may conclude that just about anyone, including themselves, can create good training materials on demand, usually in extremely short time frames. Others may also believe that IDs can create effective interventions based solely on input from a subject matter expert (SME), with no input from the learners themselves. Others may believe that just about anyone or anything can facilitate and deliver culturally relevant and equitable interventions that will produce effective learning and improved performance. Some clients and their bosses may also believe that training alone will solve all their workplace problems when people aren't performing to standard.

Clients and their bosses who've completed such observational apprenticeships may not know how to budget and plan resources for ID projects. Likewise, university

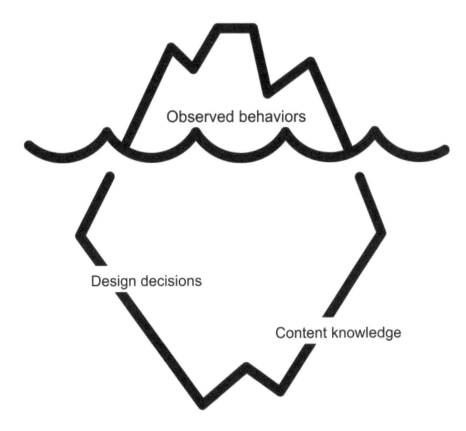

FIGURE 13.1 The iceberg of an observational apprenticeship.

professors who are clients for ID projects creating coursework may not have any idea how long it actually takes their students to complete their assignments. Or, how to plan more inclusive and equitable learning environments.

These client expectations can place IDs in a dilemma. On the one hand, IDs ideally would want to create interventions that improve performance in an organization, all while supporting diversity, equity, and inclusion. On the other hand, IDs don't always experience the level of support that's needed to achieve this ideal.

Whether they are external consultants or internal employees, IDs would want to have their clients' backs, helping them avoid bad decisions and practices that don't help them meet organizational objectives or goals. To this end, IDs would expect to work collaboratively with their clients, SMEs, organizational stakeholders, and willing learners who would perform the job and engage with the intervention, including those with identities that have been marginalized and underrepresented.

Ideally, IDs would expect clients to adequately sponsor their learning and development (L&D) projects. This means that IDs might expect clients to approve use of:

- Relevant data related to the knowledge or skills root cause of a performance gap, root causes that the intervention addresses.
- Training requirements arising from either formal or informal needs assessments that consider all of the potential root causes of a performance gap.

- Release time for SMEs to participate in task analysis and to ensure the technical accuracy, completeness, and authenticity of LeaPS deliverables.
- Release time for members of the intended population to participate in usability tests of prototypes and pilot tests of developed materials.

However, there are some clients who've formed opinions about IDs based on their observational apprenticeships sitting in school or training courses. These clients may merely want IDs to quickly create learning materials by a given deadline, without applying the LeaPS ID model or other rigorous ID model. These clients and their bosses largely expect IDs to be on board with their training requests.

What should IDs do when clients ask them to:

- Create informational training programs that IDs know won't transfer in ways that improve learners' or organizational performance?
- Create complex technical content without having access to SMEs?
- Work alone to create training materials, without access to learners or upstream and downstream stakeholders?
- Create "quick" versions of training materials that ignore accessibility standards, claiming that "those can be added in version 2.0"?
- Exclude the input of willing learners with diverse identities in ideating, creating, and testing interventions?

Developing relationships that yield better organizational intelligence can help IDs better respond to these requests.

GROW SOURCES OF USEFUL ORGANIZATIONAL INTELLIGENCE

To effectively manage these types of situations, part of real-world ID practice is to grow and maintain useful sources of organizational intelligence (Villachica, 2001). Sometimes called "business acumen," organizational intelligence (Silber & Kearny, 2009) is knowing how the organization works so you can work the organization. Organizational intelligence is about having and maintaining credible sources of information about the organization and its operations. Having good sources of organizational intelligence will then help you work the organization (James & Wallace, 2021a, b).

If you don't already know, you'll want to begin by finding out how the organization actually works. Organizations are complex systems. They usually live within larger organizational systems. And organizations themselves are composed of smaller subsystems. All of these systems interact; a change in one part of a system produces changes in other systems. If you're not familiar with the systems and subsystems affecting your organization, you'll need to learn about them. And if this information isn't already available, you'll need to create it. You can work alone, with your team, and with your boss to build and maintain sources of useful organizational intelligence.

The point is that you do your best to negotiate for what you need in any project. Your due diligence is to explain to leaders what you want to do, why it is important, how you want to do it, and ask for their advice on getting it done. When you run up against roadblocks, try to discover their root causes and ask for help from more senior colleagues to find ways to mitigate them. This takes time, perhaps as long as two or three years, before you can effectively change the level of support you receive from leaders in a large organization.

Change is hard for everyone, even when a person wants the change. If you have to convince leaders that they might want the change, you may not achieve your desired results immediately. If you do, that's fantastic. The point is that if you don't get access to what you want, you will either learn how to get it over time or you will find a new organization that will value your approach to creating more culturally responsive and equitable interventions.

Model the Organization

One way to build organizational intelligence is to use one or more models to represent the organizational system and its interactions. An understanding of how the organizational system interacts with the larger environment and how the different subsystems in the organization interact can help you better support your clients.

One useful model is Rummler's (2006) anatomy of performance, shown in Figure 13.2. This model depicts an organizational systems map by describing its processes

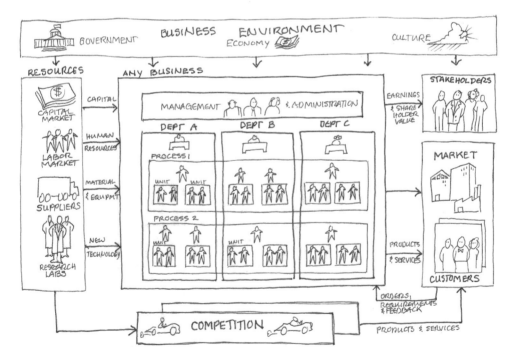

FIGURE 13.2 Rummler's (2006) anatomy of performance. ©2023 International Society for Performance Improvement. All rights reserved. Reprinted with permission of the International Society for Performance Improvement. www.ispi.org

within the larger context of the business environment. Equivalent to the first ring of the LeaPS ID model, the external environment consists of the government, economy, and culture (society). Arrows and labels depict the sources going into the organization and the outputs going to shareholders and customers. This model can also help you familiarize yourself with the major processes that cut across the organization's departments and how they provide value to their internal and external customers. Faulty handoffs as the process moves from one department to another can provide excellent opportunities to provide learning and performance support bundled with other performance solutions.

Another useful model is Kaufman's (1983) Organizational Elements model. As shown in Table 13.1, the model consists of these interlocking components:

- *Inputs*. Human labor, equipment, budgets, etc.
- *Processes*. What you do to produce the product.
- *Products*. What workgroups complete.
- *Outputs*. What the company completes as a whole.
- *Outcomes*. The product's effects on the customer and society.

Types of Organizational Truths

Gillum and Mortenson (2019) describe two types of organizational truth: official truth and ground truth. *Official truth* is what the organization formally says about itself. For example, official truth is what Pentagon officials say about a given military situation. *Ground truth* (literally the truth on the ground) is what the organization actually does. For example, ground truth is what the dirty and tired warfighters in the trenches say about the same situation. Dr. Giacumo envisions a third truth, *aspirational truth*—what the organization would ideally like to become and do. Aspirational truth can appear in an organization's vision statement and in the career plans of its employees. For example, as of 2020, the vision of US Army Medicine is to be "ready, reformed, reorganized, responsive, and relevant" (Wolf, 2020).

It's important to know the differences between what an organization says about itself, what it actually does, and what it hopes to become. These differences can help IDs

TABLE 13.1 Kaufman's (1983) organizational elements model.

	Level	Description
ENDS	Mega Level Outcomes	Impact of organizational goals on society
	Macro Level Outputs	Aggregated products and services of an organization delivered to society
MEANS	Micro Level Products	Individual products and services the organization creates for its internal use
	Processes	The methods and procedures the organization uses to create products and services
	Inputs	The raw materials and human resources required to complete processes

better understand the organization's culture. This can also help IDs navigate towards opportunities while avoiding minefields.

Most organizations specify their vision, mission, and values formally on a website and in various internal documents. These official and aspirational truths can sometimes conflict with ground truth. For example, an organization's leadership and employees might truly believe in the stated strategic objectives (i.e., official truth). At the same time, organizational leaders may implement any number of initiatives that may not align with those objectives (i.e., ground truth). These contradictions can present dilemmas for IDs, either internal or external to the organization. An important part of building organizational intelligence is determining which has priority in a specific situation—official truth or ground truth.

Organizational Truth and DEI Practices

Organizational truth also applies to an organization's DEI practices. Ideally, the official truth, ground truth, and aspirational truth about DEI are aligned. What an organization officially says about itself, what it actually does, and what it hopes to be should become the same. To determine whether this is the case, IDs should examine the organization's DEI practices. To determine the official truth, review the organization's DEI policies and procedures. Talk with human resource personnel, executives, managers, and supervisors about their views on DEI and the role of learning and performance support interventions. Interview members of underrepresented populations within the organization to understand their take on the extent to which the organization supports their work in ways that honor diversity, are equitable, inclusive, and just.

Ask people at the "doing" level about the design of learning and development interventions. Who is included? What parts do they play? Ask leaders how they support their staff members to be included, respected, and treated with dignity. If they can't point to specific objective behaviors then you might infer that they are checking the "DEI box" and might not actually embrace DEI work.

During this examination of DEI practices, ask questions that don't refer directly to diversity, equity, and inclusion in order to find out how things are actually done and how decisions are made. Examples include but are not limited to:

- Who is on a design team?
- Who else is included in the design process?
- What do each of the individuals in these roles do?
- How are design team members and other design contributors recognized?
- Who makes design decisions?
- How are design decisions made?
- How are design projects scoped?
- What milestones are included in the design process?
- What strategies do you use to approve requests for personal time off (PTO) or vacation?
- Can you tell me about a time when a decision was made to adopt a new technology? What was considered? Who was included?

- Can you show me examples of images, stock photos, and websites commonly used in your learning and development interventions?

More importantly, listen for mention of common approaches to, or stories that demonstrate efforts to:

- Build or ensure transparency and trust.
- Nurture partnerships and cooperative team relationships.
- Include representatives of diverse cultures and those with underrepresented identities in processes.
- Use participatory design or co-design.
- Include "downstream stakeholders."
- Affirm different cultural and personal identities as well as basic human needs.
- Facilitate feelings of inclusion or belonging.
- Recognize significant contributions from a wide variety of people.
- Facilitate accessibility.

Throughout the examination of DEI practices, pay attention to any contradictions between official truth and ground truth. In general, if answers don't include anything you know to be DEI-related, then you can reasonably conclude that the ground truth values likely don't center DEI.

In addition to asking specific questions, seek out as many useful individual stories as you can find. Ask about the stories, sagas, and myths that help to describe the organizational culture. Look for patterns, themes, and ways that social markers such as race, class, gender, age, ability, religion, and sexual orientation shape an individual's or group's experience. Collect as much information and as many stories as you can while recognizing that there are always limitations to time and patience. Remember that you're building organizational intelligence, and this will happen gradually.

Build and Refine Business Cases

Over time, you can apply improved organizational intelligence to develop a compelling business case that combines effective performance-based training with DEI. There are significant organizational costs for creating, delivering, and maintaining learning and performance support solutions that leave end-users out and fail to improve on-the-job performance. These costs usually take the form of continuing performance gaps, subsequent project revisions, retraining, and lower organizational performance outcomes (e.g., productivity, waste, retention, absenteeism, disengagement).

These techniques for building sources of useful organizational intelligence can help you, your team, and your boss understand the official and unofficial structure of the organization and how work really gets done and, as importantly, how work does not get done. They can help you articulate the organization's business goals and pain points and fit into the organization's culture. They can help you separate stated priorities from real ones that keep decision makers awake at night. Knowing how the organization really operates helps you figure out how to work with the organization in ways that will improve performance and benefit your clients (Marker et al., 2014).

GROW YOUR OWN CREDIBILITY SO CLIENTS CAN TRUST YOU

While you grow sources of organizational intelligence and craft a business case for culturally responsive and equitable interventions, you can use techniques to grow your own credibility as a consultant. Whether you work as an ID hired as an outside contractor or an internal employee, you are often a consultant to your clients. According to Block (2011), you are a consultant any time you are trying to change, influence, or improve a given situation while you have no direct control over the implementation or no direct reports (i.e., individuals who report to you). When you have direct control or direct reports, you are a manager. Some IDs, especially those who manage other IDs, may serve as both consultant and manager.

Consultants lack direct control and authority, and that can make their jobs difficult. IDs can lack direct control and authority over these sponsorship responsibilities that clients should meet:

- Client and stakeholder review of ID project deliverables to ensure they align with the organization's mission and strategic business objectives.
- Access to extant data that you can use to analyze training requirements and design the training.
- Ability to provide release time for SMEs to participate in task analysis and review project deliverables for technical accuracy, completeness, and authenticity.
- Ability to provide release time for a diverse, representative group of learners to participate in design reviews and tests of drafted learning and performance support materials.

Therefore, it's important to learn collaborative consulting techniques.

Techniques for Collaborative Consulting

Collaborative consulting relationships are based on trust (Block, 2011; Schein, 2016). Consultants need to trust their own abilities to provide professional advice and services, and they need to be able to trust their clients. And clients need to be able to trust their consultants and their efforts on their behalf. While responsibility to build trust occurs in both parties (i.e., clients and ID consultants), ID consultants can only be responsible for their own efforts to build trust.

So how can consultants do their part to build trust and rapport in ways that can earn their clients' support and confidence? Figure 13.3 summarizes several techniques that can be helpful.

Use actions from the list in Figure 13.3 to build rapport and trust that yield organizational intelligence. Use credible and relevant organizational intelligence to align your efforts with what your clients, their bosses, and the organization really care about. The more your efforts are aligned, the more support and trust you can expect. Collect and analyze data to show how your efforts support the organization's mission, its values, its strategic objectives, and its current strategic initiatives that support the objectives. Align your efforts with the performance goals your boss and their boss need to meet to meet their annual goals. Find out what keeps them up at night and empathize with their

Techniques for Collaborative Consulting

- ☑ Assume good intentions of others.
- ☑ Be solution-focused and customer service-oriented.
- ☑ Build sources of organizational intelligence.
- ☑ Build trust and rapport.
- ☑ Be prepared for client "thank you's" with specific asks.
- ☑ Shape client expectations.
- ☑ Ask to play with others in the organization: information technology, human relations, quality assurance.
- ☑ Employ evidence-based practices to do right by your clients and stakeholders.
- ☑ Keep your client updated regularly with status reports and planned next steps.
- ☑ Respect your client's time.
- ☑ Deliver on your promises.
- ☑ Monitor your efforts continuously.
- ☑ Don't surprise your clients.

FIGURE 13.3 Techniques for collaborative consulting.

plights. Share relevant "business friendly" articles about evidence-based practices other similar organizations have used successfully. The more clients see you as genuinely committed to helping them do what is important, the more of their trust you can earn.

To build trust and rapport with clients, begin by talking less, listening more, and asking important questions. Some of these questions should help you align your efforts. Others should help you gain insight into what the client thinks about a given situation. Ask about the characteristics that learning and performance support solutions would need to be successful. Ask about the extent to which your current efforts are helping the client at this time.

In the short term, respond to requests for training as best as you can and be prepared to ask for what you need to better serve your client in the future. For example, you might ask for:

- More release time for assigned SMEs or for access to the use cases that programmers use to test their software as they build it (useful for systems training).

- Release time for yourself to investigate learners who represent previously under-represented perspectives.
- Permission to create personas and prototypes—and for representative learners to conduct a tryout of these prototypes.
- Release time to include more underrepresented people as contributors, reviewers, and testers for ID project deliverables.

It doesn't matter what you ask for, as long as you ask for the most important thing you need at the time to better serve the client, improve workplace performance in valued ways, and create learning and support materials that are culturally responsive and equitable.

Other ways to build trust in the longer term start with working to shape client expectations. Share timely, relevant, and interesting information about best practices that could be applicable to the project you're working on. Share relevant experiences that have produced favorable and unfavorable outcomes. Avoid surprises by communicating frequently, especially about potential risks that may threaten successful project completion. Negotiate to share project status updates and progress towards milestones at frequent and regular or expected intervals. As much as possible, work with your client to identify risks to successful project completion and mitigate them.

Offer the recommendation that you believe best serves the client and provide a rationale. If the client objects, offer the next best recommendation and its rationale, and the next. Find the best recommendation that the client also believes is feasible, inclusive, equitable, and just. This technique has been called the "consultant's back-step shuffle."

Ask for permission to sit at the tables where the organization makes important decisions about performance. For example, IDs can sit with information technology staff and programmers designing large-scale software systems. IDs can provide input on user-friendly screen design, creating help systems, and where effective job aids might minimize the need for other training. IDs can work with human resource staff to specify standards, write clear policy, and formulate feedback that is timely, relevant, kind, inclusive, equitable, and actionable. IDs can work with quality assurance personnel and SMEs to create standard operating procedures (SOPs) that others can actually use to complete a given procedure in ways that meet organizational standards. IDs can work with marketing and graphic design staff to assist in multimedia design because IDs bring different but complementary insight.

WHEN YOU CAN'T CHANGE CLIENTS OR THE ORGANIZATION

There could be situations in which this kind of collaborative consulting is simply impossible. It can be particularly difficult for:

- Independent contractors who act as one-person ID shops. Moving from project, client, and from one organization to the next may not provide adequate opportunities or enough time to change consulting roles.
- IDs who work in organizations that think of IDs only as "course factories" responsible for the interventions that are asked for and nothing further. Moore (2015) notes

that "many people . . . want to leave the course factory behind but have trouble see-ing how they could actually *do* it."

Clients and organizations can become quite comfortable with the status quo. Change is hard on everyone, even when we all want it. Unless the personal and organizational pain associated with current practices is great enough for clients and their bosses to reconsider their standard ways of working, the odds may lie against IDs trying to change their consulting role to something more collaborative in nature. There are times when those who keep the organization's "official truth" are not yet ready to consider uncomfortable "ground truths" of learning and performance support materials that are not culturally responsive and equitable. In these situations, more visionary IDs may choose to use the techniques described earlier to become collaborative consultants over time. Or they may choose to take their skills, experience, and ID practices to organiza-tions and clients that are a better fit.

KEEP CLIENTS HAPPY (AND NOT ANNOYED)

Regardless of the level of collaborative consulting, there are practices IDs can use to help keep clients happy—rather than annoyed.

- *Whenever possible, employ evidence-based practices to do right by your clients and stake-holders.* As IDs, we act as consultants. As much as we can, it's our job to do right by our clients and not let them do stupid things. It's also our job to create learning and job support materials that are effective, culturally responsive, and inclusive. When we can't meet these ideals, we run the risk of adding to organizational costs without creating any offsetting benefit.
- *Do your best to shape and meet client expectations.* Some of these expectations are about the way that your ID project deliverables align with what's keeping your clients and their bosses up at night. Other expectations revolve around the overall quality of learning and job support deliverables IDs create as well as the corresponding schedule and budget. Clients who want to pay for lower-cost learning and job sup-port solutions will not be happy paying the cost of more expensive solutions.
- *Don't surprise your clients.* You don't like it when clients surprise you. Don't do it to them. To produce quality deliverables on time and on budget, make and share reasonable operating assumptions with your clients. Then collect relevant data to either verify or reject them. Create rapid, client-presentable prototypes for things that are new. Obtain client permission to test them out with representative learners before developing more.
- *Respect clients' time.* Clients are typically busy. Make it easy for them to work with you. Always be better organized than they are. Provide meeting agendas, start meet-ings on time, and send concise summaries along with any action items following the meeting. Don't waste their time talking about yourself or things that are important to you. Focus on them and their business needs. Answer their questions concisely. Usually, a "yes," "no," or "it depends" will suffice, followed by a short explanation. If

they want more information, they will ask. Be truthful. Admit when you don't have a ready answer and state when you can provide one. Don't try to "educate" them. Clients usually have no inclination to learn ID concepts or practices. Learn to translate ID jargon into language and rationale that resonate with them.

- *Deliver on your promises.* Meet any commitment you make. If you can't, provide the client with advance warning—and a darn good reason. Provide a way to make up for any inconvenience you may be causing. If possible, use formal project management change orders to specify any proposed changes to project quality, schedule, or budget. Then allow the client to review, negotiate, and approve them ("Change order," Wikipedia, 2023).
- *Monitor your efforts continuously.* To help ensure that your work is meeting clients' needs, start an ongoing dialogue with the client. Ask a stream of questions during client meetings, and as you hand off project deliverables for their review. Ask questions such as:
  - Is this deliverable meeting your expectations?
  - Is this project meeting your needs? The needs of the organization?
  - Are your bosses and stakeholders happy with our work?
  - Is there anything I need to do better?
  - Are there any emerging barriers to our shared success story that we should be concerned about?

CASE STUDY

Ocean State University (pseudonym) is a public university in a state that has recently banned the term "equity" from all instructional course books and organizational materials. Your colleague lives ten miles away and doesn't want to move out of the area. A Director of HR position became available, and your colleague applied for the job before the recent political action took place. Your colleague values equity and has reached out to you for advice on how to determine whether or not this is still a great opportunity to join a department and unit with similar values.

- Based on what you have read in this chapter, how would you advise your colleague?

REFLECTION QUESTIONS

- Pick an organization you are familiar with. What are some of the major processes it uses to meet its mission?
- Are there ways to work on supporting organizational justice, diversity, equity, and inclusion, without using those terms? If so, how? If not, why not?
- Select a given process in the organization you've picked. What departments in the organization does the process cut through? What, if any, problems arise as one group hands off the process to the next?

- Describe a job experience and the consulting role you served. To what extent were you a collaborative consultant, as described in this chapter? What were the advantages and disadvantages of the role(s) you played?

REFERENCES

Block, P. (2011). *Flawless consulting: A guide to getting your expertise used* (3rd ed). Pfeiffer.

Christopherson, K. (2019, May 14). "Apprenticeship by observation" and the role of reflection. *Teachers on Fire*. https://medium.com/teachers-on-fire/apprenticeship-by-observation-and-the-role-of-reflection-9a263f1450b9

Gillum, T., & Mortenson, K. (2019). *Performance eating rabbits: What B.O.L.D. people see and do.* Outskirts Press.

James, D., & Wallace, G. W. (2021a, December 1). *Virtual Series: L&D's pivot to performance* (interview with Steve Villachica). [video]. YouTube. https://www.youtube.com/watch?v=0LX3rIzijuQ

James, D., & Wallace, G. W. (2021b, December 15). *Virtual Series: L&D's pivot to performance panel discussion* (interview with Anne-Marie Burbidge, Steve Villachica, Dawn Snyder, and Sebastian Tindall). [video]. YouTube. https://www.youtube.com/watch?v=DPhY3X37Ff0

Kaufman, R. (1983). A holistic planning model: A system approach for improving organizational effectiveness and impact. *Performance and Instruction*, 22(8), 3–12. doi:10.1002/pfi.415022080

Lortie, D. (1975). *School teacher: A sociological study.* University of Chicago Press.

Marker, A., Villachica, S. W., Stepich, D., Allen, D., & Stanton, L. (2014). An updated framework for human performance improvement in the workplace: The spiral HPI framework. *Performance Improvement*, 53(1), 10–23. doi:10.1002/pfi.21389

Moore, C. (2015). Do you work in a course factory? Do you care? Action@Work. https://blog.cathy-moore.com/do-you-work-in-a-course-factory-do-you-care/#gref

Rummler, G. A. (2006). The anatomy of performance. In J. A. Pershing (Ed.), *Handbook of human performance technology: Principles, practices, and potential* (3rd ed., pp. 986–1007). Pfeiffer.

Schein, E. H. (2016). *Humble consulting: How to provide real help faster.* Berrett-Koehler.

Silber, K. H., & Kearny, L. (2009). *Organizational intelligence: A guide to understanding the business of your organization for HR, training, and performance consulting.* Pfeiffer.

Villachica, S. W. (2001). *Doing right by your clients: Surfing the performance improvement zone.* [video]. YouTube. http://www.youtube.com/watch?v=RU7aCDTZSAQ

Wikipedia. (2023, February 3). Change order. In *Wikipedia*. https://en.wikipedia.org/wiki/Change_order

Wolf, R. (2020, October 1). *Medical readiness to be highlighted at virtual AUSA meeting.* https://www.army.mil/article/239588/medical_readiness_to_be_highlighted_at_virtual_ausa_meeting

14

Looking Backwards and Forwards—An Afterword

INTRODUCTION

Chapters 1–12 described the elements of the LeaPS ID model along with corresponding processes and activities for each component. Chapter 13 provided guidance for real-world consulting practice. In Chapter 14, it's time to look backwards and forwards as this text comes to an end. This chapter will address the origins of the LeaPS ID model and its future potential improvement.

LOOKING BACKWARDS: ORIGINS OF THE LEAPS ID MODEL

Evolution of the LeaPS ID Model

In the beginning, there was ADDIE. Faculty members in the Organizational Performance and Workplace Learning (OPWL) department at Boise State University used ADDIE to create the Bronco Instructional Design (BID) model and began using it in 2007 when Drs. Stepich and Villachica were teaching the department's instructional design (ID) course. The BID model evolved into the Learning and Performance Support (LeaPS) ID model in 2019 when Dr. Giacumo began co-teaching the instructional design course with Villachica. This section describes this evolution.

Molenda (2003) has noted, there is no single "ADDIE Model" (p. 34). Instead, ADDIE is an acronym that refers to a "family of models that share a common underlying structure" (p. 35) made up of five core elements: Analyze, Design, Develop, Implement, and Evaluate. As shown in Figure 14.1, Gustafson and Branch (1997, 2002) arranged these core elements in a circle, and in 2002 moved the evaluation element to the center of the diagram, noting that each of the elements informs the others "as development takes place and revision continues throughout the process, at least until the instruction is implemented" (p. 22).

In 2007, Drs. Stepich and Villachica were considering whether to use a specific "ADDIE" ID model, such as Dick, Carey, and Carey (2005), Smith and Ragan (2005), or Morrison, Ross, and Kemp (2007). Instead, they chose to create a hybrid model that combined aspects of ADDIE and recent work specifying performance improvement competencies.

DOI: 10.4324/9781003360612-14

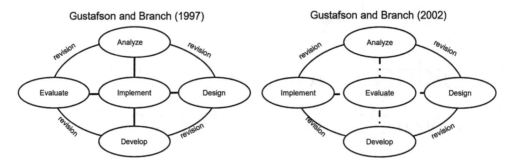

FIGURE 14.1 Comparing the core elements in Gustafson and Branch's 1997 and 2002 surveys of instructional development models. Note: These images are used with permission from Dr. Robert Branch.

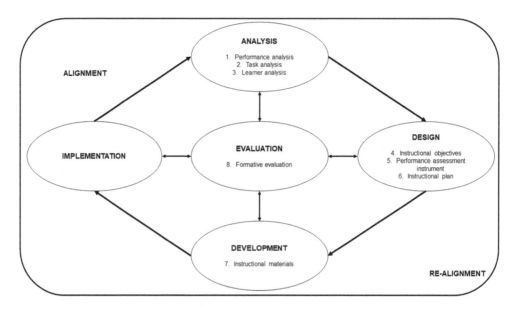

FIGURE 14.2 The Bronco instructional design (BID) model: first iteration.

Building on the work of Gustafson and Branch, Stepich and Villachica decided to create a more specialized model that was based on ADDIE and focused on the key activities that instructional designers (IDs) should be able to perform in the workplace. To this end, they created the Bronco ID (BID) model, which appears in Figure 14.2.

Using BID, instructional designers approach analysis, design, development, and implementation components largely in order. This said, revisions can occur throughout the ID process as instructional designers align and continuously re-align their work with strategic business objectives and changing contextual factors. Seen this way, formative evaluation occurs throughout the BID model, informing revisions to all its components and across its activities and deliverables.

Focusing on Employer Expectations

In creating the BID model, Stepich and Villachica included those ID activities and deliverables that corresponded to the competencies they believed an entry-level ID should possess. Villachica, Marker, and Taylor (2010) later confirmed that employers of entry level instructional designers expect them to:

- Conduct a front-end analysis or needs assessment.
- Conduct a task analysis.
- Conduct a learner analysis.
- Write performance objectives.
- Create assessment instruments.
- Sequence objectives.

The front-end analysis or needs assessment in Villachica et al. (2010) equates to the abbreviated performance analysis contained in BID. This performance analysis roughly equates to that appearing in Van Tiem, Moseley, and Dessinger's (2001) model of performance improvement (p. 43). Using BID, instructional designers complete:

- A gap analysis specifying desired and actual performance.
- An organizational analysis that aligns the gap with strategic business objectives and organizational mission, providing a compelling argument that the gap is worth closing.
- An abbreviated cause analysis indicating that:
  - Learners need to build skills in a safe learning environment where they can receive coaching and feedback.
  - Providing a job aid or EPSS alone wouldn't close the performance gap.

A²DDIE

Villachica and Stepich drew on Guerra's (2003) framework depicting key performance improvement competencies. In this work, Guerra specifies the following competencies: Assessment, Analysis, Design, Development, Implementation, Evaluation (A²DDIE) (pp. 58–59). Guerra specifies differences between "needs analysis" and "needs assessment." From a larger performance improvement perspective, the terms "needs assessment," "front-end analysis," and "performance analysis" refer to a similar set of activities, with some authors ascribing slight, but important, differences among them. Because instructional designers can mistakenly prescribe training in situations in which learners already have the skills for the required performance, Stepich and Villachica thought the addition of an abbreviated performance analysis to the ADDIE model would be useful. They believed that the name "A²DDIE" was too convoluted, so they opted to name the ID model after the Boise State University sports mascot, Buster Bronco. Hence, the Bronco ID model, or BID.

Project Alignment and Realignment

Stepich and Villachica also added the alignment/realignment components to the BID model to show that instructional design work takes place in the form of projects. They drew on an ID model from Stone and Villachica (2005) to show that ID projects—similar to other forms of project work—often shift underfoot. This makes it important for instructional designers to align their work with strategic business objectives and organizational constraints at the beginning of a project. They must then continuously re-align their efforts as constraints change during the project to ensure meeting those objectives.

From the BID Model to the Learning and Performance Support (LeaPS) ID Model

Over time, several shortcomings arose with the BID model. First, the model suggested that IDs worked through the phases in discrete order. IDs began their projects with analysis, ended them with implementation, conducted formative evaluation during the project, and conducted summative evaluation months after the organization had implemented the training. It's true that IDs in some organizations working on some types of projects may work through the phases in a linear order. It's also true that IDs in other organizations working on other types of projects may combine phases. For example, IDs creating eLearning may use rapid prototyping to combine aspects of analysis and design. Further, some IDs may spend more time developing project deliverables that other IDs have previously designed. IDs may also omit some phases.

Second, the abbreviated front-end analysis in BID proved problematic. In conducting a "mini needs assessment," practitioners could mistakenly focus on helping learners build skills and knowledge when the more significant causes of a given performance gap lay in the workplace environment. While learning interventions and job aids may address two potential causes of a given performance gap, IDs may be overlooking other environmental and individual causes of the gap.

Third, BID omitted issues related to client sponsorship. While the course would address project sponsorship as students qualified potential ID projects, this qualification of a potential training effort largely occurred within course discussions, divorced from the BID model itself.

Fourth, BID omitted any mention of the heuristics (a.k.a. "rules of thumb") that guide the work of savvy IDs in the workplace. ID is about solving design problems (Jonassen, 2004). To this end, IDs employ heuristics that give them broad decision-making latitude about what they will and will not do in different situations.

Finally, the BID model does not consider the importance of "inclusive design" and the principle of "expanded collaboration" (described in Chapter 1) throughout the life of an ID project.

To address these issues and depict a broader range of ID practice, Drs. Giacumo, Villachica, and Stepich created the Learning and Performance Support (LeaPS) ID model.

What the LeaPS ID Model Adds

In addition to addressing the shortcomings of the BID model, the LeaPS ID model and its corresponding textbook offer practitioners several advantages.

- *The LeaPS ID model is based on a collaborative and inclusive approach to design.* Instructional design is best played as a team sport. This text describes how to plan, scale, and manage such an ID project. Creating effective and just training that transfers to the workplace requires the collaboration of IDs, clients, stakeholders, subject-matter experts, trainers, eLearning developers, and learners.
- *This text provides more guidance about employing an evidence-based inclusive ID practice.* The text describes the different sources and types of data that IDs collect and analyze during an ID project. IDs may opt to use extant data the organization has already created, including any relevant needs assessments the organization has already conducted to:

  - Specify a gap between actual and desired performance.
  - Determine the gap is worth closing.
  - Identify the environmental and individual sources of the gap and how they interact.
  - Specify feasible solutions that address the causes of the gap.

The LeaPS ID model and this text provide guidance and template examples to help IDs collect and analyze data related to each major ID project deliverable.

- *This text provides guidance to create learning and performance support materials that are culturally relevant and equitable.* "Diversity," "equity," and "inclusion" should be more than empty promises an organization makes about itself. In the Empathize & Analyze component, this text provides guidance for ensuring that a learning and environmental analysis includes representatives of all the learners, including those who are typically misrepresented or unrepresented in learning and development materials. The text also provides suggestions for developing and usability testing with a wider variety of contributors than previously recommended in our field.
- *The LeaPS ID model depicts instructional design as an iterative and scalable process.* ID models commonly use feedback loops to depict the iterative nature of instructional design. The inclusion of these loops hints at iteration as tryouts, collected data, and previous drafts of ID deliverables lead to revisions of subsequent deliverables. However, these models still appear linear in nature, and these loops don't indicate the deeply iterative nature of instructional design itself. The LeaPS ID model illustrates multiple iterations that can occur throughout an ID project, both within and across each component of the model.

This text also provides guidance regarding the scaling of ID and ID deliverables. This scaling process appears in initial training requirements analysis, in which IDs select appropriate training configurations based on the nature of the job tasks that learners will complete in the workplace. IDs might support tasks requiring "awareness" using information alone. IDs can support the performance of other workplace tasks with a job aid alone. Other tasks might require minimal training and a job aid. More complex tasks will require learner practice, coaching, and feedback using extensive training with job aids. Finally, IDs can create training that supports recall performance of job tasks—without any reference to a job aid. Each of these configurations reflects an increase in scale and larger organizational commitments to create, implement, and maintain the learning and performance support materials.

- *The LeaPS ID model depicts no required start or finish points.* The text allows for flexible project scopes. IDs in some contexts will create deliverables for each component of the LeaPS ID model. In other contexts, IDs will complete deliverables for just one or a few components of the LeaPS ID model. Where input from one component is already available and shared with an ID, that input can be used to inform another component that an ID might actually do work within. In other words, IDs can simply rely on shared or pre-existing input as needed and know what to hand off to the next project contributor.
- *The LeaPS ID model and the text depict typical deliverables for both non-instructional and instructional performance-based learning needs.* The text provides guidance about creating non-instructional solutions such as job aids and mentoring systems. The model also provides guidance for creating instructional designs suitable for both instructor-led and eLearning delivery.
- *The LeaPS ID model is based on the principles of "organizational justice" and "inclusive design"* (described in Chapter 1), which create added value through expanded collaboration that deliberately includes individuals from groups that have commonly not been included in the past. This expanded collaboration begins with empathizing and analyzing at the beginning of an ID and continues throughout the life of the project. This is a more humanistic approach—navigating away from a "design for" approach to a humanistic "design with" approach.

LOOKING AHEAD: WHERE RESEARCHERS AND PRACTITIONERS CAN GO NEXT

Future LeaPS ID Research

The LeaPS ID model is an attempt to synthesize performance-based ID practice with diversity, equity, and inclusion (DEI) initiatives in ways that produce culturally relevant and equitable interventions. Future LeaPS ID-related research could investigate and share more empirical evidence related to short-, mid-, and long-term outcomes of implementing a more inclusive and equitable approach to ID processes and the design of culturally relevant and just performance-based learning. A partial list of research questions appears below.

1. What are the outcomes of using more inclusive and equitable approaches in designing culturally relevant and just performance-based learning and support? Do projects following the LeaPS ID model provide more data supporting the principles of inclusive design and expanded collaboration?
2. To what extent do potentially higher costs for inclusive and collaborative analysis and design offset costs associated with:

i. *Intervention development*? The LeaPS ID model "front-loads" costs, with extra work occurring in both the Empathize & Analyze component and the Design portion of the Design & Develop component. To what extent does front-loading lead to decreased development and implementation costs in the longer term?

ii. *Skill transfer to the workplace*? The LeaPS ID model provides guidance for supporting the transfer of learned skills to the job. To what extent will IDs be able to obtain the organizational sponsorship required for clients, managers, and supervisors to provide coaching and feedback in ways that help learners apply and hone in the workplace what they learned in their learning experiences?

iii. *Sustained workplace performance across all learners*, including those who have been discriminated against in the past? Performance-based interventions are inherently disruptive. They teach people new ways to perform their job tasks and, in some cases, new job roles. To what extent will the more inclusive population who participate in LeaPS ID efforts accept new roles and ways of performing their jobs? What is an organization's return on investment for using the LeaPS ID model to create culturally relevant and equitable interventions?

Future LeaPS ID Model Practices

The LeaPS ID model is not a static model of instructional design; it's part of an ongoing evolution of ID practice itself. The model will continue to evolve over time as IDs face new pressures from organizations that are themselves facing new pressures from governments, economies, and cultures, along with changing project management practices. IDs will also continue to try out, modify, and adapt existing ID processes to advance culturally relevant, equitable, and inclusive organizational practices and learning designs.

We believe that several longer-term trends will affect future LeaPS ID model practices.

1. Rapidly changing contexts.
2. Agile project management.
3. Design thinking.
4. Artificial intelligence (AI).

Rapidly Changing World Systems

The term "VUCA" characterizes situations that are "volatile," "uncertain," "changing," and "ambiguous" (Bennett & Lemoine, 2014). This increasing turbulence affects governments, economies, and cultures. It also affects organizational systems by changing job tasks, the role of DEI, consulting practice, change management, and organizational culture itself. Horstmeyer (2018) notes that VUCA exerts pressure on learning and development (L&D) organizations. It diminishes their resources as it simultaneously increases demands for their services. She suggests that IDs can tackle VUCA challenges using a curious mindset consisting of inquisitiveness, creativity, openness, and disruption tolerance. She claims that this mindset will enable executives and their organizations to cultivate agility, a learning culture, and operational efficiencies.

Moving forwards, we believe that IDs will be spending more time and effort supporting operations of "learning organizations" (Craig et al., 2020). IDs will create learning experiences to help leaders build both their leadership and management skills. Burkett (2022a) argues that leaders should help build resilient teams that can bounce back from adversity even stronger. Leaders will need to provide perspective to reframe tension, ensure psychological safety, show appreciation and gratitude, prioritize well-being, and amplify management support. She also suggests (2022b) that leaders will need to build skills to lead change itself. She advocates a consistent focus on strengthening individual and organizational change, continuously improving leadership development, prioritizing communication skills, creating communities and networks, shifting mindsets and experiences, and monitoring change fatigue. In addition to supporting the organization, the L&D function itself will evolve. Noonan et al. (2017) contend that L&D should focus on the following enablers: learning curation, learning personalization, social learning, and learning modalities. All of this will require IDs to focus on complex cognitive skills such as collaborative problem-solving, creative brainstorming, continuous improvement for themselves and individuals at all levels in an organization.

Agile Project Management

Chapter 2 noted that ID project managers can use different project management frameworks. One framework is called "Waterfall." Using this framework, project teams typically complete one phase of a project before moving on to another. Project teams in other organizations may use an Agile project management framework. The practitioners of this project management framework have adopted a manifesto (Beedle et al., 2001) that promotes:

- Individuals and interactions over processes and tools.
- Working software over comprehensive documentation.
- Customer collaboration over contract negotiation.
- Responding to change over following a plan.

To meet the goals in the manifesto, Agile practitioners work iteratively, moving from one "sprint" to the next. In each sprint, the Agile team will plan, design, develop, test, deploy, and then review their efforts in a retrospective. The Project Management Institute (n.d.) notes that:

> Agile approaches to project management aim for early, measurable ROI [return on investment] through defined, iterative delivery of product increments. They feature continuous involvement of the customer throughout the product development cycle. Although Agile has its roots in software and IT, Agile adoption is growing and expanding in a wide range of industries.

Use of the Agile framework is growing. Flynn (2022) reports that at least 71 percent of companies in the United States are now using Agile. One reason is that Agile projects have a 64 percent success rate. In contrast, projects using the traditional Waterfall projects only have a 49 percent success rate. In general, companies that have adopted Agile project management have experienced an average 60 percent growth in revenue and profit.

Moving forwards, we believe that use of Agile will increase, and ID project managers and teams will need to get used to it. Given the benefits accruing to Agile, organizational leadership may be unwilling to let learning and development departments use its own waterfall approaches, especially if learning and development efforts are going to be tied to the innovation of new organizational capabilities that involve the organization's information technology groups—which increasingly use Agile.

Design Thinking

The LeaPS ID model draws from Design Thinking (Brown, 2008; d.school, 2010). In particular, the LeaPS ID model stresses the importance of empathizing with learners and other stakeholders in designing learning and performance support solutions. The LeaPS ID model also draws upon Design Thinking techniques, such as journey maps, personas, and prototypes. Design Thinking also emphasizes the testing—or tryouts—of iteratively created deliverables. Malamed (2020) recommends the use of Design Thinking in learning experience design.

Moving forwards, we believe that IDs will need to become more inclusive in their Design Thinking practice. Ackermann (2023) noted shortfallings of design thinking when designers empathize with others without actually including them in the design and implementation process.

Artificial Intelligence (AI)

James (2023) notes that the GPT3 neural network machine learning model in ChatGPT requires users to input only a small amount of text to generate large volumes of sophisticated and relevant AI-generated text. The GPT3 model surpasses any similar early models for producing text that appears like humans wrote it. Users have utilized ChatGPT to create articles, poetry, and news reports. Others have used it to produce written text that employs a specified author's mannerisms.

While the ChatGPT technology is relatively new, McMurtrie (2023) notes that this technology promises to transform how people write. She maintains, "Higher education, rarely quick about anything, is still trying to comprehend the scope of its likely impact on teaching—and how it should respond." In higher education settings, students can use this tool to complete course assignments to create essays, poems, contacts, lecture notes, and software code. Students could ask this software to formulate their posts in discussion boards or write their reports. In the fall of 2023, Dr. Giacumo had her instructional design students practice using ChatGPT to assist in the creation of many of the deliverables we describe in this book and discuss its limitations.

McMurtrie (2023) maintains that higher education's response to the disruption arising from this new technology is mixed. Some academics can see this, and similar tools based on artificial intelligence, as dangers to learning. They fear students will use these tools as shortcuts to the difficulties inherent in formulating original ideas, organizing their thoughts, or demonstrating their knowledge. They can see the use of this tool as "cheating." Rudolph, Tan, and Tan (2023) state that one of the earliest and more prevalent concerns about students using ChatGPT is that it threatens professors' use of essays as an assessment method. Academics worry about students outsourcing their written assignments to this software tool. And they worry that these essays will pass muster when examined by automated plagiarism detection tools. Such concerns may be rendered moot if Microsoft (owner of ChatGPT) includes it in the next release of their MS-Office software. Rudolph et al. (2023) report that some academics maintain that tools like ChatGPT will become as commonplace as calculators and computers.

Other academics see this technology as intriguing. McMurtrie (2023) reports that these academics can see students using this tool to draft essays, explain confusing ideas, and smooth out awkward first drafts. These academics also argue that it's their responsibility to prepare students to use these technologies in the workplace and in everyday life. Rudolph et al. (2023) note that ChatGPT can help students learn via experimentation and experience. They recommend that academics alter their use of written assessments. Academics can avoid using assignments and examinations "that are so formulaic that nobody could tell if a computer completed them" (p. 14). Instead, they recommend using assessments that foster students' critical thinking and creativity.

Turning to instructional design in particular, James (2023) argues that ChatGPT could challenge learning content production by removing humans from much of the process. Users could simply use this tool to pose their own questions about how to respond in specific situations. He does see a significant opportunity to use ChatGPT's ability to be trained. He foresees ID teams large and small training this tool to use internal organizational data to contextualize learning and development. He suggests that this tool could be trained to understand the dynamics of a specific organizational culture, its customers, its team dynamics, and implicit expectations. Users could then employ this now-contextualized tool to answer questions, obtain advice, and provide guidance about achieving their desired outcomes.

AI is developing rapidly. ChatGPT is one example of AI that could influence the future of IDs and the work they do. We foresee that other AI tools could be similarly disruptive, changing the nature of ID work while opening new opportunities. IDs could conceivably find themselves part of efforts involving:

- Recommender systems (used on Netflix) to produce individualized learning paths for new employees and career paths for experienced ones.
- Advanced analytics to provide better information for measuring the effect of learning and performance support on the organization—and how to improve its impact.
- Chatbots and online tutors to promote learning at a lower cost than other eLearning approaches.
- Other forms of AI tools for creating digital graphics and voice-overs.

Much has already appeared in the literature regarding the rise of AI and its effects on DEI, Design Justice, and Organizational justice. Recently, Watkins and Human (2023) noted that practitioners and researchers in our field have a role in ensuring that AI conceptual boundaries, or what people can imagine AI to do, evolve in a way that ethically and equitably serves human needs. Without this deliberate work, AI applications may be profitable but likely shortsighted thus putting societal, organizational, and individual needs in conflict, and increasing existing inequities. For example, thoughtful AI approaches combined with non-AI approaches can augment individual learning and performance (Yorks et al., 2020), AI algorithms can be programmed to prevent bias by discounting physical attributes, specific behaviors, and affinities in documentation reviews (Jora et al., 2022). However, when AI efforts are focused at supporting individual learning and performance, they also cost organizational learning and systems development by funneling finite human resources away from systems-level work (Wilkens, 2020), which can affect issues of equity. AI itself is a tool with limited capacity. It can provide L&D support based on previously documented explicit knowledge and not tacit knowledge, social norms, or values (Wilkens, 2020). This means that diverse cultural perspectives, voices, and associated outputs, which have been historically missing from products created by researchers and practitioners, are often missing from AI outputs (Jora et al., 2022). Thus, it's imperative that IDs become familiar with the potential of AI tools in consideration for use in interventions to help ensure inclusive and equitable interventions.

REFLECTION QUESTIONS

- This chapter has briefly described four emerging trends that the authors feel will impact ID practice.

  - Rapidly changing contexts.
  - Agile project management.
  - Design thinking.
  - Artificial intelligence.

  What other trends have you noticed? Why are they important?

- What changes related to these trends have you noticed within your workplace? Have they influenced your work, as an ID or in any other job?
- How have you experienced AI, including and excluding diverse expert voices, colleagues, and learners, in your organization?

REFERENCES

Ackermann, R. (2023, February 9). Design thinking was supposed to fix the world. Where did it go wrong? *MIT Technology Review*. https://www.technologyreview.com/2023/02/09/1067821/design-thinking-retrospective-what-went-wrong/

Beedle, M., van Bennekum, A., Cockburn, A., Cunningham, W., Fowler, M., Highsmith, J., Hunt, A., Jeffries, R., Kern, J., Marick, B., Martin, R. C., Schwaber, K., Sutherland, J., & Thomas, D. (2001). *Manifesto for Agile Software Development.* https://agilemanifesto.org/

Bennett, N., & Lemoine, G. J. (2014). What VUCA really means for you. *Harvard Business Review*, 92(1/2), 27. https://hbr.org/2014/01/what-vuca-really-means-for-you

Brown, T. (2008). Design thinking. *Harvard Business Review*, 86(6), 84–92. https://hbr.org/2008/06/design-thinking

Burkett, H. (2022a, March 29). Building team resilience at the speed of change. *Talent Management*. https://www.talentmgt.com/articles/2022/03/29/building-team-resilience-at-the-speed-of-change-%EF%BF%BC/

Burkett, H. (2022b, August 2). Building change leadership from the ground up. *Talent Management.* https://www.talentmgt.com/articles/2022/08/02/building-change-leadership-from-the-ground-up/

Craig, S. D., Li, S., Prewitt, D., Morgan, L. A., & Schroeder, N. L. (2020). *Science of learning and readiness (SoLaR) exemplar report: A path toward learning at scale.* Defense Technical Information Center. https://apps.dtic.mil/sti/pdfs/AD1104999.pdf

Dick, W., Carey, L., & Carey, J. O. (2005). *The systematic design of instruction* (6th ed.). Pearson.

d.school. (2010). *Bootcamp bootleg.* http://dschool.typepad.com/files/bootcampbootleg2010.pdf

Flynn, J. (2022, November 27). *16 amazing Agile statistics [2023]: What companies use Agile methodology.* https://www.zippia.com/advice/agile-statistics/#:~:text=Conclusion,U.S.%20 companies%20using%20it%20today.

Guerra, I. J. (2003). Key competencies required of performance improvement professionals. *Performance Improvement Quarterly, 16*(1), 55–72. doi:10.1111/j.1937–8327.2003.tb00272.x

Gustafson, K. L., & Branch, R. M. (1997). *Survey of instructional development models* (3rd ed.). http://www.eric.ed.gov/ERICWebPortal/detail?accno=ED411780

Gustafson, K. L., & Branch, R. M. (2002). *Survey of instructional development models* (4th ed.). https://eric.ed.gov/?q=gustafson%2c+kent&id=ED477517

Horstmeyer, A. (2018). How VUCA is changing the learning landscape—and how curiosity can help. *Development and Learning in Organizations, 33*(1), 5–8. doi:10.1108/DLO-09–2018–0119

James, D. (2023, February 24). Mediocrity is over: The ChatGPT threat to average instructional design. *Forbes.* https://www.forbes.com/sites/forbeshumanresourcescouncil/2023/02/24/mediocrity-is-over-the-chatgpt-threat-to-average-instructional-design/?sh=68f33fb63109

Jonassen, D. H. (2004). *Learning to solve problems.* John Wiley & Sons.

Jora, R. B., Sodhi, K. K., Mittal, P., & Saxena, P. (2022, March). Role of artificial intelligence (AI) in meeting diversity, equality and inclusion (DEI) goals. In *2022 8th International Conference on Advanced Computing and Communication Systems (ICACCS)* (Vol. 1, pp. 1687–1690). IEEE. doi:10.1109/ICACCS54159.2022.9785266

Malamed, C. (2020). How to use design thinking in learning experience design. *The eLearning Coach.* https://theelearningcoach.com/elearning_design/design-thinking-for-instructional-design/

McMurtrie, B. (2023, March 6). ChatGPT is everywhere: Love it or hate it, academics can't ignore the already pervasive technology. *Chronicle of Higher Education.* https://www.chronicle.com/article/chatgpt-is-already-upending-campus-practices-colleges-are-rushing-to-respond?

Molenda, M. (2003). In search of the elusive ADDIE model. *Performance Improvement, 42*(5), 34–36. doi:10.1002/pfi.4930420508

Morrison, G. R., Ross, S. M., & Kemp, J. E. (2007). *Designing effective instruction* (5th ed.). John Wiley & Sons.

Noonan, M., Richter, G., Durham, L., & Pierce, E. (2017). Learning and the digital workplace: What? So what? Now what? *Strategic HR Review, 16*(6), 267–273. doi:10.1108/SHR-09–2017–0061

Project Management Institute (n.d.). *Agile practices.* https://www.pmi.org/learning/featured-topics/agile

Rudolph, J., Tan, S., & Tan, S. (2023). ChatGPT: Bullshit spewer or the end of traditional assessments in higher education? *Journal of Applied Learning and Teaching, 6*(1), 1–22. doi:10.37074/jalt.2023.6.1.9

Smith, P. L., & Ragan, T. J. (2005). *Instructional design* (3rd ed.). John Wiley & Sons.

Stone, D., & Villachica, S. (2005). *Want reliable metrics for your organization? Use prototyping!* [conference session]. ISPI Instructional Systems Conference, Las Vegas, NV, United States.

Van Tiem, D., Moseley, J. L., & Dessinger, J. C. (2001). *Fundamentals of performance technology: A guide to improving people, process, and performance* (1st ed.). Silver Spring, MD: International Society for Performance Improvement.

Villachica, S. W., Marker, A., & Taylor, K. (2010). But what do they really expect? Employer perceptions of the skills of entry-level instructional designers. *Performance Improvement Quarterly, 22*(4), 33–51. doi:10.1002/piq.20067

Watkins, R., & Human, S. (2023). Needs-aware artificial intelligence: AI that "serves [human] needs." *AI and Ethics*, 3(1), 49–52. doi:10.1007/s43681-022-00181-5

Wilkens, U. (2020). Artificial intelligence in the workplace—A double-edged sword. *The International Journal of Information and Learning Technology*, 37(5), 253–265. doi:10.1108/IJILT-02–2020–0022

Yorks, L., Rotatori, D., Sung, S., & Justice, S. (2020). Workplace reflection in the age of AI: Materiality, technology, and machines. *Advances in Developing Human Resources*, 22(3), 308–319. doi:10.1177/1523422320927299

Glossary

Advance organizer. An instructional technique to connect what learners already know to what they will be learning. The advance organizer must present the new information at "a higher level of abstraction than the new content itself. [It] may be represented visually or verbally by a picture, diagram, story, chart, or oral description" (Bruegge & Widlake, 2001, p. 179).

Affinity groups. A deliberate and often cultivated structure where groups of people sharing common identity group characteristics, interests, or goals, come together in a flat or hierarchical organization. These groups can allow individuals from diverse backgrounds to influence more inclusive and equitable policies, practices, and innovation; access networking opportunities across functional departments; access informal mentoring relationships (Geist, 2023). Some organizations nurture these groups to meet organizational goals and strategic outcomes related to social responsibility, organizational justice (e.g., policies, procedures, interactions), talent development (e.g., knowledge, skills, abilities, competencies), or retention (i.e., attitudes, relationships). Affinity groups can foster diversity, equity, and inclusion by giving group members a collective voice (Hirsch, 2021).

Analyze. To inform an approach to an ID project by collecting multiple data points, aggregating them, and making meaning of them.

Assessment strategies. The different types of assessments IDs might incorporate into an instructional environment (e.g., performance assessments, knowledge assessments).

Assessments. The way an instructor or eLearning will determine if learners have built the desired knowledge, skills, capabilities. IDs create assessments that enable learners to show they have met specified standards for performing their job tasks. IDs can also aggregate assessment results across groups of learners to conduct either formative or summative evaluations to reveal where instructional strategies have fallen short, or where additional practice and feedback could be useful.

Authentic assessment. Learners are required to "demonstrate their ability to analyze the task and synthesize, from the range of skills and knowledge that they have acquired, those which will be necessary for the completion of a specific outcome, where the approach to the potentially correct response may not always be clear cut or obvious" (Ashford-Rowe, Herrington, & Brown, 2014). Authentic assessments measure the performance of learners performing their job tasks—or as close as possible.

Blueprint. A type of design document used in eLearning projects that documents the ID team's design decisions. It communicates the features and functions of the completed eLearning. It serves as a reference ensuring the team applies the same design rules as the blueprint. Design blueprints often contain these components: project specifications, course features and components, design strategies, technical specifications, and other relevant information such as relevant individuals' names and schedule information (ELDAPT Instructure, 2022).

Change management. "The application of a structured process and set of tools for leading the people side of change to achieve a desired outcome" (Prosci, n.d.). A change is the project, initiative, or solution being introduced in the organization to improve the way work gets done, solve a problem, or take advantage of an opportunity (Prosci, nd).

Chunking. Some instructional design work is figuring out how to split large amounts of content into smaller, bite-sized pieces and what pieces to fit together.

Coaching. Ongoing relationships that facilitate an already competent learner achieving a specific professional goal or objective, performance-based management tasks, or leadership effectiveness. Coaching can also be the provision of real-time error detection and correction as learners are practicing job tasks in an instructional setting.

Cognitive apprenticeship. An instructional approach for teaching cognitive skills that are otherwise invisible (Collins, Brown, & Holum, 1991). Provides guidance for creating learning environments composed of content, method, sequence, and methodology. Suggests characteristics for each dimension. Cognitive apprenticeships facilitate cognitive and metacognitive learning experiences that may gradually increase in complexity through expert demonstration or modeling, coaching, and faded support in authentic contexts (Arianto & Nikmah, 2017).

Communities of Practice (CoPs). Groups of people who are informally bound together by shared expertise and passion for a joint enterprise. Some CoPs meet regularly. Others communicate asynchronously. People in CoPs "share their experiences and knowledge in free-flowing, creative ways that foster new approaches to problems" (Wenger & Snyder, 2000).

Contextualized learning. This builds job skills by situating them in workplace practice. Essentially, learners build workplace skills by practicing them in a safe and authentic learning environment. Because the context of the learning environment matches the context of the workplace environment, learners will be able to apply their learned skills in ways that should meet organizational standards. To create contextualized learning and performance support materials, IDs should collaborate with clients, learners, supervisors, managers, and stakeholders, who can represent, include, and advocate for the diverse identities of the intended learner population experience.

Continuous improvement. "Continuous improvement, sometimes called continual improvement, is the ongoing improvement of products, services or processes through incremental and breakthrough improvements. These efforts can seek 'incremental' improvement over time or 'breakthrough' improvement all at once" (American Society for Quality, n.d.).

Critical tasks. The tasks—or specific parts of tasks—that an L&D intervention will address. These critical tasks are often first identified in needs assessments and in client conversations when clients request an L&D intervention. IDs iteratively refine these critical tasks throughout the E&A component.

Culturally responsive design. Choices that designers make, ideally in partnership, or input, with learners of diverse cultural backgrounds to feel included, affirmed, or represented, in various environments (e.g., organizations, communities, products, services) (Garner et al., 2023).

Culture. "Culture should be regarded as the set of distinctive spiritual, material, intellectual and emotional features of society or a social group, and that it encompasses, in addition to art and literature, lifestyles, ways of living together, value systems, traditions and beliefs" (UNESCO, 2001). This "includes knowledge, beliefs, arts, morals, laws, customs, and any other capabilities and habits acquired by [a human] as a member of society" (Government of Samoa, 2019). Dickson-Deane et al. (2018, p. 310) remind us that it "is not merely a proxy for race, minoritized or marginalized communities, or any singular aspect." Culture is a combination of our identities and the identities of organizations that informs our human perspective and is imbued in learning environments and technology (Dickson-Deane, 2023).

Curated content repositories. A collection of informational resources relating to a topic or domain, that have been manually or machine-selected, organized, and managed, to facilitate just-in-time learning and performance support. Individual items in the repositories are sometimes recommended, reviewed, or rated by users. Such repositories are also called "information systems" and "knowledge bases."

Design. The process of using outputs from the Empathize & Analyze phase as inputs to plan for the actual development of materials and files used by learners and other stakeholders such as instructors or administrators. Design involves planning and depicting the look and functions of the learning and performance support materials.

Design affordances. The possible abilities enabled by the design of a learning or performance support environment, thus determining the possible actions a potential learner can take (Bower, 2008).

Design deliverables. Documents that IDs create during the design phase and submit to clients and project stakeholders for review, testing, and approval.

Design disaffordances. The abilities that are prohibited by the design of a learning or performance support environment, thus limiting the possible actions a potential learner can take.

Design document: provides plans, graphics, specifications, and samples to show the look and workings of the instruction, largely before it is built or made.

Design thinking. A method IDs use to generate empathy for learners; bring learners into the collaborative design process; iteratively frame a problem; try out prototypes; and create innovative and effective learning, instructional, and performance interventions (Rogers, 2003; Svihla, 2017). "Design thinking" can guide all aspects of a learning and performance support project, from the initial analysis through development and implementation.

Development. The process of building the actual learning and performance support materials that learners will use to complete their learning experiences.

Disaggregated data. "Data that can be broken down and analyzed by race, ethnicity, gender, disability, income, veteran status, age, or other key demographic variables"

(Equitable Data Working Group, 2022). These data enable ID teams and stakeholders to understand the ways in which people who belong to multiple underserved and underrepresented populations can experience discrimination or disadvantage.

Distractors. The "wrong answer" items that appear in a multiple-choice question. Ideally, each distractor should represent a common misconception and provide feedback to correct it.

Diversity. When a group of people comprises individuals from different backgrounds including: socioeconomic status, cultures, ethnicities, genders, abilities, orientations, ages, nationalities, languages, and religious, thereby exhibiting a multitude of both similarities and differences amongst all individuals (Mulu & Zewdie, 2021).

Downstream stakeholders. Stakeholders inside or outside the organization who are customers receiving outputs (products or services) that other groups in the organization produce.

Electronic Performance Support System (EPSS). "A computer-based system that improves worker productivity by providing on-the-job access to integrated information, advice, and learning experiences" (Raybould, 1990, p. 4).

Empathize. To care for the learners, users, and stakeholders, recognizing their emotional and body responses to situations as indicators of each person's unique experience. Trying to understand learning and performance support experiences through the eyes of the learners, users, and stakeholders, knowing many will have very different experiences, rather than understanding only through one's own ID eyes and one's own personal lived experience.

Empathy. The ability to perceive or understand others' emotions and perspectives (Baaki et al., 2021; Melo et al., 2020).

Empathy mapping. A facilitation technique IDs can use to collaborate with learners to build and articulate insights into learners' experiences, motivations, and wishes (Boller, 2022).

Equity. Consistent, systematic, fair, just, impartial, treatment of all individuals, which ensures access to resources and process-enabling opportunities to succeed and grow, including those who belong to underserved communities, regardless of their demographic, sociocultural, ethnic, gender, abilities, orientations, religious backgrounds, rural location, or socioeconomic status (Looney, 2021; Diversity, Equity, and Inclusion Definitions, 2023).

Fidelity. How closely learning designs and learning environments represent authentic performance contexts. Expert learners and performers can sometimes do better with lower fidelity. Novice learners and performers often do better with higher fidelity. However, the degree to which that's an accurate statement is dependent on the level of complexity and factors associated with any given specific intended learner and performance context.

Formal instructional events. Components of units, lessons, modules, courses, sessions, and other organized events that an instructor, mentor, eLearning, coach, facilitator, or technology delivers. These components can include presenting the purpose or problem, activating prior learning, demonstration, practice and feedback, and integration of learning into the workplace.

Formal learning environments. The structured and organized contexts where instructional strategies are implemented to help learners build new knowledge, skills, abilities in ways that meet specified performance requirements. These environments also contain specific systems for learner accountability and assessment.

Formative evaluation. The process of obtaining feedback from clients, subject matter experts (SMEs), learners, trainers, supervisors, managers, and other stakeholders to guide ongoing project activities. IDs then use this feedback to make revisions and iterate L&D interventions, making them more engaging and effective (McDonald & West, 2020).

High-level and detailed design documents. Complex solutions like learning and performance ecosystems often require two sets of design documents to adequately describe these solutions for the clients, ID teams, learners/users, SMEs, and other stakeholders who will create, implement, and maintain them. In these situations, a high-level design document describes the major components of the ecosystem and how users will interact with them. This document may also describe the development and integration of these components into a system that satisfies the performance and technical requirements for the ecosystem project. Detailed design documents for each major component describe their contents, operation, development, and testing in greater detail.

ID roles. IDs can potentially play many roles during Design & Development. The Association for Talent Development (ATD, n.d.) states that an instructional designer: "applies learning theory and a systemic approach to design and develop content, learning activities, training, and other solutions to support the acquisition of new knowledge or real-world skills. Instructional designers develop all instructional materials of a training program, including presentation materials, participant guides, handouts, and job aids or other resources. They are also responsible for evaluating training, including assessing what was learned and whether the learning solution led to measurable behavior change. Prior to course design and development, an instructional designer conducts a needs assessment."

ID templates. They are reusable forms that IDs use again and again, typically created by senior IDs and project managers. Template files are formatted with the appropriate styles with blanks or placeholder text where IDs can insert the information relevant to a given project deliverable (Wiley, 2022).

Implementation (rollout). Planning and executing the logistics and resources required to deliver instructional and non-instructional learning experiences to learners and ensure the adoption of newly learned skills, knowledge, and performance support in the workplace.

In-person classroom instruction. Traditional instructor-facilitated learning interventions that occur in a classroom.

Inclusion. Promotion, appreciation, and integration of all people regardless of identities and characteristics, which welcomes everyone so they feel valued, respected, and supported by organizational processes and resource allocation (Kuknor & Bhattacharya, 2021; Diversity, Equity, and Inclusion Definitions, 2023).

Informal learning environments. Contexts that prioritize self-selected observations, curated content, discovery, community-based or network activities, and social interactions, within which learners develop new knowledge, skills, and build competencies, to do their work and become more effective in an organization.

Information dumps. The Cambridge Dictionary defines information dumps as "The practice of giving too much information at the same time, or a piece of writing that does this" (Cambridge Dictionary, n.d).

Inputs. People, resources (e.g., money, time, materials, tools, technology), and activities used to complete parts of a process.

Instruction. "A set of events or activities presented in a structured or planned way, through one or more media, with the goal of having learners achieve prespecified behaviors" (Dick, Carey, & Carey, 2004).

Instructional design (ID) projects. Planned pieces of work in which instructional designers clarify opportunities, plan for, create, implement, or maintain learning and performance support materials for learners in a given organization.

Instructional materials. Any materials that support a formal learning intervention. They can include participant guides, instructor guides, eLearning, online courses, curated content, slide decks, videos, etc.

Instructional strategies. The ways an instructor, mentor, coach, some other individual, or eLearning will facilitate learners' building new knowledge, skills, abilities.

Instructor guides. Standardized materials to support the instruction an instructor facilitates in traditional classrooms, virtual classrooms, and on the job. In this case, standardized means aligned with learning objectives and also usable by different instructors with varying levels of experience. Use of instructor guides helps ensure a given course produces standard learning outcomes from one instructor to the next. Instructor guides are generally professionally packaged for easy handoff, for use during instructor-led events, and usually include a review of the learning objectives, domain information, scripts, prompts, activities, facilitation, and guidance.

Intersectional bias. Bias that is found when looking at subgroups of samples defined by two or more identity features in nexus when compared with a reference group (Russell, Szendey, & Kaplan, 2021).

Intersectional learner subgroups. A group of intended learners who share the same intersectional demographic and differ from other groups who share different demographics (e.g., Black women, Black men, white women, white men) (Costanza-Chock, 2020).

Iterative design process. An approach to design in which IDs make revisions to an existing deliverable as new information becomes available and collaborators bring new ideas into the project. This iteration incrementally changes and improves ID project deliverables.

Iterative ID processes. Verstegen, Barnard, and Pilot (2006) contend that iteration involves IDs returning to a design activity they have already worked on before to correct errors and improve the design of project deliverables. Using an iterative process, IDs design a piece of a project deliverable, submit it to others for review and/or testing, and use the resulting data to revise the deliverable. They may then repeat these steps several times, until the deliverable seems to meet the needs of clients, learners, and project stakeholders.

Job aids ("cheat sheets"). An external standardized device that can enhance memory and reduce guesswork, guiding individuals' performance in organizations with just-in-time information (Mutambo, Shumba, & Hlongwana, 2021). When provided as a component of instructional systems they "provide information to support per-formers on specific job-related tasks" (Willmore, 2018). Common formats include reminders, model, step, checklist, worksheet or template, process table or flow-chart, decision table, troubleshooting diagram, data array, scripts, or combinations of these formats.

Job shadowing. Learners follow a more experienced performer as they perform their job tasks.

Journey map. "A journey map is a visualization of the process that a person goes through in order to accomplish a goal. In its most basic form, journey mapping starts by compiling a series of user actions into a timeline. Next, the timeline is fleshed out with user thoughts and emotions in order to create a narrative. This narrative is condensed and polished, ultimately leading to a visualization" (Gib-bons, 2018). In ID settings, journey maps commonly depict either a process a learner completes in a workplace setting or a learning experience that a learner completes.

Just-in-time learning. When individuals are able to immediately access and apply learn-ing experiences in their job tasks.

Knowledge workers. Employees who think for a living. Their job tasks involve sup-porting processes, where they recognize situations, make complex decisions, and solve problems. Their main capital is knowledge (Gao et al., 2020). Examples include programmers, physicians, pharmacists, architects, engineers, scientists, design thinkers, public accountants, lawyers, editors, and academics. Line workers who can shut down an assembly line and serve on quality teams are performing knowl-edge work. Owing to the nature of their work, knowledge workers can often benefit from performance support solutions.

Learning and performance ecosystem. Also called "learning ecosystems." The space where learners access information and generate knowledge or build competencies derived from multiple experiences, including formal and informal learning activi-ties as well as performance support systems that are meaningfully selected, inten-tional, curated, interconnected, diverse, authentic, cooperative, and constructive (Bannan, Dabbaugh, & Walcutt, 2019). In organizations, learning ecosystems can be facilitated for learners in partnership with their advisors, mentors and/or man-agers. They can be conceptualized by learning and development professionals in partnership with input from stakeholders ranging from learners to line managers, and executive leaders.

Learning management system (LMS). "[A] powerful training and professional devel-opment software resource that organizations of all sizes can incorporate . . .. Many LMS platforms are hosted in the cloud, allowing for remote access. An LMS com-bines database management within a digital framework to manage curricula, training materials, evaluation tools, course scheduling, regulatory compliance and more" (Uzialko, 2023). LMS software enables organizations to provide learning, development, and training while monitoring learner progress.

Learning portal. "[A] learning portal is a centralized digital hub through which employees can access eLearning content and other important resources. These edu-cational hubs allow learning and development (L&D) teams to provide consistent, engaging, and high-quality training materials for employees to complete when it works best for them" (Gupta, 2023).

Learning resources. Any inputs that enable learners' control of their own knowledge, skills, and competencies acquisition. These can include but are not limited to professional learning and development plans, content repositories, personal learning networks.

Logistics. Planning, implementing, and maintaining the flow of goods, services, and information, from origin to end users (Ahrens et al., 2015).

Maintenance. The process to ensure learning and performance support materials remain current after they've been initially implemented. ID teams work with other stakeholders to collect data regarding potential updates to the learning and performance support materials, make decisions about what to update, report the decisions, revise the materials, formatively evaluate the materials, and release the revised materials. The maintenance process starts anew with each release.

Mentoring. Ongoing relationships that facilitate general organizational acumen, positive attitudes, and psychosocial (e.g., principles, metacognition) skills growth, which are often nurtured by organizations to meet organizational goals and strategic outcomes related to knowledge management, talent development (e.g., knowledge, skills, abilities, competencies), or retention (i.e., attitudes, relationships) (Giacumo, Chen, & Seguinot-Cruz, 2020).

Microlearning. A short, concise learning unit that can often be used by individuals in job settings.

Minimum viable product (MVP). An early, basic version of a learning experience that will meet the minimum necessary requirements. Given feedback from clients, learners, and other stakeholders, the organization could then adapt and improve the product as needed in the future (EnSpire Oxford, 2022).

Mobile performance support system (MPSS). "A mobile system with information, tools, methodology, and perspectives to provide easy access to workers with minimal help from others" (Huang & Klein, 2023, p. 150). MPSSs employ portable technologies such as handheld and wearable devices that are small and easy to carry. They connect to wireless networks to exchange data with other systems.

Multifaceted intervention programs. A collection of multiple interventions, which may be both instructional and non-instructional, that are required to adequately support learners' knowledge and skill development.

Needs assessment. A process to determine gaps between current and desired organizational systems performance, whether they are worth closing, their corresponding root causes, and potential solution sets that align with the root causes.

Non-extractive design. Sustainable co-design methods that create value for a community, and its members, centers their needs, builds on their existing solutions, recognizes their contributions, provides economic rewards, builds their capacity, incorporates concrete mechanisms for community accountability, produces outputs that are effective and maintainable (Costanza-Chock, 2020).

Organizational communities of practice. A deliberate and often cultivated learning structure where a group of people share their functional practices, so they can learn to do better (Nithithanatchinnapat et al., 2016) and may exist within one organization or across multiple organizations (Mavri, Ioannou, & Loizides, 2021).

Organizational culture. "A set of shared values, beliefs, and key understandings among members that influence work patterns and organizational management patterns" (Tarmizi, Lian, & Puspita, 2021, p. 110).

Organizational justice theory. A theory that can be used to measure organizational members' perception of the level of fair treatment they've received, equitable access to resources, and transparent processes (Greenberg, 1987). It's often modeled with three constructs: procedural justice (e.g., outcomes or decisions regarding policies, procedures, processes), distributive justice (e.g., resource access and allocation, equity, needs), and interactional justice (e.g., relationships, respect, dignity) (Greenberg, 1990).

Participant guides. Materials to support learners in standardized learning environments. They are generally professionally packaged and can include job aids, learning activities, references, and logistical information.

Performance assessments. A collection of performance criteria usually associated with specific knowledge and skills that, when applied to a performance, can determine the level to which one has demonstrated mastery (McGrath & Navarro, 2022).

Performance gap. A discrepancy between the way the organizational system is performing and the way the organization leaders would like it to perform. Ideally, IDs only create learning and performance support materials to aid knowledge and skill development or provide adequate guidance, when they are inadequate or missing from the organizational L&D system and it's a root cause of the performance gap.

Performance support. A tool, or process, or system, that helps people learn something, or do something (e.g., perform a task, make a decision), or remember something, exactly when they need it.

Performance support system (PSS). "An optimized body of coordinated online and offline methods and resources that enable and maintain a person's or an organization's performance. The goal is to give performers what they need, when they need it, and in the form in which they need it so that they perform in a way that consistently meets organizational objectives" (Villachica & Stone, 1999, pp. 443–444).

Personal learning networks. Flexible learning contexts deployable in organizations, which center the learner, integrate project-based learning, progress based on learners' performance, allow for coaching, are facilitated through online social knowledge exchanges, incorporate recommender algorithms, and are usually located on an LMS or social media tool (Fake & Dabbagh, 2020).

Personas. Fictional representations of different types of learners, that represent intended groups of learners. Personas depict learner knowledge, skills, attitudes about a given job task, and any associated learning and performance support materials. Schmidt and Tawfik (2022) share a persona example with a name, role, quote, demographic information, goals, attitudes, behaviors, motivations, and barriers.

Processes. A series of repeatable steps, actions, or procedures, taken to achieve a goal, change, or purpose.

Project budget. An aggregated set of costs for completing each task specified in a project scope by the deadlines specified in the project schedule. Project managers calculate the cost of each task by multiplying the hourly rate the ID completing it is paid by the estimated time to complete the task. The total budget reflects the aggregated costs of completing all the tasks in the project scope.

Project deliverables. Plans, reports, draft materials, or other tangible things (either print or electronic), given to clients at various points during the project. IDs create project deliverables for clients and other project stakeholders to review and approve.

Project scale. The overall size and complexity of ID projects and their budgets can range between small, medium, and large. Depending on the scale of a given project, IDs may use all or parts of the LeaPS ID model. A given project may involve many project deliverables, iterations, and formative evaluation feedback loops, or very few. They may use many formative evaluation techniques or a few. They may work with a large cast of people playing different project roles or a few.

Project schedule. An aggregated set of dates on which IDs will start and end project-related tasks. The schedule can also specify when IDs submit deliverables for review, testing, and approval. Ultimately, a project schedule needs to provide an adequate amount of time to complete the project scope and meet the needs of the sponsor, client, and organization.

Project scope. The collection of tasks required to complete a given ID project, listed roughly in their order of completion during the project. Because ID projects vary in size, the number of tasks in a given project scope will also vary.

Prototype. A first draft of some object, tool, or technology, that may be semi-functional, semi-complete, or even fully functional, used to demo a design concept and test it with users.

Quizzes. A form of knowledge assessment intended to provide feedback regarding comprehension and basic application of conceptual knowledge.

Scope creep. An undesirable project management situation where the number of tasks in the project scope have unexpectedly increased, the quality of the deliverables has increased, the actual time to complete the tasks has exceeded the estimated time, or the cost of completing the project has exceeded the budget. Scope creep breaks both project budgets and project schedules, resulting in missed deadlines for project deliverables and cost overruns.

Scripts. Used in creating eLearning and videos, scripts provide an outline of the program in the form of program title, section titles, and often slide titles. They specify the audio voice-over and the on-screen text that coordinates with the voice-over script. They may also contain notes about any graphics, text related to helping the viewer find their way through the program, and other text relevant to any viewer interactions (eLearning Art, n.d.).

Self-assessments. A form of knowledge assessment that learners can use to reflect on their own past, current, or future understanding and performance.

Sequencing. Some instructional design work is figuring out what content chunks and support systems learners need to access and in what order.

Situated learning. A social process in which learners co-construct the norms, behaviors, values, relationships, and contextual understanding that are required to participate in an organization and make authentic decisions according to their roles (Lave & Wenger, 1991). In other words, adults learn to authentically perform job tasks, or make authentic decisions in a safe learning environment by performing the tasks themselves. This can be achieved through a variety of learning activities such as simulations, case studies, project-based learning approaches, or cognitive apprenticeships.

Skill transfer. When individuals use what they learned previously in new settings. Transfer can occur from one module in a curriculum to the next and between training and the workplace. For L&D interventions to improve performance, they must transfer to the workplace.

Stakeholders. In organizations, "stakeholders" have an interest in the overall organization or intervention. They are either involved in or affected by the actions the organization takes or intervention. They have a voice in determining whether interventions the organization implements are successful or not. They may also be people in the organization who have a voice in determining whether a given ID project is successful. Some stakeholders are upstream—the suppliers. For example, they can be the supervisors and managers of the learners or the people who supply the things that learners use to perform their job tasks. Upstream stakeholders could also include a sponsor and client's bosses—as well as the people in the organization's executive suite. Other stakeholders can be downstream—the receivers. They can be recipients of the work products that learners produce—or the organization's customers.

Storyboard. A graphic organizer that guides development of video or multimedia. It often includes scene or slide content-sensitive titles, story sequencing, text for any required script, and mock-up images or simple text descriptions of visual content. It can also include functionality instructions for learner interactions, usability, accessibility, and objectives, as needed. The fidelity may be low (e.g., mostly text, some functionality indicated), moderate (e.g., multimedia that's more fleshed out, likely semi-functioning), or high (e.g., includes all information necessary for someone else to fully develop the final object).

Structured on-the-job learning (SOJT). Planned instructor-facilitated learning interventions that occur in the workplace setting. The instructor works with individual or small groups of learners to facilitate all learning activities on the job (Jacobs, 2003; Smith, 2018). Learners often receive crafted explanations or demonstrations from instructors who are successful performers, while they are performing critical tasks in an authentic environment. The instructors also provide opportunities for practice and coaching. Learners then try to imitate more-experienced behaviors through trial and error (van Pamel, 2013). The instructors use checklists to verify learners can perform tasks in ways that meet specified criteria (van Pamel, 2013).

Summative evaluation. A way to determine value in instructional, non-instructional, and performance support materials, learners, instructors, instructional strategies, facilities, or the L&D function itself (Tshilongamulenzhe, Coetzee, & Masenge, 2013). Summative evaluations answer questions regarding "how good is it?" or "did it meet our needs?"

Task characteristics. Information that provides a high-level overview of a given workplace task or set of tasks. Information may include critical tasks, goals, cues, resources, task frequency, task duration, standards, prerequisite skills, and what is critical/difficult/complex about task performance.

Task list. A hierarchically decomposed list of activities comprising a given workplace job task, consisting of tasks, subtasks, steps, and additional information about key steps.

Templates. Blueprints or patterns that can guide actions required to design or develop something. They can save lots of time when designing and building standardized L&D interventions by providing parameters for creativity.

Tryout. An implementation of a prototype or full version or an object, tool, or technology, with a small group of potential intended users with the goal to observe actual performance and make improvements.

Unstructured on-the-job training (UOJT). An unplanned instructional solution where learners receive impromptu explanations or demonstrations from more experienced employees. Learners then try to imitate more-experienced behaviors through trial and error (van Pamel, 2013). Unstructured OJT can arise organically as learners seek out help from others doing similar work. This approach is sometimes called "Work with Joe."

Upstream stakeholders. Stakeholders inside or outside the organization who either provide inputs that a given group in an organization uses to create a product or service for customers either inside or outside the organization; or leadership that sets direction, manages, and monitors the performance of subordinates in the organization.

Virtual classroom instruction. Instructor-facilitated learning interventions that occur using video conferencing software such as Zoom or MS-Teams, enabling remote learners to interact synchronously with the instructor and each other (Barron, 2020).

What keeps executive and senior leaders up at night. These individuals worry about whether the organization is bringing in sufficient revenue and controlling costs in ways that keep the organization financially viable. They worry about meeting the terms of their bonuses. They also worry about timely issues that can affect the organization's strategic objectives.

Wireframes. Low-fidelity graphic organizers that communicate structure and navigation. They are usually made up of lines and text that indicate screen layouts indicating different media types and functional element behaviors of an eLearning object, app, or web page. They do not typically include color, styling, or graphics. Wireframing results in prototypes that are of higher fidelity than paper prototyping, but lack the functionality and visual elements of high-fidelity prototypes (Earnshaw, Tawfik, & Schmidt, 2018).

Workflow. "The sequence of steps involved in moving from the beginning to the end of a working process" (Merriam-Webster, 2023). IDs specify and complete workflows as part of their project management responsibilities.

References

Ahrens, A., Zaščerinska, J., Purvinis, O., & Andreeva, N. (2015). Criteria for qualitative decisions in business logistics: Conceptual framework. In *10th International Conference Intelligent Technologies in Logistics and Mechatronics Systems* (ITELMS) (pp. 11–20).

American Society for Quality. (n.d.). *Continuous improvement.* https://asq.org/quality-resources/continuous-improvement

Arianto, F., & Nikmah, U. (2017, September). Cognitive apprenticeship model in the aesthetics and ergonomics material of entrepreneurship subject on students' creativity in vocational higher school. In *9th International Conference for Science Educators and Teachers* (ICSET 2017) (pp. 561–563). Atlantis Press.

Ashford-Rowe, K., Herrington, J., & Brown, C. (2014). Establishing the critical elements that determine authentic assessment. *Assessment & Evaluation in Higher Education, 39*(2), 205–222. doi:10.1080/02602938.2013.819566

Association for Talent Development (ATD) (n.d.). What is instructional design? https://www.td.org/talent-development-glossary-terms/what-is-instructional-design

Baaki, J., Tracey, M. W., Bailey, E., & Shah, S. (2021). Graduate instructional design students using empathy as a means to an end. *Journal of Design Research, 19*(4–6), 290–307.

Bannan, B., Dabbaugh, N., & Walcutt, J. J. (2019). Instructional strategies for the future. In Walcutt, J. J., & Schatz, S. (Eds), *Modernizing learning: Building the future learning ecosystem* (pp. 223–242). *Advanced Distributed Learning Initiative.* Retrieved from https://adlnet.gov/assets/uploads/Modernizing%20Learning.pdf

Barron, S. (May 5, 2020). What is a virtual classroom? *Education Technology.* https://resources.owllabs.com/blog/virtual-classroom

Boller, S. (2022). Design thinking for TD. In Biech, E. (Ed.), *ATD's handbook for training and talent development.* ATD.

Bower, M. (2008). Affordance analysis–matching learning tasks with learning technologies. *Educational Media International, 45*(1), 3–15. http://dx.doi.org/10.1080/09523980701847115

Bruegge, C. V., & Widlake, D. E. (2001). Advance organizer. In Medsker, K. L., & Holdsworth, K. M. (Eds), *Models and strategies for training design* (pp. 175–192). International Society for Performance Improvement.

Cambridge Dictionary. (n.d.). Infodump. Retrieved from https://dictionary.cambridge.org/us/dictionary/english/infodump

Collins, A., Brown, J. S., & Holum, A. (1991). Cognitive apprenticeship: Making thinking visible. *American Educator, 15*(3), 6–11.

Costanza-Chock, S. (2020). *Design justice: Community-led practices to build the worlds we need.* The MIT Press. https://library.oapen.org/bitstream/handle/20.500.12657/43542/external_content.pdf

Dick, W., Carey, L., & Carey, J. O. (2004). *The systematic design of instruction* (6th ed.). Allyn & Bacon.

Dickson-Deane, C. (2023, March 10). How Should We Define Culture in Research? [Webinar] CLT Division professional development program, Virtual.

Dickson-Deane, C., Bradshaw, A. C. & Asino, T. I. (2018). Recognizing the inseparability of culture, learning, and technology. *TechTrends*, 62, 310–311. doi:10.1007/s11528-018-0296-3

Diversity, Equity, and Inclusion Definitions. (2023). Retrieved from https://www.washington.edu/research/or/office-of-research-diversity-equity-and-inclusion/dei-definitions/

Earnshaw, Y., Tawfik, A. A., & Schmidt, M. (2018). User experience design. In West, R. E. (Ed.), *Foundations of learning and instructional design technology: Historical roots and current trends.* EdTech Books.

ELDAPT Instructure (2022). *Elearning design blueprints—How does it [sic] works?* https://www.linkedin.com/pulse/elearning-design-blueprints-how-does-works-template-/?trk=pulse-article_more-articles_related-content-card

eLearning Art (n.d). *Structure and script your eLearning projects: 6 practical tips to write better eLearning scripts.* https://elearningart.com/development/script/

EnSpire Oxford (2022). What is an MVP (hint: it's not the most valuable player)? Retrieved from https://eship.ox.ac.uk/what-is-an-mvp-hint-its-not-the-most-valuable-player/#:~:text=%E2%80%9CThe%20minimum%20viable%20product%20is,customers%20with%20the%20least%20effort.%E2%80%9D

Equitable Data Working Group. (2022). A Vision for Equitable Data: Recommendations from the Equitable Data Working Group. https://www.whitehouse.gov/wp-content/uploads/2022/04/eo13985-vision-for-equitable-data.pdf

Fake, H., & Dabbagh, N. (2020). Personalized learning within online workforce learning environments: Exploring implementations, obstacles, opportunities, and perspectives of workforce leaders. *Technology, Knowledge and Learning*, 25(4), 789–809.

Gao, Z., Zhao, C., Cooke, F. L., Zhang, B., & Xie, R. (2020). Only time can tell: Whether and when the improvement in career development opportunities alleviates knowledge workers' emotional exhaustion in the Chinese context. *British Journal of Management*, 31(1), 206–220.

Garner, S. L., Young, P., Fendt, M., Koch, H., George, C. E., Hitchcock, J., Green, G., Kulaba, P., & Kingsley, R. G. V. (2023). Effectiveness of a culturally responsive health gaming application to improve diabetes health literacy in India: A randomized controlled trial. *CIN: Computers, Informatics, Nursing*, 41(10), 796–804. doi:10.1097/CIN.0000000000001009

Geist, S. (2023, March 28). The benefits of affinity groups in the workplace. McGregor Boyall, *Human Resources & Talent Management Blog*. https://www.mcgregor-boyall.com/resources/blog/the-benefits-of-affinity-groups-in-the-workplace/

Giacumo, L. A., Chen, J., & Seguinot-Cruz, A. (2020). Evidence on the use of mentoring programs and practices to support workplace learning: A systematic multiple-studies review. *Performance Improvement Quarterly*, 33(3), 259–303.

Gibbons, S. (2018, December 9). Journey mapping 101. Nielsen Norman Group. https://www.nngroup.com/articles/journey-mapping-101/

Government of Samoa. (2019). *National Culture Framework and Policies: 2018–2028*. Ministry of Education, Sports and Culture. https://unesdoc.unesco.org/ark:/48223/pf0000367587

Greenberg, J. (1987). A taxonomy of organizational justice theories. *Academy of Management Review*, 12(1), 9–22.

Greenberg, J. (1990). Organizational justice: Yesterday, today, and tomorrow. *Journal of Management*, 16(2), 399–432.

Gupta, D. (2023, March 10). 8 Best Learning Portals in 2023 (+Features, Use Cases). *The Whatfix Blog*. https://whatfix.com/blog/learning-portals/

Hirsch, A. (2021). An Inside Look at Workplace Racial Affinity Groups. https://www.shrm.org/resourcesandtools/hr-topics/behavioral-competencies/global-and-cultural-effectiveness/pages/an-inside-look-at-workplace-racial-affinity-groups.aspx

Huang, Y., & Klein, J. D. (2023). Mobile performance support systems: Characteristics, benefits, and conditions. *TechTrends*, 67, 150–159. doi:10.1007/s11528–022–00804-y

Jacobs, R. L. (2003). *Structured on-the-job training: Unleashing employee expertise in the workplace* (2nd ed.). Barrett-Koehler.

Kuknor, S., & Bhattacharya, S. (2021). Exploring organizational inclusion and inclusive leadership in Indian companies. *European Business Review*, *33*(3), 450–464.

Lave, J., & Wenger, E. (1991). *Situated learning: Legitimate peripheral participation*. Cambridge University Press.

Looney, J. D. (2021). Diversity, equity, & inclusion: Why does it matter to leadership development? *Journal of Character and Leadership Development*, *8*(2), 59–67. https://jcldusafa.org/index.php/jcld/article/view/38/38

Mavri, A., Ioannou, A., & Loizides, F. (2021). Value creation and identity in cross-organizational communities of practice: A learner's perspective. *The Internet and Higher Education*, *51*, 1–20. doi:10.1016/j.iheduc.2021.100822

McDonald, J. K., & West, R. E. (Eds.) (2020). *Design for learning: Principles, processes, and praxis*. EdTech Books. https://edtechbooks.org/id

McGrath, B., & Navarro, J. C. M. (2022). Beyond high-stakes assessment. In Ramlall, S., Cross, T., & Love, M. (Eds), *Handbook of research on future of work and education: Implications for curriculum delivery and work design* (pp. 193–212). IGI Global. doi:10.4018/978–1-7998–8275–6.ch012

Melo, Á. H. D. S., Rivero, L., Santos, J. S. D., & Barreto, R. D. S. (2020, October). EmpathyAut: An empathy map for people with autism. In *Proceedings of the 19th Brazilian Symposium on Human Factors in Computing Systems* (pp. 1–6).

Merriam-Webster. (2023). Workflow. Retrieved from https://www.merriam-webster.com/dictionary/workflow#:~:text=noun,end%20of%20a%20working%20process

Mulu, A., & Zewdie, S. (2021). The effect of diversity management on organizational performance: The case of Ethio-Telecom South West Region. *European Journal of Business and Management Research*, *6*(2), 134–139. https://doi.org/10.24018/ejbmr.2021.6.2.813

Mutambo, C., Shumba, K., & Hlongwana, K. W. (2021). Exploring the mechanism through which a child-friendly storybook addresses barriers to child-participation during HIV care in primary healthcare settings in KwaZulu-Natal, South Africa. *BMC Public Health*, *21*, 1–15. doi:10.1186/s12889-021-10483-8

Nithithanatchinnapat, B., Taylor, J., Joshi, K. D., & Weiss, M. L. (2016). Organizational communities of practice: Review, analysis, and role of information and communications technologies. *Journal of Organizational Computing and Electronic Commerce*, *26*(4), 307–322. doi:10.1080/10919392.2016.1228357

Prosci (n.d.). Change management defined. https://www.prosci.com/resources/articles/definition-of-change-management

Raybould, B. (1990). Solving human performance problems with computers—A case study: Building an electronic performance support system. *Performance & Instruction*, *29*(10), 4–14. doi:10.1002/pfi.4160291004

Rogers, E. M. (2003). *Diffusion of innovations* (5th ed.). Free Press.

Russell, M., Szendey, O., & Kaplan, L. (2021). An intersectional approach to DIF: Do initial findings hold across tests? *Educational Assessment*, *26*(4), 284–298.

Schmidt, M., & Tawfik, A. (2022). Activity theory as a lens for developing and applying personas and scenarios in learning experience design. *Journal of Applied Instructional Design*, *11*(1). https://edtechbooks.org/jaid_11_1/activity_theory_as_a

Smith, P. (2018). *Learning while working: Structuring your on-the-job training*. Association for Talent Development.

Svihla, V. (2017). Design thinking and agile design. New trends or just good designs? In West, R. E. (Ed.), *Foundations of learning and instructional design technology*. EdTech Books. https://edtechbooks.org/lidtfoundations/design_thinking_and_agile_design

Tarmizi, A., Lian, B., & Puspita, Y. (2021). The influence of organizational culture and motivation on employee performance. *Journal of Social Work and Science Education*, *2*(2), 109–116.

Tshilongamulenzhe, M. C., Coetzee, M., & Masenge, A. (2013). Development of the learning programme management and evaluation scale for the South African skills development context. *SA Journal of Industrial Psychology*, *39*(1), 1–14.

UNESCO (2001). UNESCO Universal Declaration on Cultural Diversity. https://en.unesco.org/about-us/legal-affairs/unesco-universal-declaration-cultural-diversity

Uzialko, A. (2023, February 21). What is an LMS (Learning Management System)? *Business News Daily*. https://www.businessnewsdaily.com/4772-learning-management-system.html

van Pamel, M. (2013). On-the-job training: Best practices: Structured v unstructured on-the-job training. https://onthejobtraingingbestpractices.blogspot.com/2013/04/structured-v-unstructured-on-job.html

Verstegen, D. M. L., Barnard, Y. F, & Pilot, A. (2006). Which events can cause iteration in instructional design? An empirical study of the design process. *Instructional Science*, 34(6), 481–517. https://www.jstor.org/stable/41953724

Villachica, S. W., & Stone, D. L. (1999). Performance support systems. In Stolovitch, H. D., & Keeps, E. J. (Eds), *Handbook of human performance technology: Improving individual and organizational performance worldwide* (2nd ed., pp. 442–463). Jossey-Bass/Pfeiffer.

Wenger, E. C., & Snyder, W. M. (2000). Communities of practice: The organizational frontier. *Harvard Business Review*, 78(1), 139–145. https://hbr.org/2000/01/communities-of-practice-the-organizational-frontier

Wiley, D. (2022). *Project management for instructional designers* (3rd ed.). EdTech Books. https://edtechbooks.org/pm4id

Willmore, J. (2018). *Job aid basics* (2nd ed.). ATD.

Index

References to tables and figures are indicated by an italic *t* or *f* following the page number.